An Anthology On
# The Ror Caste
### Ishwar Singh Mehla

B.Sc. Engineering- Electronics & Communication Engg. (Hons)
IB(E)S, FIETE, FIE, Charted Engineer (IETE)
Former; Dy Director General (Engineering);
AIR & DD, and Director of Board; BECIL

# रोड़ समाज
### के बारे में एक संकलन
ईश्वर सिंह महला

## The Rors of Northern India from Haryana, Uttar Pradesh & Uttarakhand

उत्तर भारत के हरियाणा, उत्तरप्रदेश व उत्तराखंड का
रोड़ समाज

INDIA · SINGAPORE · MALAYSIA

ISBN 979-8-88975-966-9

1st Published; May 16, 2023
Edition-1; October 8, 2024
Edition-2; October, 2025



**Disclaimer:** I, Ishwar Singh Mehla, author-An Anthology On The Ror Caste, hereby notify, Proverbs & Sayings on the Castes in the book is without malice & not to demean any caste .
> Published in Sunday Times of India Delhi NCR vol. 36 No. 29 New Delhi page-18 Sunday July 20, 2025.
> Published in Nav Bharat Times Delhi NCR, Varsh 79, No. 173 page-6 Tuesday July 22, 2025.

# श्रीमद् भगवद् गीता

कर्मण्येवाधिकारस्ते मा फलेषु कदाचन।  
मा कर्मफलहेतुर्भूर्मा ते सङ्गोऽस्त्वकर्मणि॥

तुम्हारा अधिकार तो केवल कर्म करने का है, कर्म के फल पर नही।  
इसलिए ना तो कर्म से भागना उचित है, ना ही कर्म के फल की  
आशा रखना उचित है॥

श्रीमद भगवद्गीता; अध्याय-२, श्लोक ॥४७॥

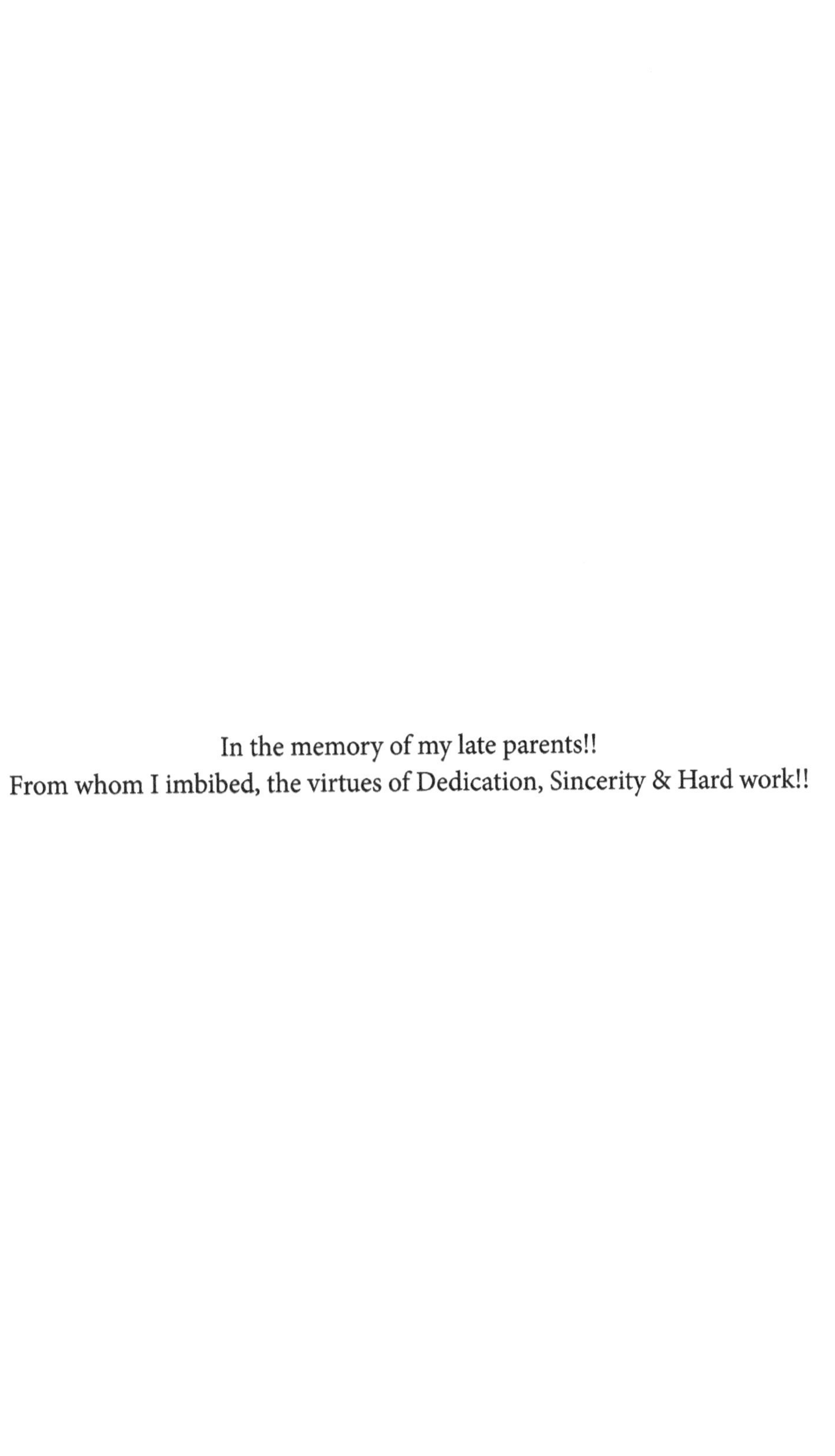

In the memory of my late parents!!
From whom I imbibed, the virtues of Dedication, Sincerity & Hard work!!

# Contents

# Foreword......

*"No distinctions of Caste and Creed should hamper us. All are the sons and daughters of India. We should all love our country and build our destiny on mutual love and help."* ............... "Sardar Patel"

This book Titled "An Anthology on the Ror Caste" authored by Er ISHWAR SINGH MEHLA has been compiled on perusal of voluminous authentic documents from various reliable sources.

The book elucidates the measurable attributes of the Races, and the Postulations of Origin of Rors from other castes have been logically described based on recorded data. The author has also given an overview of physical characteristics of Rors and their socio-economic status, caste councils, associations, welfare bodies, habitats in Haryana, UP, & Uttarakhand, contribution to Nation through professions in agrarian fields, sports, education, employment in civil and military organisations, business, politics etc.

The prevailing shortcomings being faced by the Ror community have been briefly described for introspection. The Way Forward for its development and upliftment has been suggested to make a positive impact in social, economic, educational, political, and other fields.

The author being an inquisitive and well-wisher of the Ror Community has carried out years of extensive research on perusal, collection, compilation, and analysis of reliable published literature. He has acknowledged the contribution and opinion of almost all the authors on the origin & evolution of Rors.

The book is laced with illustrations, tables, photographs and written in a simple language to make it a pleasurable reading for the Patrons.

I am sure you will find this book as one more tool in the armamentarium for enhancing the awareness and knowledge about the origin, evolution and progression of Ror Community based on the facts.

I wholeheartedly compliment the author for his hard work, dedication, and devotion in the quest of his journey to publish an informative, educative, motivational, and authentic book for members of the great Ror Community.

**Dr (Brigadier) Zile Singh (retd)**

Why a book on caste in modern times? A well-known quote of the East India Co officer, "To understand the people of India, to enter into & understand their point of view, and to realise how the things strike them, cannot be understood without understanding the caste system & their caste." In the words of Bamfylde Fuller that, "Nothing wins the regard of an Indian so easily as a knowledge of the facts connected with his religion, caste, prejudices, & his habits."

Caste is deeply ingrained in Indian social system. Though there is not much emphasis on the caste in metros & cosmopolitan cities, but it is prominently ingrained in the minds of masses in villages, where 70% of the population still inhabit. In normal times caste identity is immaterial in workplace, especially in metros & cosmopolitan cities. People use, reuse, hide, & play with their own caste identities as per their requirements. They use it to garner social, & political support in the localities where they live. Sometime they hide it, if they find that their caste may create trouble for them. Sometimes (in many cases), they claim higher identities as their clever strategy for survival.

In Indian society everyone should know his caste as starting with the birth, entire social life, upbringing, all customs & rituals, social relations with other castes, betrothal & marriage, final rites etc depends purely on caste only. Say to initiate marriage alliance; everyone must know his own, his mother's, grandmother's (paternal & maternal) gotra. All these are embedded in every Indian's mind & are to be told without hesitation as and when needed.

Caste system is very necessary to prevent the further disruption of a particular lineage (Diversity necessary). No person, community, society, country can remain disconnected from its past, as they take inspiration from their glorious past and endures to avoid the past mistakes. A saying by the English writer Stuart, "if you want to enslave and govern a country or a state or a community, first attack its self-respect, and cut it from its glorious past history, caste & pride."

History of the origin of every caste/class has umpteen ambiguities, uncertainties, myths & difficulties. These difficulties rise to a higher level when there is prejudice of connecting a caste to a national or a well-established caste. Earlier classification of people of India as per Manu, was Varna. In fact, caste (should be called Jaati) arose not due to the purity of the blood but due to the Varna evolution, and more precisely perhaps because of cross-breeding. This is the reason there is no definite & justified cause of the origin of a caste.

History of a race is narrated based on the written documents, archaeological findings, folktales, words of mouth, coins, artefacts, ruins of their forts etc, but in case of 'Ror caste,' there is dearth of this basic material and as such the history remains enigma, incomplete, unauthenticated, and loose. Hence the need for a book on the Ror Caste, to apprise it's who's who & masses from diverse domains, on all aspects of their community, so that they connect to it, identify with it, participate in caste welfare activities & work for its upliftment & development in all spheres including the most important sphere the socio-political, & feel proud about their caste.

This book differs from all previous ones on the Ror caste as it describes their profile almost in every aspects from old & the modern write-ups, regarding their customs, birth & marriage rituals, inheritance system, acceptability in professional parlance, their present living conditions, education, means of livelihood, day to day life, and socio-political standing in the society vis-à-vis other Agricultural Dominant land-owning Martial castes.

This book, has been compiled after sieving more than 30 varied documents, and the books penned by few writers up to 2011 on the history of The Ror Community. I am not a trained historian but a technocrat, and this venture of mine was induced by the pain & zeal to set the records straight and undo the wrong done & disrepute brought to my community by a handful of self-serving elements through conflicting versions of the history of Rors.

I invite readers to send me their constructive feedback, by email at id; ismehla@gmail.com, for improvement by a revised version, if found inevitable. Further, a Hindi version of the Book also can be thought of if there is popular demand, though main aim of the book is for literate Rors, who are proficient in English language but are not conversant with their caste identity.

**Ishwar Singh Mehla**

# Introduction......

The book lucidly proceeds with 1st chapter briefly describing the attributes of Races & methods to measure such attributes as Race is main constituent of a caste.

Chapter-2 Describes various theories on the origin of castes by eminent writers, and most common definition in addition to the actual as in the treatise of The Hindu Law book; The Manusmriti, in modern times as given by: Herbert Risley, & Senart etc.

Chapter-3, Describes famous proverbs & popular sayings on the castes; taunting or cajoling or demeaning type as prevalent in the society that time and are equally in currency even now being sort of universal truth for each caste, depicting a humorous life-line of the society.

Chapter-4, Lists all the castes found in pre-partition Panjab, as detailed in the Book, 'Panjab Castes', by Denzill Ibbetson, with special emphasis on Ror Caste & briefly describing other dominant agrarian castes including their origin & clans.

Chapter-5, Details the socio-political, socio-cultural & economic status of the People as described in the British era District Gazetteers. Later part, verbatim describes archaeological ruins of the Kagarol fort, & fifty-two Gadhis/Kasaundigadh etc of Raja Ror or Raja Gaj (or Dhaj?), based on the ASI report-1871-72 Vol-IV.

Chapter-6, Describes then Panjab castes in every aspect, as in Census reports, & Glossaries of Tribes & castes of N-W Provinces & Oudh; by Crooke. Castes like Rajput, Jaat, Arora, & Khatri, etc also have been described, in order to let Rors know that theirs Vs these castes, & that Rors have not evolved from them.

Chapter-7, is an extract on the Anthropological Profile of the Rors, from the 1st post-independence 'The People of India-Haryana & UP' series Book - prepared by various Sociologists & Anthropologists as part of the Govt of India project under the department of Anthropological Survey of India. This latest govt authenticated source, touches every aspect of the Ror caste.

Chapter-8, is an overview of various postulations on the origin of Rors, from almost all available writeup on the Rors, including from Bhaats.

Chapter-9, is the critical evaluation of some paradoxes about the Ror caste, to understand the psyche of its people & the truth about the paradoxes from the facts available in the public domain or as the Rors claim.

Chapter-10 describes presently socio-political position & district wise habitats in all the three states including international sports-persons, freedom fighters, educational & economic status, and civil award winners.

Chapter-11 describes the social & religious life of Rors in r.o. Daily life, Clothing & Ornaments, Birth, marriage & related rituals, family structure, status of women, life-cycle rituals, food habits, Art, craft, & festivals, Re-marriage of widows, economic status, Social-division, & including social-intercourse of Rors with similar status castes, and the Caste welfare bodies etc.

Chapter-12 throws light on the occupations & professions, excluding the main ancestral Agrarian & Pastoral, taken up by the Rors covering almost all spheres of earning of livelihood from the service sector starting with Civil, Military, Govt, Semi-govt, Public & Corporate sectors to self-business.

Chapter-13 takes up the most important issue of the way forward for the community to make a mark in the social scenario of the habitat region and describes the ailments plaguing it, and also the ways & means to remedy the ailments for an all-round development & upliftment of the community.

Chapter-14 records & tabulates Ror Gots, district wise villages inhabited by them, and the Gots they share with other castes including the comparison of their Traits with Marathas in order to clear the confusion created in the psyche of unsuspecting youths about their evolution.

The last chapter-15, "To connect the dots," wherein some threads/hints as extracted from, "The Annals of Rajasthan," penned by Col James Tod and from the Material for Research on 'Raja Ror' by Col Ram Chander (Retd) & Clarification to Unification: by Major M.S. Keshwar (Retd) etc, are detailed for further critical study to clear the ambiguities & to know the evolution of the Ror caste, which is an elusive & enigma as of now.

The summary concludes the subject matter of the origin of The Ror Caste, which based on the facts mentioned in this book and as brought out by various documents Rors are said to be of Kshatriya origin. However it needs to be established once for all by a book written & authenticated by academic/ historians in coordination with an apex committee consisting of subject matter expert members of Ror community.

**Ishwar Singh Mehla**

# Acknowledgements......

This book has been compiled, after consulting varied govt, semi-govt, and private documents from wide spectra multiple sources. It also incorporates an overview from all the books penned by independent writers up to 2011 on the history of The Ror Community of the Northern India.

To start with, I express & acknowledge my sincere thanks and gratitude in using the material from the following documents, books, & reports;

1. People of India, by Sir Herbert Risley; 1st Published 1913; a LPP edition
2. Panjab Castes by Sir Denzil Ibbetson, published in 1916
3. Origin and Growth of caste; Narender Kumar Dutt
4. District gazetteers of British era written from 1872 onwards
5. Census 1868 of Punjab; source: jstor.org
6. Census 1881 of Punjab Vol-I; source: jstor.org
7. Census of India-1891: Punjab; source: jstor.org
8. Census Report -1891, Punjab & its Feudatories, Part-I; source: jstor.org
9. Census 1891: Punjab & its Feudatories, Part-III; Imperial tables & supplementary returns for native states.
10. Census of India 1901; Vol.17, Punjab; its feudatories & the North-West Frontier Province. Pt-1
11. Census of India 1911; Vol.14, Punjab: pt. 3, Appendices
12. Census of India 1921; Vol. 15; Punjab & Delhi: Part 2
13. Census of India, 1931, Vol. XVII; Punjab Part-I
14. A Glossary of Tribes and castes in Punjab & NWFP; Vol-I
15. Tribes and Castes of North-Western Provinces & Oudh (4 volumes) compiled by William Crooke in 1896,
16. Archaeology Survey of India Report 1871-72, Vol IV; by A. Cunningham
17. 'People of India' series: Haryana, Vol-XXIII;
18. 'People of India' series: Uttar Pradesh & Uttarakhand Vol-XLII part-III.
19. Ror Etihas ki Jhalak: Dr Rajpal Singh; ed1987.
20. Ror Maratha-Etihas Part1 & 2; Ek Jhalak; 2002: By Prof. Om Prakash, and Mahender Singh Arya.
21. Ror-Udhbav and Vikas; Dr Surender Singh Kadiyan; ed 2003.
22. Ror Maratha History; Dr. Vasant More; ed 2009.
23. Ror Maratha Spirit in Haryana by: Uday Mahurkar (Ex India Today).
24. Ror Vansh Ka 5000 Varsh ka Etihas: Ram Das Rode; ed 2009.
25. Clarification to unification: Major (Retrd) M.S. Keshwar; ed 2011.

26.   DNA based study; 2012; by Anurag Kadian & others.

27.   The Annals of Karnal; 1914; by Major C H Buck DC Karnal.

28.   Annals and Antiquity of Rajasthan by col James Tod; edited by William Crooke 1920.

29.   Material for Research on Raja Ror; Col Ram Chander Rasina.

30.   MOAs of; Ror Mahasabha, Ror Employee Association, Ror Chetna Manch, & website of Mahasabha.

31.   Directory-2011; by Ror Employee Association & village map prepared by Mr Zile Singh Chauhan of Raipur Rodan.

32.   Final report on settlement of land Revenue of Delhi District in 1878-80 by R. Maconachie.

33.   Settlements in The Yamuna-Hindon Doab, An Archaeological Perspective; by Rewant Vikram Singh.

I acknowledge gratefully all other sources also, whom I have not specifically mentioned above, but I have used their material/work in this book. Also, I do not claim originality for some material in this compilation, even though I have spent lot of valuable time on searching/locating the resources and then gleaning, abridging, & adapting them to make the narration more interesting to read, lucid and comprehend the matter more systematically so that it appeals to the readers. Readers are free to use, but caveat is to use with due acknowledgment only, the material of this compilation for furthering the cause of knowing & gleaning the history of the Origin of The Rors.

I also, acknowledge the community individuals like; Sh S P Verma former Jt. Director DRDO for loaning the first two books of the above list, Dr Devinder Singh scientist working in NGRI for making available pdf copy of few books on Rors & Marathas, & Dr Balkar Singh for 'People of India' Book series for UP & UK Rors from the Parliament of India library, Sh Ram Das Rode a copy of his book; Ror Vansh Ka 5000 Varsh ka Etihas, Brig Randhir Singh & Lt Col Multan Singh for an updated list of Défense persons, Dr Pal Singh Mehla for book Clarification to Unification & his input on academicians, Dr Rishi Pal Singh, & Sh Dila Ram ji for the list of Agriculture Scientist & Diploma Engineer Rors, Col Uady Singh for Ror logo & the earliest Rors who enrolled in the army, & photographs of 3rd Gen Rors from his village in the Military & Sh Suresh Rode of Kalamajra for a photograph of Late Lt Col Dei Chand ji, the 1st commissioned Ror officer in the Army, and also prof Mehar Singh Khanchi of Shera, for making available handwritten material of the Sauram Khap Panchayat on Rors.

Finally, I am indebted with gratitude on the gesture of Dr (Brigadier) Zile Singh who not only kindly agreed to write a befitting concise foreword for this unique book of mine on the Ror community but did a proof check of the published book also for removing some missed out edit & errors. Further also my gratitude & many thanks to Col Uday Singh, S P Verma, Hukam Singh Chaudhary, Dr Balkar Singh, Dr Mehar Singh Khanchi, R D Mehla, Dila Ram, and Mukesh Chaudhary for their views on the book, and Sanjay Dabur & Col Ajay Dabur for their feedback about my book. Also I am thankful to Dr K S Kadian for his feedback about his village Katladi (Katlahedi) & some Gots, and info given by Commandant Satyavan Khanchi on the Rors working in BSF. Use of photos of public figures & outstanding sportspersons of the community in the book, from the open sources are purely for the literary purposes & for the better cause of the community only without any other aim or commercial consideration by me.

My express apology for any error in factual data, abridged matter from the original, or in the name, rank or citation of the defence personnel, politicians, sportspersons, professionals, or any other luminary of the community, as it is inadvertent, & unintentional or might have crept in due to autocorrect function of the MS word software.

In the end, I acknowledge the unstinted support of my wife Shashi Mehla, which enabled me to devote time on my book writing work, and also my children; daughter Isha Mehla (Spouse Aarjav & their adorable sons Vivaan, & Vihaan), and son Ishan Mehla (spouse Chetna & their adorable son Mudit and daughter Bhumi) for their love and affection.

**Ishwar Singh Mehla**
Former: Dy. Director General (ENGG) - AIR & DD, and
Director of Board of CPSE-BECIL
Place; Delhi, March 2023; Native Place; Gudha (Gharaunda)

# Explanatory Notes......

Spelling of many words like; names of persons, places, castes, & rivers etc in this book at number of places may look wrong, but it is not, as these have been written as spelled that way by the Britishers that time in their documents; District gazetteers, Glossaries etc, & by the Enumerators in the Census Reports etc. or other writers in their write-ups. Initially while compiling the data Britishers followed the accent of natives, which was much different than theirs, hence the originality retained in transcribing. Also, many alphabets of Hindi, which do not have any equivalent English Alphabets, are now being spelled differently than these were initially spelled by them. Few examples & other explanations are as below.

1. The syllable; ā; has the sound of 'aa' like in Sāmbhar. So, I have spelled राम as Raam at places instead of; 'Ram.' Few more such words spelled are; जाट as Jaat instead of Jat; भाट as Bhaat instead of Bhat भट etc.

2. There are many words, in few chapters specially wherein matter from District Gazetteer, census or Glossary has been taken, which were spelled by Britishers as per the accent of natives & such words are;

Umbala for Ambala, Dehli/Dahli for Delhi, Daia/Dahia for Dahiya, got in place of gotra or as the natives call & pronounce it in villages even as of now, Hariana/Haryana for Hariyana, Jamna/Jumna for Yamuna, Sunpat for Sonipat, Sarusti for Saraswati, Tahsils/Tahsildars; Tehsil/Tehsildar etc.

I preferred to retain the old spelling to maintain the originality of the text.

3. For many alphabets of Hindi like ड़, ड़ा, ढ, ढा etc., which do not have any equivalent English Alphabets, I preferred to go for the better sounding replacements as;

Dhankhar by Dhankhad, Kheri (a) by Khedi (a), Garh by Gadh, Rangar by Rangad रांगड़, Ror by Rode रोड़ and not Rod रोड which means a metal bar (as used by Maratha Writer), Rorni by Rodni रोड़नी etc.

4. Spelling of the Caste Ror; Though the spelling of the caste name; Ror (Hindi; रोड़) has been the main version, but it has been spelt differently by different census enumerators or the govt staff etc, such as: Raur, Raud, Roar, Rod, Rode, Rohad, Rora, Rore, Rour etc. Now also different Ror community people as per the area, or as spelled at the time of their school admission by teachers etc as per their knowledge or idiosyncrasies, or the general public & also by the Ror themselves, in day-to-day use, are spelling it their way.

So, it is imperative, to select the most acceptable, logical, less prone to misspelling & sounding dignified with no ambiguity, & without any inadvertent chance of wrong spelling or interpretation by the public; Say Raud or Rodes or even Rohd or Rohad (रोहड़ like जोहड़ spoken with half/short sound of ह or h) instead of Ror etc. Also, it is stated that the name of the caste in Hindi is रोड़ and not रोड, which means, the Road i.e., सड़क, but many from the community also writes it as रोड or रोर and not as रोड़. So, to avoid all ambiguities or deliberate or inadvertent spelling mistakes, like Gaud (गोड़) is spelled, let it also be spelled as Raud (रोड़) or Rohd or Rohad or Rodes. Pronunciation & articulation wise also it augurs much better and looks logical. Rode, also would have been a preferable choice but being a verb, & name of a sub-caste even in Aroras, Arain, & Jat etc & even some Ror have started writing it that way, it is not suggested.

**Ishwar Singh Mehla**

# Views & Messages...

Delhi, February 23, 2023

Yes, it is different and interesting approach to decipher the mystery or enigma called रोड़ and other matching sounding names of many other Castes and Sub castes. It is your hard labour that produces this new work. Now acceptance by community vis a vis, it would come under Scholarly Work rather than an Interesting History Non-Fiction category.

Personally, I would like to prefer it initially as a PhD Thesis and then later to be published as Non-Fiction Book. This way may be English version will work fine and later may be Hindi edition. May be under new Education Policy you can register for PhD.

– Col Uday Singh (retd), Delhi; Dadupur Rodan

* * * * *

Karnal, March 9, 2023

A good and painstaking effort on the part of the author. Deserves kudos for it.

– Satya Pal Verma, Karnal (Saanch), Former; Joint Director, DRDO

* * * * *

Delhi, March 18,2023

This book offers a balanced interpretation on the multiple perspectives available regarding the history of Ror community. It is capable of inspiring them to shake off their caste centric inhibitions and reconcile with vagaries of past. In essence, the community is expected to continue playing a dominant role towards social harmony and nation building, with a renewed vigour and confidence.

– Dr Balkar Singh, Bastada (Delhi); (Deputy Director, Parliament of India)

* * * * *

Delhi, March 20, 2023

This is an innate human yearning to know about his/her past regarding every aspect of living/existence and seems that our brain needs it to put things in proper perspective. Diving deep in all available sources, this scholarly work about history of Rors is truly commendable; while fulfilling the yearning of fellow Rors to know about their past, would most certainly act as a strong foundation for future historical research on the subject.

– Hukam Singh Chaudhary, Bastada (Delhi)<br>
Former Dy Chief Engineer (Delhi Metro), Presently Director-Rail, egis

* * * * *

Kurukshetra, March 18, 2023

It is human nature to know about one's caste, race, & gotra, so, that one, without hesitation, can explain his credentials. The origin of the Rors is a matter of great controversy & in spite of the efforts by some writers from time to time, there is still no unanimity of opinions on the issue.

It is a matter of great satisfaction & immense pleasure that Mr Ishwar Singh Mehla has taken the task to bring out a book on Ror history, An Anthology on 'The Ror Caste.' Though some authors have already written books on Ror history but I do hope the efforts made by Mr Singh will be an improved & valuable version leading to almost truth.

The book contains 15 chapters, and author has tried a systematic description of the origin & functioning of Indian caste system with special reference to Rors. He has given the bird eye view of almost all theory of origin of Ror caste, briefly describing each, either from official govt documents or penned by independent/standalone writers till date including, Bhaats, ASI report & Annals of Rajasthan by Tod.

I along with Dr Raj Pal Singh, the author of 'Ror Itihas Ki Jhalak,' visited the places near Agra & Fatehpur Sikri i.e., Kagaroll, Kasaundi Garhi, Fifty-two forts etc. The discussions with local populace revealed that the remains of old forts in Kagaroll & near by areas belongs to Raja Ror son of Khangar. ASI report 1871-72 Vol-IV also authenticate this, which establishes the existence of Rors in the places nearby Agra during 2$^{nd}$ BC.

The book may be of immense use for Ror masses to know about the inter-caste dynamics of their community, & a reference material for scholars as author has pieced about the social & religious life of Rors, & their relations with other castes.

I congratulate Mr Ishwar Singh Mehla for the efforts he has put to fill the gaps in Ror history. It is hopped that the readers in general & research scholars in particular will be benefited from the present write-up.

Signed – Dr M S Khanchi;
Former Principal, Babu Anant Ram Janata College, Kaul, Kaithal (Haryana)

* * * * *

Kurukshetra Sept 15,2023

Your book is so inspiring, it seems, whatever written in it, are words of a well reputed historian.

– R D Mehla Kurukshetra (Jadaula)
Former; Librarian ICARI PUSA Delhi

* * * * *

Gurugram August 2, 2023

Author, 'Ishwar Singh Mehla,' a broadcast Engineer, Whom I know since 1979 being in the same department, enjoys high reputation in the Engineering Fraternity of All India Radio, took up on himself the herculean task of bringing the book, 'An Anthology on The Ror Caste.' He left no stone unturned in collecting, compiling, and analyzing the pertinent data in a systematic manner so that it covers all aspects (traditions, rituals, habits, traits, socio-economic conditions, professions, relations with other castes in same professions etc.) from origin to present status.

The book gives detailed information about the progress made by The Ror caste post-independence in general & particularly in the field of education (Technical, academic, scientific, agriculture, medical, military etc.), & sports, which is very encouraging, & is matter of pride for every, 'Ror'.

The author has done really very hard work with devotion & deserves appreciation. He has laid solid foundation for further research by the research scholars.

Signed – Dila Ram, Delhi NCR (Taraodi)
Former; Director Engg, AIR & Doordarshan

* * * * *

Delhi NCR August 20, 2023

Sir, First of all, congratulations to you for publishing your book – "An Anthology On The Ror Caste," I have read your book on our ROR Samaj and would like to Thank You for your hard work and great efforts for compiling all the chronicles for ROR Samaj. I have read other books on ROR Samaj history also but found that most of other books have been written under a prejudice mind set towards a particular theory about our ROR Samaj. I found your book as an encyclopedia comprising all theories of other books on ROR Samaj plus incorporating established government records. This book is a, "Must Read Book", for all, especially the young generation of our Samaj. It is surely a Gem for Home as well as Samaj Library.

Thanks & Regards

– Mukesh Chaudhary
CEO Broadcast Media Communications

* * * * *

# Chapter-1. Races and Physical Features

## 1.1 Racial Division of Indian People

Modern science of ethnology defines various physical types, w.r.t their distinctive characteristics to determine, & establish their connection with one or other family of the mankind. Mr Herbert Risley states, the data ordinarily available are of three kinds; Physical characteristics, Linguistic characteristics, and religious/ social usages. As per William Flower; *Physical characteristics are the most trustworthy; in fact, the only true test of a race*, and most Anthropologists agree to this postulate. Language, customs, etc., may give indications, but they are often misleading. (This chapter is an extract from People of India," Herbert Risley Page 1 to 66)

## 1.2 Language and Race

As stated by Sir Henry Maine, the study of Sanskrit, after the translation of *Kalidasa's Shakuntla* in 1789 & *Manusmriti* in 1794, by William Jones, gave the world, "the modern science of Philology & the modern theory of race."

The belief; 'linguistic affinities' prove community of descent, commended alike to populations struggling for freedom & to rulers in search of excuses for removing a neighbour's landmark. (The idea of tribal sovereignty almost revived when Napoleon-III, justified annexation of Savoy saying the territory where French is spoken ought to belong to France).

The linguistic data are easier to collect & examine than physical observations which form the main basis of ethnological conclusions. 2ndly, languages lend more readily to the classification than the minute variations of form & features, leading to an ethnic type. 3dly, *most important*; while there are practically no mixed languages, there is hardly any pure race. Words may be borrowed on any scale, but essential structure of a language remains unchanged.

Races, normally mixes freely; produces endless variety; and even now it is very difficult to arrive at as to as per which system such varieties should be classified. So, the question arises; within what limits can we argue *from the similarities of language to commonalty of the race or from the differences of language to the diversity of race*? Schwiker & Hale states that, *language is the only true test of racial affinity*; but Sayce opines that, *"identity or relationship of language can prove nothing more than social contact"*? The latter view may be too absolutely expressed keeping in view that speech is a physiological function depending upon the structure of the larynx box. Some races produce sounds which other races can only imitate imperfectly, is a matter of common observation, and may reasonably be ascribed to vocal cords. (This is proved by the differences in phonetic capacity even among Indian races e.g., Bengalis cannot pronounce clear "*S*" but make it "*Sh*," the Maharashtrians speak "*V*" as "*W*"; & nearly all native of UP find difficult to speak words starting with 'S', like "*Smith* "without prefixing a vowel & turning it to *"i-Smith".) Even within a single language, dialectic variations occur due to physical causes.* So, there can be four (4) cases for the relation between race and languages;

(1)   Where both language & physical type have changed by contact with other races e.g., Bengali speaking Kochh; lost their tribal language but their original Mongoloid type still clearly visible in Assam; modified by intermixture with Dravidian element;

(2)   Where language has changed but the racial (physical) type has remained same e.g., Ahom's, Bhumij, etc in India;

(3)   Where the original language remains same but the racial (physical) type has changed, e.g., the Khas in Nepal, and a large proportion of Rajputs all over India;

(4)   Where, both language and the physical types are unchanged, e.g., Andamanese, Santhals, Mundas, Manipuris etc.

In the first 2 cases an appeal to the language would clearly be ineffectual unless historical evidence is available as to what the original language has been. In India, the only instance where historical evidence & ancient records throw lights is of the **"Ahom's,"** a **Shan** people, who entered Assam in early13th century; within 300 years conquered & gave their name to it. By the end of 17th century, they embraced Hinduism, lost their original language. For remaining two (2) cases, it can be further elaborated as below;

(1)   In areas where several languages are spoken, one or more will usually be found to be gaining, while others stationary or declining; the equilibrium is rare. The former may be dominant, & the latter as subordinate. What language belongs to either class is a matter of observation.

(2)   The fact that a particular tribe uses a dominant language does not suggest any inference as to its origin.

(3)   The fact a group speaks decadent or subordinate language indicate proof of their origin; value depends on circumstances.

Ex; 1. *Rajbansi-Kochh & Bhumij,* both speak Bengali but not of Indo-Aryan descent. For such cases their Physical Type is conclusive. 2.; *Vaidu* herbalists of Poona, speak Marathi, are *Canarese* brought from *kanara* by a Peshwa & settled in Khirki. Similarly, *Kasar copper-smiths* of Nasik speak Gujarati at home & Marathi outside. The man dresses like Marathas, but women still wear traditional petticoat of Gujarat instead of Marathi sari. Both these cases of linguistic evidence point to *migration.* Nor do linguistic criteria throw any light on the question that *Mundas* and *Oraons,* two distinct tribes of identical Physical Type, speak languages which differ widely in structure and vocabulary.

## 1.3 Physical Characteristics and Race

For ethnological purposes physical characteristics are said to be of two types; Indefinite Characteristics, which can be described only, and; Definite Characteristics, which can be measured and reduced to numerical expressions.

**(a)  Indefinite Physical Characteristics:** Descriptive or secondary *characteristics* includes color & texture of skin; color, form & position of eyes; color & type of hair; form of face & features. It is extremely difficult to observe, define, & record these traits. Color is most striking of these but is the most evasive also. The skin, exhibits extreme divergence of colour which any one can detect at a glance. Starting with dead black Andamanese at one end, the other end is ivory skin of typical Kashmiri & very light transparent brown, "wheat-colored" of higher caste of upper India. But less variety is traceable in the eyes & hairs. From one end of India to other end, hair of most of the population is black or dark brown, except tawny shade of higher castes. Throughout India, eyes are invariably dark brown, except grey of Konkani Brahmins, & combination of blue eyes, auburn hair, reddish blonde complexion in north-western frontier.

**(b) Definite Physical Characteristics:** Definite characteristics are more authentic & firm ground for identifying a race. So, measurement of human body parts with a standard scale, usually expressed in terms of a particular part, of which rest are to be in multiples or in fractional parts of the entire stature. The Egyptian canon is based on the length of the middle finger with 19 times for full stature, the Greeks expresses limbs in 1000 parts and Roman in Vitruvius.

## 1.4 Measurements Methods for Definite Physical Characteristics

Measurement of the skull is most accurate & conclusive way to decide the racial characteristics (Bernard de Palissy). Anders Retzius (Swedish naturalist), founder of "craniometry" (science of measuring of skulls) suggested one of the chief characteristics of the skull by the relation of its maximum breadth to its maximum length, the latter as 1000 parts.

**(a) Measurement of Shapes of Skulls:** (1) Dolicho-cephalic or **long-headed**, in which the length exceeds the breadth by about one-fourth; (2) Brachy-cephalic or **short-headed**, in this length exceeds the breadth from one-fifth to one-eighth; and (3) Mesati-cephalic or **medium-headed** and ranging from 77.7 to 80%, between two diameters.

**(b) Measurement of Shapes of Face;** Mr Retzius based on measurements of faces classified races as; (1) The Orthognathic; jaws & teeth project either not at all, or very little beyond a line drawn from the forehead. (2) The Prognathic; in which, the above-mentioned projection is very clear and marked.

## 1.5 Application of classification to India

The caste system of India has remarkable variations of physical type, differences of grouping and social position. The process of fusion among Indian people has long been arrested. The physical characteristics of the groups are.

**(a) Shape of Head:** Form of the head is ascertained by measuring it in a horizontal plane; the greatest length from a definite point on the forehead to the back of the head, and the greatest breadth, a little above the ears. The proportion of breadth to length expressed as a percentage, is called the cephalic index; the length taken as100. Heads with index of 80 and above, are categorised as **broad or brachy-cephalic;** between 80-75, as **medium** heads (**mesati-cephalic**); index below 75 are called **long ordolicho-cephalic** heads.

**A test of Race:** The form of head is an extremely constant & persistent character, which *resists the effect of climate & physical surroundings, and* is *not liable to be modified by the action of artificial selection.* The intermixture of races of different head-forms will, affect the index, but it tends to revert to the original type when the effect of crossing is withdrawn. *The form of the head, especially when combined with other characters, is a good test of racial affinity.*

**Indian's Head Shape:** Indian are mainly *long-headed* people separated by Himalaya & from the broad-headed Mongolian people. *Broad-headed* are found in Assam & Burma on the east, and in varying degrees in the lower Himalayas & in a belt on the west coast of India extending from Gujarat through the Deccan to Coorg. *Long heads* predominate in Punjab, Rajputana, & United Province. *Medium heads* prevail in Bihar, but certain groups of Bengal (Muhammadans & Chandal's of East Bengal, Kayasths, & Bengali Brahmins) have distinct tendency towards *broad-head.* In south of Vindhya ranges, the prevalent type seems to be *mainly long or medium-headed, short-headed* appearing only in the western zone. Coastal areas are affected by foreign influence, Malay, or Indo-Chinese on the east, Arab, Persian, African, European, & the Jewish on the west. Thus, these mixed types cannot be brought under any general formula.

**(b) Shape of the Nose:** Indisputably accurate, Nasal index is measure of length & breadth from the specified points, expressed in percentage of the former. If a man's nose is as broad as long-his index is100.These are grouped in three types; *Narrow or fine noses* (leptorrhine) in which width is less than 70% of the length; the *medium noses* (mesorrhine) with an index between 70 to 85 %, and *broad noses* (platyrrhine) with proportion above 85%. A nose thus, represents very distinctly, the personal impression which a particular type looks to an observer, *like the broad nose of the Negro or of the typical Dravidian is his most striking feature.* For intermixed races with different nasal proportions, it records a large range of variations; & enables group types in a serial order corresponding to that suggested by other characters. *For these reasons the nasal index is accepted by all anthropologists as one of the best tests of racial affinity.*

**Grouping as per shape of Nose;** Generally, *broad type of nose* is most common in South, Central Provinces, Chhota Nagpur; *fine noses* are confined to Punjab & Baluchistan; population of the rest of India fall in *medium type.* Range of the index is very large & it varies from 123 to 53. The average nasal proportion of Mal Paharia tribe of Bengal is a 94.5, pastoral Gujars of Punjab 66.9, Sikhs of 68.8, & Bengali Brahmins & Kayasths of 70.4. *If pan-India castes, with finest nose at the top, coarser at the bottom, are arranged as per averaged nasal index, it will be found that this order substantially matches with the accepted order of social group prevailing in the society. Thus, the social status of the members of a particular group varies in the inverse ratio to the mean relative width of their noses.*

**(c) Shape of Face:** Measured by *Orbitonasal index,* is the percentage of distance between the two orbital dots measured in a direct line, forming the base of a triangle & the distance from each of these to the dot on the bridge of the nose as its two sides. If, the bridge of the nose is so low that it does not project beyond the level of the orbits, then the two sides will be equal & index is 100. If the elevation of bridge of nose is marked, the index may be as high127 to 130. This index is grouped into three; **Platyopic:** below 107.5, **Mesopic:** 107.5 to 110 and **Pro-opic:** above 110.

In case of India these are; *Platyopic:* below 110, *Mesopic:* between; 110 to 112. 9, *Pro-opic:* 113 and above. A comparative flat Mongolian face is a peculiarity which cannot fail to strike even to a casual observer as it is connected with the formation of cheek-bone, margins of the bony sockets of the eyes, & the root of the nose.

**(d) Statures in India:** As per Topinard; 4 categories are: *Tall Stature*; 170 cm (5'7") & more, *above Average*; 165cm (5' 5"), & under; 170cm (5'7"), *below Average*; 160 cm (5' 3") & under 165 cm (5' 5"), & *small stature*; 160 cm (5' 3").

The stature is affected by; climate, soil, elevation, food supply, habits of life, occupation, and natural or artificial selection. The influence of city life, tends to reduce the stature & produces physical degeneracy, but is comparatively small in India, where 50 to 80 % of the population is engaged in agriculture and lives an outdoor life. The Hill dwellers are generally shorter than the people of the plains. Within the hill region it may in either case be observed that stature is often greater at high than at moderate altitude–a factor ascribed to the downstream.

## 1.6 Race Vs Caste Vs Ethnicity Vs Culture

Race; A Race, is an ascribed status, and biologically inherited. It is grouping of humans based on shared physical traits like nasal index, hair texture, skin color, shape of head, & face etc.

Caste; A caste originates from tribes, & tribes consist of different races. Due to lot of cross or inbreeding & intermixing Indians are completely different in appearance though their skull is Caucasoid. But still SC, ST & OBC are distinguishable as they contain less ANI (Ancestral North Indian) gene, in SC/ST it is still less. So, there is distinct difference in appearance as compared to General (almost all cases), even it is evident in psychology & behaviour also.

Ethnicity; It refers to factors like food habits, regional culture, common ancestry, or physical attributes & language.

Culture; Culture is a social behaviour or customary traditions of social life style being followed by the people.

* * * * *

# Chapter-2. The Origin of Castes

## 2.1 The word Caste and Definition

The word 'Caste' is not of Indian origin, but derived from the Latin 'Castus,' meaning purity of blood, & in India 1st time it was coined by Portuguese. It came from Portuguese adventurers who came with Vasco-de-Gama to the West Coast of India at Kozhikode Kerala in 1498. "The ancient Indian system of classification of society was *Varna* system & Jaati, but not the caste. Caste 1st time was created in 1881 census by Ibbetson. (Ref; H Risley "People of India," PP 67)

(a) As per Herbert Risley; "A caste is a group of families having a common ancestor:(human or divine); same hereditary; regarded as a single homogeneous community." Generally, is associated with a specific occupation also. (ibid68)

(b) As per M. Emile Senart: "It is a close corporation; with a chief & a council; observing common rituals relating to marriage, food; ruling its members by power of final or revocable exclusion authority of the community." (ibid68 & 69)

## 2.2 Transformation of Tribes into Castes

Ethnographic survey describes the singular course of evolution by which a large mass of people surrendered their comparative freedom & took in exchange a caste having more bindings as its status is higher. Several such distinct processes, which happened independently in different places & times, are as below. (ibid72 to 75)

(a) **By Self-Declaration**: Somehow few tribe men, became independent land owners, managed to enrol as Rajput, institute a Brahmin priest, who invents for them a mythical ancestor, arms with a family miracle, & declare they belong to a some hitherto unheard-of clan of great Rajput. Initially they face difficulty in marriages of their females as they will not marry them in their original tribe, but after a generation or two they inter-marry, if not with pure Rajputs, at least with manufactured ones. (Ex. *Nagbansi Rajputs of Chhota Nagpur,* who trace their origin from the *Takshak Raja,* the king of snakes)

(b) **By Adoption**: When a group embraces a particular tenet of Hinduism, & becomes *Vaishnavas, Lingayat,* etc. Whether there is any mixture of blood or not will depend upon local circumstances & the rules of the sect regarding inter-marriage. Such cases are actually absorption as identity of the converts is invariably lost.

**(c) By Mass Enrolment**: When a tribe enrol under a new caste, claim an origin of antiquity, & is readily distinguishable from any of the recognized castes. The Kochh inhabitants of Jalpaiguri, Rangpur, & part of Dinajpur tell them as Rajbansis or Bhanga-Kshatriya (To escape wrath of Parshu-Ram fled to Northeast Bengal; claim descent from Raja Dasharath).

**(d) By Mass Conversion**: A whole tribe without abandoning their tribal titles convert to Hinduism, like Bhumij of west Bengal, who lost their original language & now speaks only Bengali; worship Hindu Gods in addition to their own & the more advance among them employ Brahmins as family priests. (Now they are a caste in full sense, & has stopped all customs of its true descent. Their physical characteristics only survive. Now they are more strictly endogamous than they were as a tribe.)

**(e) By mutability of caste**: When a Brahmin, a Pujari, or Levites, drops his sacerdotal character, stops to receive alms, and becomes a cultivator, he ceases to be a Brahmin, and he also has to employ other Brahmins as priest e.g., Taga Brahmins. Similarly, a Mahajan is so long till he is a Merchant, but a Kayasth when he becomes a clerk.

## 2.3 Types of Castes

By a variety of complex social forces, whose working & processes, cannot be precisely traced, a number of and types of castes as given below have formed.

**(a) Tribal type caste**: A tribe; Bhumij, convert into a caste, preserving its original name & its characteristic customs, but modifying, its animistic practices & ordering its manner of life in tune to that of Hinduism. (ibid75)

**(b) Occupational type caste**: Almost every caste has a traditional occupation, though many of its members might have abandoned it, but the adoption of new occupations may give rise to sub-divisions of the caste which ultimately develop into entirely distinct castes. (Ex. Ahirs as herdsmen; Chamar & Mochi leather workers etc.) (ibid76)

**(c) Sectarian type castes**: Few having evolved some metaphysical ways for a speedier relief from the *taedium vitae* became *religious sects*, but as the time passed, found their group unduly heterogeneous. So, faced with practical difficulties in realising their ideals, reorganised them on the lines of an ordinary caste. Example; *Lingayat* community, founded as a sect, developed into an endogamous sub-castes based upon the social distinctions which their founder had expressly abjured. Another examples; Jogi, Bishnois & Sadhs of the United Provinces. (ibid78)

**(d) Castes formed by Crossings**: The castes; which were compact or had the distinction between fishing & hunting, agriculture & handicrafts, were supposed to have evolved by cross or inter-breeding. A man may marry a woman of another tribe; the offspring of such unions do not become members of the either group, but a distinct endogamous aggregate, the name of which often denotes the precise cross by which it was started. Nine tribe of Mundas; Khangar-Munda, Kharia-Munda, Konkpat-Munda, Karanga-Munda, Mahili-Munda, Nagbansi-Munda, Oraon-Munda, Sad-Munda, Savar-Munda; all from inter-marriages between Munda men & women of other tribes. (More examples; Khas of Nepal; offspring of the marriages between Rajputs or Brahmins immigrants with native women, the Rajbansi Barua's of Chittagong; believed to be offspring of Burmese father & Bengali mothers, the Vidurs of the Central Provinces; claim Brahmin parentage on male side, though now marrying among themselves, still admit children of mixed union between Brahmin & women of other caste into their community, and the Boria caste in Nowgaon district of Assam, who are offspring of Brahmin & Ganak widows & their descendants, and the female child of Brahmins who attained puberty before marriage, and so, as per tradition had to be married to men of lower caste. Boria is derived from Bari, a widow, but prefer to call them *Sut* or *Suta*; Shastric designation of the children of a Brahmin woman by a Kshatriya or a Vaisya father). (ibid82 to 86)

**(e) National Castes:** The history & traditions of Marathas stamp them as a national caste. "Marathas," have two divisions; Maratha & Maratha Kunbi-the formers are hypergamous to the latter, but were not originally distinct. Kunbi consists of two divisions, Desh Kunbi & Konkani Kunbi; inter-marriages between these are not usual. The highest class of Marathas consist of 96 Gotra/kulas, & claims Kshatriyas Rajput descent. (They wear sacred thread, marry their daughter before puberty, & forbid widow re-marriage. Their Rajput claim is refuted by anthropometric data & by the practice of worship of Kuldevta/Totems, such as sun-flower, Kadam & mango tree, conch shell, peacock feather, & turmeric, during marriages & house-warming ceremony. Paradox is that they take Kunbi girl as wife, but do not give their daughters to Kunbi men. A wealthy Kunbi, however can gain promotion as Kshatriya & marry into higher grade.) Similarly, Newars (both Hindu & Buddhists) of Nepal, were a national caste & dominant race until it was conquered by Gurkha Prithvi Narayan in 1768.) (ibid86-88)

**(f) Castes formed by Migration:** Some members of a caste, who settle permanently in another part have tendency to detach from the parent group. It is assumed they eat forbidden food; worship alien gods, & enters into relations with strange women. Consequent to this, when they wish to take wives from their parent group, they find their social status lowered, & they have to pay heavily for marrying. With the passage of time this becomes unaffordable; emigrants start marrying among themselves & thus becomes a sub-caste distinguished by territorial name, such as Jaunpuria etc.

Ex; Nambudiri Brahmins of Malabar; who came to west coast from Kathiawar & Northern Deccan. (a separate caste now, different from Brahmins of other parts of India, as they practice of polygamy; no infant marriage; restrict marriage to eldest son, other brothers entering into polyandrous relations with Nair women, & custom of ceremonial fishing as part of their marriage rituals). Owing to this loss of identity, the instances of formation of caste by migration is comparatively small. But occasionally social promotion, rather than degradation also can happen. (In Chanda district of Central Provinces, the helot weavers & basket makers wrote them as Barwaiks, it being unknown in census office, was referred to district officer for clarification, who replied; Barwaiks is a clan of Rajputs from Odisha who had come to Nagpur with Bhosle Raja in military service). (ibid88-92)

**(g) Castes formed by changes of customs:** The neglect of established or adoption of new customs or secular occupations, has been the main reasons from the earliest times for formation of a new caste. As per Manusmriti, the men of three higher Varna, if do not receive sacrament of initiation at proper time or who follows forbidden occupations, becomes Vratyas or Outcastes. (Ex. Tyagi & Babhans or Bhuinhars of United Province & Bihar, supposed to be Brahmins; lost their status by taking to Agriculture). Similarly, Chauhan Rajputs of Delhi, Gaurwa Rajputs of Delhi & Gurgaon, for all purpose of equality, or inter-marriage, ceased to be Rajputs due to the practice of widow-marriage. *A crucial test of relative social position between others martial castes & Rajputs is; former practise Karewa but later do not.* (ibid92-94)

**(h) Castes formed by political stature:** In Panjab there is tradition among Jats & Gujars that they descended from Rajputs who married below them, stopped to seclude their women, or began to practice widow re-marriage. So, one & same tribe is Rajput where it has, & Jat where it has not risen to political prominence. (Ref; Panjab Castes; D Ibbetson, PP-6)

**(i) Castes modified by Rajas;** It has been habitually modified by the action of Rajas, who claimed the right of promoting or demoting members of various castes, as per the faithfulness of a particular group/tribe.

## 2.4 Origin of the Caste System

The Indian tradition as to the origin of caste is so widely diffused; it forms so large a part of the working consciousness of the Hindus that it can hardly be ignored merely because it has no foundation in facts. It is indeed a fact in itself which has played, continues to play, a large part in shaping of Indian society. (ibid257 to 277)

(a) **The Indian theory:** Tenth chapter of Manusmriti tells, how the *Anima Mundi* (supreme universal inconceivable soul), *"produced by a golden egg, in which "He Himself was born as Brahma, the progenitor of the whole world".* Then, "for the sake of the prosperity of the world, He created Brahmin, Kshatriya, Vaisya, & Sudra and allotted them their distinctive duties. Brahmin was enjoined to study, teach, & receive alms; the Kshatriya to protect the people & abstain from sensual pleasures; the Vaisya to tend cattle, trade, lend money, and to cultivate land; the Sudra to serve the three higher groups. (The classification in this book of dharma, for regulating & guiding the social and spiritual life of Hindus, was strictly as per the division of the labour and in no way as per the birth of the person as propagated and believed).

Starting from this basis of Manusmriti, the standard Indian tradition proceeds to trace the evolution of the caste (Jaati) system from a series of crosses, 1st between members of 4 main Varnas & then between descendants of these initial unions. (The men of 3 higher groups may marry women of any of the group below them. If the wife belonged to the group just next in order, the children took her rank, & *no new caste is formed.* But if mother is from a group further lower down in the Varna, her children belonged neither to her group, nor to father, *but formed a distinct new caste.* Ex; son of a Brahmin by a Vaish woman is an Ambastha; bestowed with art of healing, while if mother is a Shudra-the son is a Nishad; must live by killing fish). *The son of a Kshatriya father & Shudra mother is, "an Ugra, resembling both, a Kshatriya, & a Shudra, ferocious in his manners & delighting in cruelty."* All above cases are unions of anulom or "in the hierarchy," as father is of higher rank than mother. Unions of Pratilom or against hierarchy are wherein woman belongs to higher group, & man to a lower group. The extreme instance of this is a *Chandal; son of a Shudra by a Brahmin woman;* who is described as "that lowest of the mortals," condemned to live outside the village, to wear cloths of Dead, to eat from broken dishes, execute criminals, & to carry the corpses of the destitute. Similarly, the *Ayogavas,* from a Shudra father, & a Kshatriya mother, are branded as wicked who eat reprehensible food. Unions between the descendants of these first crosses produce among others, the Sairandhra, skilled in adorning his master, & pursues occupation of; the art of snaring animals; and "the sweet voiced Maitreyak, who ring the bell at dawn to raise the great man.) (ibid258-259)

**(b) The Historic elements:** It is small wonder that European critics were so impressed by the intricate complex structure & characteristics of this unique social evolution, that some of them made a mistake of putting it aside without further examination, branding it a mere figment of the systematizing intellect of the ingenious Brahmins. But fantastically it opens indirectly & unconsciously an instructive glimpse of pre-historic society in India. It shows that when Manu's treatise was compiled, there existed an elaborate & highly developed social system including tribal or national groups like the Magadha, Vaideha, Malla, Licchvi etc; the functional groups such as Ambastha; the physicians, the Suta; the charioteers, the Nishad; boatman etc. (ibid259-260)

**(c) Process of Caste Making:** The Inter-marriages under hypergamy represent castes in the making. Few families discover some quality of social distinction, refuse to give their daughters in marriage to other members of their caste, but continue to take wives. After a time when they have enough women for a jus connubii of their own, they close their ranks, marry only among themselves; pose as a superior sub-caste of their main caste. Lastly, they break-off all links with parent stock, assume a new distinct caste name; e.g., educated Pods of Bengal. (ibid263)

**(d) Denzil Ibbotson's theory:** As per hypothesis in his book 'Punjab Castes' followings are the steps in the process of evolution of caste; The tribal divisions common to all primitive societies; the guilds based upon hereditary occupations common to the middle life of all communities; the exaltation of the priestly office, & of the Levitical blood by a special insistence upon the necessarily hereditary nature of occupation; and the preservation & support of this principle by a set of rules, regulating marriages & intermarriages, declaring certain occupations and foods to be impure and polluting, and prescribing the conditions and degree of social intercourse permitted between various castes.(ibid263-64)

**(e) Herbert Risley's Theory:** A caste in its modern, rigid form is of comparatively recent origin? The older Varna system & customs, for instance, recognised the possibility of a Kshatriya becoming Brahmin, or vice-versa; and although a man was supposed to take his 1$^{st}$ wife from his own class, but there was no binding rule to this effect, while in any case he was free to take 2$^{nd}$ wife from lower class.

**(f) Nesfield Theory:** He assumes; the Aryan race was absorbed by the indigenous population completely as the Portuguese of Goa have been absorbed into Indians. The homogenous people thus formed are divided by Nesfield into seven groups (121 castes), as enumerated in the census of 1881;

| 7 Groups for distributing 121 castes of Agra & Oudh of United Province | |
| --- | --- |
| I. Casteless Tribes | III. Artisan Castes |
| II. Castes connected with lands | A. Preceding Metallurgy |
| A. Allied to hunting state | B. Coeval with Metallurgy |
| B. Allied to Fishing state | IV. trading castes |
| C. Allied to Pastoral state | V. Serving castes |
| D. Agricultural | VI. Priestly castes |
| E. Landlords and Warriors | VII. Religious Orders |

(The function only was the basis on which caste system of India was build up. The order of groups is determined by the principle that, "each caste represents one or other of those progressive stages of culture with marked industrial development. The rank of any caste was dependent upon whether the industry represented by it is an advance or backward stage of culture. Thus, the natural history of human industries affords the chief clue to the gradations as well as to the formation of Indian castes"). (ibid265-66)

**(g) M. Emile Senart Theory:** As in 'The Tribes and Castes of Bengal,' "a caste is the normal development of ancient Aryan institutions, which assumed this form in the struggle to adapt themselves to the conditions with which they came into contact in India". In developing this proposition, he relies mainly upon the general parallelism that may be traced between the social organisation of Hindus and that of the Greeks & Romans in the earlier stages of their national development. He points out close similarities that exist between the three series of group in r.o. family, it's gotra & caste. (He puts forward the records of classical antiquity that the leading principles which underlie the caste system forms part of a stock of usage and tradition common to all branches of *Aryan people i.e., Roman, Greeks and Indians,* in almost all respect of marriage, social customs, jus-connubii or hypergamous rights, food habits and acceptance/prohibition of it from other castes, funeral feasts even the shraddha, way of expulsion from caste etc). (ibid267-68)

* * * * *

# Chapter-3. Proverbs and Popular Sayings on Castes

## 3.1 Definitions

A 'proverb' is a short saying that is widely used to express an obvious truth but it is brief, simple, & popular saying, that gives advice & effectively embodies a common place truth based on practical experience or common sense. Few essential features of the proverbs are: brevity, their bearing on the practical conduct of every-day life, & these are in the local dialect. John Russell says, a proverb is, *"The wisdom of many & wit of one."* Mr Borchart, a German also says, a proverb is a saying current among the people in popular language, with studied brevity, a truth of all. 'Proverbs' on the other hands are vulgar, for the common man, whom, "One meets in all ranks of the society." A modern writer impressed by the brevity & the heartless tone of many proverbs describes them as, *"the algebra of materialism."* However, to call it, the algebra of "Popular Pessimism" is nearer to truth. (Ref; "People of India H Risley–PP 128 to 153)

## 3.2 General and Particular Proverbs

There are many proverbs, which contains a truth of general application which holds good for all times & stands its ground in the face of social change and political or economic revolutions. Such proverbs are based on universal experience and embody the common-sense of mankind. Their form may differ, but the underlying idea is everywhere the same & everywhere has given rise spontaneously to some telling phrases. Like British proverb, *"To carry Coals to Newcastle"*, figures in delicate irony of the Greeks as *"Owls to Athens"*, and in India, *"Ultey Bans Bareilly ko"*, *"उल्टे बाँस बरेली को"!* The saying in which it is summed up is colored by the spirit of the time when these were coined & of the nation which produced them. They hold good for their place of origin, but not for the whole world.

## 3.3 Proverbs and Sayings on few selected Castes

An exhaustive list of proverbs and Sayings about majority of the Indian castes are detailed in book 'People of India', by H Risley (ibid128 to153 & Appendix-I ibid 305 to 333). One finds a truth of universal experience rendered in terms of caste relations, and it bears witness to the supremacy of the caste sentiments in India & the prominent place it occupies in the daily life of the people. Proverbs and

Sayings relating to almost all the castes are covered in the above book except few castes like; Rors, Kambohs, Saini etc. Proverbs & Sayings relating to few selected Panjab castes as extracted from chapter-III, & appendix-I of book, 'People of India', and on Ror caste as prevalent in society & also given in book-Clarification to Unification & Ror Udbhav evam Vikas, are as below;

**(a) Brahmin (Priest):** A very popular saying is; "A Chaube set out to become a Chhabbe! But returned as a Dube"!! The irony of the saying is directed at the ignorant Brahmin, who wants to know six Vedas whereas there are only four Vedas. There are many more such proverbs & sayings, for which interested readers can refer the book, People of India, by Herbert Risley, who formally listed the Caste System of India 1st time in modern times. (ibid 130 & 305 to 307)

**(b) Baniya (Money-Lender):** Few Sayings; A proverb of impossible: A Baniya is no one's friend, if he takes a walk, it is only for gain. If a Baniya's son tumbles down, he is sure to pick something. A Baniya's terms are indefinite as he says one thing at night & another in the morning. For more sayings refer (ibid 131, & 311-313)

**(c) Rajput (Warrior and Landholder):** Few Sayings are; Grudge not the Ghee; the horse will be useful in battle (Rajput's answer to his wife: when she demurred to his wasting Ghee on his horse, instead of grass). He starves himself but keeps a Bhat to sing his exploits at his door: Rajput pride. There is no end to clans of Rajputs and the varieties of rice. The Baghel & the Gohel are the two fiercest clans of Rajputs. For more ref (ibid308)

**(d) Jat (Landowner and cultivator):** A Jat's baby has a plough - handle to play with. The Jat stood on his corn-heap and called out to king's Mahavats, "Hi, there, what you will take for those little donkeys?" Another Saith the Jat, "Listen wife, as we got to live in this village: if the folk says a cat walked away with a camel, we must chime in." refer (ibid 309-10)

**(e) Gujar (Minor Landowner and cultivator):** There is a saying, "A Gujar's daughter is a box of Gold." (The bride-price is high among Gujars). Sense for a Gujar: a sheath for a harrow (Two impossibilities). In no man's land one makes friend with Gaddis & Gujars. for more refer (ibid317)

**(f) Ror (Minor Landowner & cultivator):** Like other cultivators & landowning castes,Rors have proverbs like; "Kahin ki Int Kahin ka Rora, Bhanumati ne Kunba Joda", Appears to have emanated due to so many surnames. (ref page-(xv) preface of book, "Ror Udbhav and Vikas" by Dr Surinder Singh Kadian). Another is "Rode ki Marod, not willing to yield, even after requests & cajoling.

Another prevalent is, "Rode Handi Fod". It means spilling the beans to reveal the secret for the better cause., even fully knowing that it may even invite trouble for him. This shows how dare-devil they are. (It appears to have some historical background of restoration of Kota/ Bundi principality in 1342 AD, wherein how the Rors (consisting of Hurda, Khichi, Maniyal, Thardak, Bodle,) & few others from the stock of Bundi & Kota, helped to retain principality, & came to be known as "Handi Fod". (Ref: Col Tod; Annals of Rajasthan Vol-II, PP-373 to 374 footnotes no; 3: sub ref: para 26, page; 66 to 68 of book;Clarification to unification; Major: M.S. Keshwar (Retd)). Another proverb about Rors is, "Rode ki Naa",. That is; once a Ror says, 'NO', He means 'NO', he sticks to it and does not change, come what may. It's a sort of obstinacy (Hath). (This appears to have sprung from the premise that Rors are Guhilas of Mewad, wherein a word once uttered or promise made, cannot be taken back / compromised, come what may. Also might have emanated from the 'NO' Dola to Aibak in 1208. Two more instances of this; Obstinacy of Rawal Chanda of Chittor on the sally (a witty remark) by his own father for not marrying princess of Mandore; and another is obstinacy of Korma Devi, daughter of Chief of Mahillas / Mohillas Manik Rao of Nagore, who married, 'Sadoo', son of the chief of Jaisalmer, instead of betrothed prince of Mandore).(Ref: ibid;Annals of Rajasthan Vol-I, Page; 223 to 224; sub ref: para 34 page 86 to 88 of book Clarification to unification).

* * * * *

# Chapter-4. Punjab Castes and Rors

## 4.1 Category of castes

This section describes the castes found in Panjab as enumerated in the Census-1881. Mr Denzil has grouped the castes in four categories e.g., (1) The Jats, Rajputs, and allied Castes; (2) The Minor Land-Owning and Agricultural Castes; (3) Religious, Professional, Mercantile and Miscellaneous Castes; and (4) Vagrant, Menial and Artisan castes. Few related castes vis-a-vis Rors are described briefly herein. (NB.1. Number within the bracket after the caste is the serial number assigned by the enumerator in the census tables. 2.This chapter is an extract of 'Panjab Castes' by D Ibbetson; pp-97to163)

## 4.2 The Jat, Rajputs, and Allied Castes

Abstract no.71 of census 1881 details their distribution. The distinction between Jats & Rajputs in many parts is so indefinite, that their separate figures had no significance & they together constituted nearly 28 % of total population.

(1) **The Jat** (Sno.1); The details of origin of Jat race, is found in; ASI Report, vol-II, (pp 51-61); Tod's 'Rajasthan', vol-I, (pp 52 -75 & 96-101; Madras reprint; 1880); Elphinstone's History of India, (pp 250-253); & Elliot's Races of NWP, vol-I, (pp130 -137). For more details on Jats & their tribes; refer paras 421 to 440, part-III-The Jat, Rajputs, and Allied Castes of Panjab Castes (ibid97 to 131). Socially *Jats* occupy a position which is shared *by Rors, Gujars, & Ahirs*; in fact, all four eat & smoke Hukka together. They stand at the head of castes that practice *Karewa/ widow-marriage*. (ibid103)

**The Jats tribe of south-eastern districts:** Jats of Jamuna districts, Jind, Rohtak, & Hisar, are of slightly finer physique. They are mostly Hindu; few Musalman are known as "Mulla." They *have come either from Bikaner or Rajputana, or northwards* along the Jamuna valley. Very few of them appear to have come from Panjab to the Jamuna. (ibid126)

**Main clans: Ghatwal:** Claim descent from Saroha Rajputs, headquarter; Ahulana in Gohana; **Dagar:** numerous in Delhi & Gurgaon, small colony in Rohtak.; **Jakhar & Sangwan:** Said to be descended from a Chauhan Rajput of Bikaner; 20 generations back; 4 sons founded Jakhar, Sangwan, Piru, & Kadiyan Jats; **Sahrawat:** Claims descent from Sahra; a son or grandson of Raja Anangpal Tunwar; confined to Delhi, Gurgaon, Rohtak from 25 generations back, & Patiala territory; **Dahiya:** Claims descent from a Chauhan Rajput Manik Rai (founder of Hansi); by a Dhankhar Jat wife; found on NE of Sampla & Sonipat tehsil;

**Golia:** Claims originally Brahmins of Indore; 30 generations ago; lost caste by inadvertently drinking liquor from gol kept outside a distiller's house; found in Rohtak, & Karnal only; **Rathi:** Claim origin from Tunwar Rajputs; found in Delhi, Gurgaon & Rohtak; **Khatri:** found in Delhi, Rohtak & Patiala; **Dalal:** Descent from a Rathor Rajput & a Bargujar Jat wife; 30 generations back; had 4 sons from whom Dalal, Deswal, Maan, & Sehwag Jats sprung; found around Delhi, Rohtak, Hisar; **Ahlawat:** Descent from a Chauhan Rajput of Sambar; 30 generations ago; Sprang Ahlawat, Olian, Birma, Mare, & Joon Jats; do not intermarry; found in Rohtak, Delhi,& Karnal; **Deswal:** or, "men of the country", sprung from Dalal stock; are numerous in Rohtak, Gurgaon, & Karnal; **Dhankhar:** of same stock as Rathi; almost confined to Jhajjar in Rohtak; **Phogat:** Found in Jind, & portions of Gurgaon & Rohtak; do not inter-marry with Deswal; **Sangwan:** Claim descent from Jakhar ancestor; head-quarter in Jind; also found in Rohtak & Hisar; **Pawania:** A Hisar tribe, also found in Rohtak, Sirsa, Jind, portion of Patiala, & Ambala; **Bahniwal:** Found in Hisar division, Patiala, & Montgomery; claim Bhatti Rajputs by descent; had given much trouble in 1857; and **Nain:** Found in Patiala, Hisar & Dehli. (ibid127 to 131)

(2) **The Rajput** (Sno.2); Broadly a tribe of any caste, which had in ancient time supreme power throughout any fairly extensive tract of country, would be classed as Rajput. The distribution as shown in abstract no.71 of the census-1881 is almost same all-over Northern India. More has been published about them than any other Indian caste. Tod's Annals and Antiquity of Rajasthan is the master piece. Rajputs of Panjab are fine brave men; retain their feudal instinct more strongly than any other non-menial caste. The tribe heads wield extraordinary authority. They are very tenacious of the integrity of their property in the village land, seldom admit strangers to share it with them. *Pride of blood, being the essence of their Rajput hood, is their strongest characteristics.* They are lazy & poor husbandmen; prefer pastoral to agriculture pursuits, look upon all manual labour as derogatory & the ploughing as degrading; it is *only the poorest class of Rajputs who himself ploughs.* They, in most parts of the Panjab plains, *are* cattle-stealers by ancestral profession; but they exercise their calling in a gentlemanly way, as there is honour among Rajput thieves. (ibid131-132)

**Main tribes of Rajputs: Tunwar:** Gave India Vikramaditya; & Delhi its last Hindu ruler Anangpal (founder of Delhi on the ruins of Indraprastha in 792 AD). When ejected from Delhi, settled at Pundri in Karnal, once the seat of Pundirs, and then spread to both north & south. **Chauhan:** One of the agnikula tribes; moved to Delhi & Ajmer from Sāmbhar near Jaipur; on ejection from Delhi, moved to Sambhal in Moradabad-UP; their central village is Jundla in Karnal; occupy all the tract lying immediately to the east of Tunwar tract in Ambala, Karnal & adjoining part of Patiala, Nabha, & Jind; which was held by the Pundir

Rajputs till the Chauhans migrated from Sambhal under **Rana Har Rai** some 20 generation ago, probably in Bahlol Lodi's time, & drove the Pundir across Jumna. **Mandahar:** came from Ajodhya to Jind; driven out Chandel & Bra Rajputs from the tract into the Shivalik & across the Ghaggar respectively; were almost confined to Nardak of Karnal, Ambala, & part of Patiala; their capital was Kalayat in Patiala, with minor centres at Safidon in Jind & Asandh in Karnal; and more recently spread down the Jumna riverain of Karnal district, with Gharaunda as local centre. **Pundir:** Dahima race, a most powerful vassals of *Chauhans* of Delhi, commanded the Lahore frontier for Prithvi Raj Chauhan, original seat was Thanesar/ Kurukshetra & Ambala, with local capitals at Pundri, Rambha, Habari, & Pundrak. **Gaurwa & Gaur:** Rajput kings of Bengal belonged to it & found in the central Jumna-Ganges doab. **Bargujar:** claims descent from Luv son of Shriram, old capital was Rajor, the ruins of which are still to be seen in the south of Alwar, held Alwar, & the neighbouring part of the Jaipur till displaced by Kachhwaha. **Jadu:** or Jadubansi of lunar race, "the most illustrious of all the tribes of India, by Tod. Bhatti is their dominant branch. **Jatu:** Tunwar of Haryana are divided into 3 clans from 3 brothers; Jatu, Raghu, & Satraula. Jatu were largest & most important, who ruled from Bhiwani to Agroha. **Bagri:** Bagri is Bhatti or Rathore Rajput, south west of Sirsa & Hisar. **Baria:** Confined to Patiala & Nabha; Suryavanshi Rajputs; claim descent from Raja Karan of Mahabharata. **Rathor:** Solar Rajputs; old seat Kanauj, but their modern dynasties are found in Marwar & Bikaner, are in many districts in Panjab, but not numerous. (ibid135 to139)

**Rajput tribes of the western Plains:** Rajputs tribes in this part have spread up the river as conquerors. Abstract 80, shows their distribution. **Punwar:** A Agnikula Rajputs; found in whole tract of Satluj, along lower Indus, had spread along the Beas into Jalandhar & Gurdaspur also; are plenty in Rohtak & Hisar; once held the entire Rohtak, Dadri, & Gohana. **Bhatti:** A Jadubansi, lunar race, founded Jaisalmer; their territory greatly circumscribed after the advent of Rathors. Sirsa; adjoining Hisar etc was known as Bhattiana; as it was their abode. (ibid139-144)

**Rajput tribes of the Satluj; Wattu:** Raja Junhar of Bhatner, a descendant of Bhatti raja Salvahan of Sialkot, had 2 sons Achal & Batera; formers had 2 sons; Jaipal ancestor of Bhatti proper, & Rajpal of Wattu; from the latter sprang Sidhu & Brar Jats. **Joya:** "the Lords of the Jungle-desh," comprising of Haryana, Bhattiana, Bhatner, & Nagore. **Khichi:** a Chauhan clan originally from Ajmer, then to Delhi; to lower & middle Satluj during Mughal rule, along Ravee from Multan to Lahore; few along Chenab, & considerable in Dehli district. (ibid145-146)

**(3) The Castes Allied to the Rajputs: Thakkar, Rathi, and Rawat** (S no. 60, 39, & 82); Thakurs & Rathi are the lowest class of Hill Rajputs who though are admittedly Rajputs, give their daughters to Rajputs, however do not reach the standard which would entitle them to be called Rajputs, but are above Rawat. *Rathi's do but Thakkar's do not practice widow marriage.* (ibid98-99)

## 4.3 Minor Land-Owning and Agricultural Castes

In this category Denzil has roughly grouped the tribes & castes into three heads; (a) Minor Land-owning Dominant Tribes, (b) Minor Agricultural, and (c) Pastoral Tribes & Foreign Races, & described as below. (1st group includes caste/tribes which were not so numerous or of general importance as to rank with 4 main races, yet occupied a social position somewhat similar to theirs, & either are or have been politically dominant in their tribal territories The 2nd group includes those cultivating tribes who though are very large & important element in the agricultural sector, but occupy a subordinate position, & have not risen to political prominence. The 3rd group includes misc. assorted titles; Shekh or Mughal, which are of foreign origin). (ibid164 to 213)

(1) **Minor Land-Owning Dominant Tribes:** The tribes or castes, which are like Rajputs & Jats, dominant in parts of Panjab, but are not so numerous or of general importance as to rank with 4 main races, yet occupied a social position somewhat similar to theirs,& either are or in recent times have been *politically dominant in their territories*, & divided into 4 groups are; Karral, Gakkhar, Awan, & Khattar of salt–range tract; Khokhar, Kharal, Daudpotra of western plains; & *Dogar,* **Ror, Taga***, Meo, Khanzadah of Eastern Plains*; while **Gujar,** who are more widely distributed than the rest, comes in the last. A part abstract as below indicates the strength of Rors. (ibid166 to 67)

| Part Abstract no; 83; Showing Distribution of Minor Dominant Tribe of Eastern Plains in Districts and states; Ror Caste | | | | | | | | | | | | |
|---|---|---|---|---|---|---|---|---|---|---|---|---|
| Dist./states | Figures-census 1881 | | | | | % Population per 1000 of total population | | | | | | |
| Caste S. No | 46 | 55 | 86 | 34 | 8 | 46 | 55 | 86 | 34 | Total | 8 | G. Total |
| Caste Name | Dogar | Ror | Taga | Meo | Gujar | Dogar | Ror | Taga | Meo | | Gujar | |
| **Delhi** | 48 | **666** | 9954 | 9567 | 25836 | -- | 1 | 15 | 15 | 31 | 40 | 71 |
| Gurgaon | -- | -- | 140 | 103678 | 20955 | -- | -- | -- | 161 | 167^ | 33 | 200 |
| **Karnal** | 1960 | **34094** | 4162 | 351 | 21898 | 3 | 55 | 7 | 1 | 66 | 35 | 101 |
| **Ambala** | 1417 | **4861** | 4 | 889 | 51077 | -- | 4 | -- | 1 | 5 | 48 | 53 |
| **Ludhiana** | 2214 | **26** | -- | 9 | 30759 | 4 | ? | -- | -- | 4 | 50 | 54 |
| British Territory 1 | 49338@ | **39467** | 14305 | 115899 | 553417@ | 3 | 2 | 1 | 6 | 12 | 29 | 41 |
| **Patiala** | 8475 | **36** | -- | 62 | 35359 | 6 | -- | -- | -- | 6 | 24 | 30 |
| **Jind** | 189 | 1048 | -- | 6 | 1740 | 1 | 4 | -- | -- | 5 | 7 | 12 |
| Total East Plain 2 | 14095 | 1084 | -- | 828# | 55872$ | 6 | -- | -- | -- | 6 | 22 | 28 |
| Total Hills-3 | 4 | -- | -- | -- | 17445 | -- | -- | -- | -- | -- | 23 | 23 |
| **Total 1+2+3** | 63437 | **40731** | 14305 | 116227 | 626734 | 3 | 2 | 1 | 5 | 11 | 18 | 2 |

Legends: @ Includes population in many other districts of Rohtak, Hisar, Sirsa, Jalandhar, Hosiarpur Gurdaspur, Amritsar, Lahore, Rawalpindi, Multan, Jhang, Hazra & many more–see details in original table; # Includes 374 Nabha+335 Faridkot+25 Kalsia; $ Includes Gujars of Nabha: 5456+ Kapurthala: 5805+ Faridkot: 645+Malerkotla: 2376+Kalsia: 4491; and ^ Includes 6 % Caste no.123 Khanzadah of this group which has not been shown in the part abstract table.

**The Ror** (Caste S.No. 55); (*Verbatim as in census 1881 report*) The real seat of Panjab Rors is in the great Dhak Jungles south of Thanesar on the border of Karnal & Ambala districts, where they hold a Chaurasi (84), of which the AMIN village, where Pandavs are said to have arranged their forces before their last fight with Kauravs, is the Tika or Head village (*Never heard & not true?*). *But Rors have spread down into the lower parts of Karnal & into Jind district in considerable numbers. They are also said to hold 12 villages beyond Yamuna and Ganges in UP.*

The Rors, are fine stalwart men, of very much the same type as the Jats, whom they almost equal as husbandmen, their women also work in the fields on equal footings. They are more peaceful and less grasping in their habits than the Jats, and are consequently readily admitted as tenants whereas the latter would be kept at arm's length.

Of their origin Mr Denzil Ibbetson, say nothing certain. He says that, "They have the same story as the Aroras, of them having been Rajputs who escaped fury of Parshu Ram by stating that their caste as *AUR or ANOTHER.*" The Aroras are often called Roras in the east of Panjab; yet I (Mr. Denzil) can hardly believe that the frank and stalwart Ror is of the same origin as the Arora. (ibid178 to179)

| S No | Clans | Nos | S No | Clans | Nos |
|---|---|---|---|---|---|
| 1 | Sagwal | 1848 | 3 | Khichi | 1207 |
| 2 | Maipla | 1567 | 4 | Jogran | 1193 |

As written by Ibbetson their sub-division seems to be exceedingly numerous. A few of the largest sub-divisions are given in the table on LHS.

Ambala Rors appears to be mostly Sagwal. (ibid179)

The Amin Ror says that, they came from Sambhal in Muradabad; but this may also be in order to connect themselves with their neighbours, the Chauhan Rajputs, who certainly came from there. *But almost all Rors point to Badli in the Jhajjar Tehsil of Rohtak district as their immediate place of origin, though some of them say that they came from Rajputana.* Their social status is identical to that of the Jats; and they practise *Karewa or widow-marriage*, though only, within their own caste. As seen from part abstract No. 83 tabulation, Rors; a Minor Dominant Tribe, were found in district of Delhi, Karnal, Ambala, and Ludhiana;

total 39647 in British Territory, and in Native States of Patiala, & Jind; total 1084. Thus, total Population of Rors as per 1881 census in Panjab (both Native & British Territory) was **40,731.**

**NB:** Intriguing & surprising the largest & the main Ror clan found in 66 villages (about 20 %); **Mehla** does not find mention in 'Panjab caste' by Denzil Ibbetson? Or is it **Maipla & Mual**, came to be called as Mehla later on?

**The Taga** (Sno 86); An agrarian caste, said to be Gaur Brahmins by origin, the oldest inhabitants of Jamna Khadar of Delhi & Karnal, in which they are found. (Ref; H. Elliott's; Races of the North-West Provinces, vol-1page106-115). They are of superior social standing & seclude their women, but are bad cultivators, especially the Mahomedans (about 3/4th of Tagas has adopted Islam). (ibid179)

**The Gujar** (Caste Sno. 8); Gujars an 8th largest in Panjab, are a fine stalwart man of same physical type as the Jat. They are of same social standing as the Jat; both eat & drink together without any scruple. But Gujar is far inferior in both personal character and repute to the Jat. He is lazy to a degree, and a wretched cultivator; his women though not secluded, will not do field work; while his fondness for cattle extends to those of other peoples. Mr Maconachie says, "*A Gujar have two qualifications of a highlander (a hilly home) and a constant desire for other people's cattle*". He never seems to have had the love of fighting & the manly character for independence which distinguishes this class elsewhere. On the contrary he is generally a mean sneaking cowardly fellow." (ibid182-88)

## 4.4 Minor Agricultural and Pastoral Tribes

Are divided into 3 classes; 1st class consists of market Gardeners or growers of vegetables; e.g., Mali, Saini, Arain, & Bagban, all 4 are closely connected; even some of them almost undistinguishable; 2nd class is Kanet & Ghirath, a low-class cultivator of the hills, and the Kambohs, Ahir, and other misc. cultivators; and 3rd constitute of the Ghosi and Gaddi, which are Pastoral rather than agricultural.

**The Mali and Saini** (Sno.45 & 31); Are found as Mali only in the Jamna zone, eastern portions of Hisar. Are called Saini in the eastern sub-montane districts, Arain or Bagban in the remaining province. About 10 % of Saini are Sikhs, & rest Hindus. Malis & Sainis, like all vegetable growers occupy a very inferior position among the agricultural castes; but of the two Sainis are probably the higher, as they often own land/even whole village, & generally are less mere market gardeners than are the Malis. (ibid188-89)

**The Kambohs** (S.No.33); Jamna Kambohs (claim descent from Raja Karan) seems to have come from the west, & has quite lately been a very large influx of Kambohs from Northern tract of Patiala into great Dhak Jungles between Thanesar & the river. Kambohs of

Bijnor trace their origin to trans-Indus. A fact that 40 % of them are Hindus & 23 % Sikhs is conclusive proof of them not having any extra-Indian origin. Denzil in section 486 of his book has noted that Arains (Rains) and Kambohs are supposed to be closely related. (ibid201)

**The Ahirs** (Sno.27); Though pure Pastoral caste, but in Panjab they are exclusively agricultural, are 1st rank as husbandmen, as good as Kambohs but somewhat superior to Jats. Their social standing is same as of Jat & Gujar, who eat & smoke together. They had dominant position in Rewari & the country to the west of it still locally known as '*Hirawati*,' where they held nearly 3/4th of it in 1838. (ibid202)

## 4.5 Religious, Professional, Mercantile, and Miscellaneous Castes

A heterogeneous collection of castes which includes some of the highest & the lowest, yet there is a connection between the priestly Brahmin & semi-priestly Nai, between the merchant Khatri & the pedlar Maniar. Mr Ibbetson, have divided these castes into six (6) groups. **1. Priestly castes**: Brahmins (3), Pujaris (120), Saiyads (24), Ulama (70), Chishti (116), & Bodla (172): **2. Ascetic & Mendicant:** Hindus; Bairagi (53), Sanyasi (95), Gosain (102), Sadh (155), Jogi, Aghori; Sikh; Suthra Shahi (163), Udasi (84), Nirmala (152), Akali or Nihang, Diwana Sadh; Musalman; Bharai (48), Madari or Malang (63), Benawa (111), Darvesh (136), Jalali (143), Husaini (160), and Qadiri (175): **3. Minor Professional Castes:** Nai (21), Bhaat (62), Dum & Mirasi (25), Jogi, Rawal & Nath (40 & 80), Behrupia (128), and Bhand (141): **4. Mercantile & Shop-keepers:** Baniya (14), Dhunsar (173), Bohra (124), Pahari Mahajan (112), Sood (75), Bhabra (88), Khatri (16), Khakha (179), Bhatia (69), Arora (10), Khojah & Paracha (44 &104): **5. Carriers & Pedlar Castes:** Untwal (144), Maniar (47), Bhatra (174), Kangar (180), Kunjra (114), Tamboli (165): **6. Misc. Castes:** Kashmiri and Dogra (26 & 182), Dogra (181), Gorkha, Parsi, & Bangali (148, 184 & 168), Kayasth (90), Bishnoi (106), Chazang (138), and Kanchan/Muslim Kanjars (96). (ibid214 to 265; Part V)

## 4.6 Vagrant, Menial and Artisan Castes

These castes divided into 11 groups, though of lowest strata, but are one of the most important sections. Politically they are unimportant; but are great mass of work force as industries are entirely in their hands & hardest part of the field work also, is performed by them.

**1. The Vagrant & criminal tribes:** Od & Beldar (85 & 129), Changar (64), Bawaria (71), Aheri & Thori (91 & 100), Sansi (72), Pakhiwala (117), Jhabel (107), Kehal or Mor (161), Gagra (133), Mina (166), Harni (159), Biloch (18), and Bangali (168); **2. Other Criminal tribes:** Tagus/kanjars (135), Dumna & Chuhra (41 & 44), & Rawals (64); **3. Gypsy Tribes:** Nut, Bazigars (88 & 89), Perna (164), Hesi (167), Garris (177), Qaladari (121), Baddun (150), Gandhila (158); **4. Scavenger castes:** Chuhra (4), Dhanak (43),

Khatik (87); **5. Leather–workers & Weavers:** Chamar (5), Musalman Chamar/Mochi (19), Chamrang (113), Dabgar (169), Koil (66), Julaha & Paoli (9), Gadaria (73), Kanera (170); **6. Watermen, Boatmen, and Cooks:** Jhinwar (15) - Kahar–Mahra (28), Bhatyara & Bharbhuja (92 & 108), Mallah & Mohana (42); **7. Workers in Wood, Iron, Stone, & Clay:** Lohar (22), Sikligar (157), Dhogri (153), Tarkhan (111), Kamangar (132), Thavi (149), Raj (93), Khumra (171), & Kumhar (13); **8. Workers in Other Metal & Minerals:** Sunar (30), Nyaria (131), Daoli (134), Thathera (115), Agari (109), Nungar & Shoragar (76 & 154), Churigar/Kanchera/Glass worker (139); **9. Washer-men, Dyers,& Tailors:** Dhobi & Chhimba (32 &33), Lilari & Rangrez (67&110), Charboa (54), Darzi (61); **10. Miscellaneous Artisans:** Penja, Teli, & Qassab (83, 23 & 38), Kalal or Distiller (56); **11. Menials of Hills:** Barwala & Batwal (49 & 78), Meg (57), Dumna (41), Barara (137), Sarera (97), Koli & Dagi (68 & 50), Rehar (176), Dosali (178), Hadi (185), Ghai (151); and **Purbia Menials:** Kori (99), Kurmi (119), Jaiswara (127), Pasi (156), Purbi (146). (ibid266 to 338, part vi)

*  *  *  *  *

# Chapter-5. Rors in Gazetteers and Raja Ror

## 5.1 History of District Gazetteers

The Board of Directors of East India Co to govern their newly acquired territories in India, on June 24, 1803, desired its officers to collect & supply them details on the "chronology, geography, Government laws, social setup, agriculture, industries, flora & fauna, animal kingdom, minerals, political revolutions, status of arts & sciences, and the state of internal & foreign trade," of each district. Based on this, they compiled the history of their possessions in India in the form of District Gazetteers. Publishing starting from 1872 was spread over 10 years interval, & revision of gazetteers was undertaken in 1901 to update & weed the outdated information, by a separate volume for each district.

## 5.2 What is a District Gazetteer?

A District Gazetteer is a miniature encyclopaedia, a multifaceted compendium of the strategic important informations about the district. It is a repository of authentic information as it not only deals with geographical data but contains valuable narrations of socio-economic changes which takes place in the district. These are in fact a mirror of society which reflects a picture of life in the district as is lived by its people. It is a resource of immense importance to administrators, research workers and also to general readers.

## 5.3 District gazetteers and Rors as Principal Community

A dist. Gazetteer under Principal Communities in its Chapter on People; describes political profile, social customs/rituals, socio-economic condition, & social intercourse among various castes. Herein Rors as one of the principal communities in that districts as described that time, vis-a-vis equally placed status castes shall be described.

(a) **Karnal District Gazetteer:** *(An extract from Karnal District Gazetteer-1883-84, as of 1872)*

**Physical Aspects:** Karnal district of 1872, comprised of 4 tahsils; Panipat, Karnal, Thanesar, & Kaithal.

**History and Archaeology:** District have archaeological remains of highest values, which unfortunately lie buried under towns & villages where investigation is difficult and liable to misinterpretation. The environs of *Thanesar & Pehowa, the Polar mound on Sarusti*

*(Saraswati) Kaithal town, lofty eminence of Amin,* and numerous villages in Nardak, if explored, would fill up many blanks in the early Hindu history. Villages on the edge of Bangar tract, high above the surroundings, such as *Indri, Churni & Kohand,* mark the position of old forts guarding the fords (Ghaats) of the Jamna when its course was further to the west than at present. (ibid1to 5)

**The legendry period:** Kurukshetra, the battle ground of epic: Mahabharata is a folk tale in Nardak tract. This area is full of tiraths & holy tanks; Village *Bastali (Vyas + Asthali);* the legendary author *Vyas of the Mahabharat,* & that the Ganges flowed underground into his well to save him from the trouble of going to the river to bathe, bringing with it his *Iota & loin-cloth,* which he had left in the river, to convince him that the water was really of Ganges. The well is still there to shame the sceptic. It was at *Gyondar* that *Gautam Rishi* censed the spot in the moon & gave *Indra* his thousand eyes. Parasir tank at *Bahlolpur* is where warrior *Duryodhan* hid till Krishna's jeers brought him unwillingly out to fight. *Phalgu tank in Pharal,* is where Kaurav & Pandav observed the funeral rites of their warriors. (ibid13 to25)

**Tribal distribution:** The agricultural tribes of the dist. are *Jats, Rajputs, Gujars,* **Rors,** *Kambohs, Syed & Pathans.* Jats are found in all parts of the district, particularly numerous in Kaithal tehsil. Rajputs predominate in Nardak of Karnal & Kaithal, and in Bet Markanda circle of the Thanesar tehsil. Gujars are numerous in the Khadar circle of Panipat & the Nardak and Bangar circles of the Kaithal tehsil. The **Rors** are chiefly to be found in the Indri Nardak and the adjoining tract of Kaithal. Of minor tribes, *Kamboj* of Khadar tracts are remarkably industrious. *Arains of Panipat & Malis* of Thanesar, though not numerous, but their cultivation is unequalled. Of the non-agricultural tribes, *Brahmins & Banias* (important families of Panipat, Karnal, Ladwa, & ordinary village shopkeeper) are the chief landowners. (ibid81)

**Former Inhabitants:** Tagas are probably the oldest inhabitants; who originally held a great part of the Khadar, now hold most of the pargana Ganaur. *Chandel* Rajputs held *Kaithal & Samaana,* with local headquarters at *Kohand,* from where they ruled the neighbouring tract. The *Brah Rajputs* held the country around *Salwan, Asandh, and Safidon;* while the *Pandirs* held *Thanesar and Nardak,* with capitals at *Pundri,* Ramba, Habari and Pundrak close to Karnal. The Mandhar Rajputs from Ajudhia, settled in Jind, expelled the Chandel & Brah Rajputs and took over their country, the former going towards the Siwaliks, and the latter beyond the Ghaggar: Mandhars made Kalayat in Patiala their capital, & settled in the local centres of *Asandh, Safidon and Gharaunda.* Mandhars expelled by Chauhan Rajputs under Rana Har Rai, fled beyond Jamna. The Chauhans made Jundla their headquarters and held a great part of the Nardak. The Tunwar Rajputs originally held Panipat & adjoining country around it but seems to have been displaced by Afghans. They now hold the country beyond Thanesar, and still own a section of the city of Panipat. The old boundary of the Tunwars, & Mandhars in Kaithal used to meet in *Pai* village, which belonged to Mandhars. *Habari* to the east was and is a Chauhan village, and Mundri, which is now a **Ror** village was *Tunwar. Tunwars* also held *Korana, Pharal and Rasulpur,* in which they had a large fort. Pharal is the only village they now hold. Probably they once held the whole Nali tract and were expelled by Mandhars. The Chauhans & their former dependents held 6 to7 villages around Habari. Rajput chiefs (Ranas & Rais) subject to payment of tribute to Delhi, were almost independent authority till the consolidation of Mughal Empire. Aurangzeb, forcibly converted many to Muslim faith, & degraded them to mere village chiefs.

**Arrival of Rors to this area**; In *Ain-e-Akbari*; principal castes of Pargana Karnal are stated to be *Chauhans & Rangad* (Mandhar Rajput who had converted to Islam). Those of Pargana Panipat were *Afghans, Gujars & Rangads*. The surrounding castes were Tagas in Ganaur; Afghan & Jats in Sonepat; Jats in Gohana; Rajputs, Rangads & Jats in Safidon; Rangads in Pundri; Rangads & Jats in Habari; Rangads & Tagas in Indri. The Pandirs held Bhatinda, and the Brahs the country about Samaana. A rough tribal distribution Map no V, prepared by Mr Ibbetson in his Settlement Report on Panipat Tehsil and Karnal Pargana, at the time of Ain-e-Akbari (1590AD), shows Afghans held a large part of the lower Khadar and also formerly held a part of Bangar, which was occupied at the time by Gujars. At present there is only one Afghan village, besides partly Panipat city. The total disappearance of Afghans must be due to changes in the river-course. It is noticed that they have been *replaced very largely by Gujars*; and I (Ibbetson) do not think *Gujars were ever in a position, as Jats most undoubtedly were,* to acquire territory by conquest in this part of the country, especially from Afghans. Probably Afghans left their Bangar villages for the more productive Khadar soil as it was left available by change of course in the river. They were again, after the time of Akbar, driven out by the branch of Jamna sweeping over the parts held by them. The parts near Rakashera & Barana have, escaped river action altogether, and are still largely occupied by the original Taga inhabitants. But in the intermediate parts of Khadar the people have only been settled for some eight (8) generations, which, at the usual Indian estimate of 25 years a generation, would bring their first 'arrival well this side of the date of the Ain-e-Akbari."

**Gujars**; As usual were intimately connected with Rajputs & *settled by them in portion of their territory*. Gujars who originally held the area about Naraina were Chokar; those about *Sutana & Nain* were Chamain, while those of *Kohand & Bapauli* were Rawals. *The two first* *clans have been largely replaced by **Jats** & **Rors**;* while the last has spread over parts of the Khadar formerly occupied by Afghans. (ibid81 to 83)

**Main Tribes of Karnal district: (1) Rajputs:** A principal tribe, they are fine, brave, & retain the feudal instinct more strongly developed than any other non-menial caste, the heads wielding extraordinary authority. They are very tenacious of the integrity of their property in the village land, and seldom admit strangers to share in it. They are lazy but proud, look upon manual labour as derogatory, much preferring the care of cattle, whether their own or other people's. *In the Nardak a great part of the actual work of cultivation is done by other castes. They are cattle-stealers by ancestral profession,* but they exercise their calling in a gentlemanly way, & there is certainly honour among Rajput thieves.

The principal clans are *Chauhans & Mandhars.* Mandhars had settled in early days about Samaana. Safidon branch obtained villages now held by them in Nardak by inter-marriage with Chauhans. They expelled *Chandel Rajputs* from *Kohand & Gharaunda* when they first came here, but Chandel re-conquered them. Finally, Mandhars reoccupied these two places, when they came directly from Kalayat in Patiala. All *Chauhans,* sprung from original people who settled at *Jundla* & claim descent from *Rana Har Rai.* Their origin is from Sāmbhar in Ajmer; but Rana Har Rai came from Sambal in Moradabad. The Chauhans of Moradabad took this departure about 19 generation (475 years) ago during Bahlol Lodhi (1451-89) time. *Tunwars,* of lunar race, have almost wholly disappeared from the district, & now chiefly represented by the Rajputs of Panipat. Pharal in Kaithal is a large Tunwar village, & in neighbourhood is called Tunwaron ki. The Nardak in Kaithal is to a considerable extent used to designate the limit of the tract occupied by Mandhars and Chauhans. (ibid90-92)

**(2) Jats:** Jats are pre-eminently agricultural caste, and, *with the exception of **Rors,** and of **Arains, Malis, & Kamboj;*** who are practically market gardeners, are best cultivators. They are a fine stalwart race, and are notorious for their independence, acknowledging to a less degree the authority of their headmen. They hold several tribal groups of villages; but they also own parts of villages almost all over the tract save in the Gujar and Rajput portions. Jats of the district seems to have come partly from *Bagad,* where they were in force 700 years ago. In no case have Jats settled from across the Jamna. *Jats are not mentioned as a prominent caste of the tract in Akbar's time, and probably gained footing during breaking up of Mughal dynasty, when they became an important element in the politics of the time.*

**Principal clans: Jaglan;** Jagla from Jaipur, **Ghanghas;** Ghatwal or Malak; from Ahulana, **Deswal;** from Rohtak, **Sandhu;** Gagsina, Khotpura; Phul Patiala, **Ahlawat;**

Babail, from Dighal in Rohtak. **Other clans;** Rathi, Ahlawat, Sahrawat, Mehlawat, Narwal, Dehia, Kanda, kundu, Dhaliwal, Maan, Beniwal, Nain, Lather, Kadian, Duhan, etc (ibid92 to 94)

**(3) Gujars:** Gujars are a notorious thieving tribe; as a rule, their cultivation is of the untidiest type, though in many Khadar and canal villages they have really applied themselves in earnest to agriculture. They have a habit of breaking up far more land than their numbers and appliances can properly cultivate. Though their women will go to the well, bring food for the field workers, pick cotton, and do other light work. The difference between a Gujar and a Rajput thief was well put by a villager as follows; "A Rajput will steal your buffalo; but he won't send his father to tell that he knows where it is and will get it back for Rs 20/-, and then keep both Rs 20/-, and buffalo, but a Gujar will."

The Gujars like Rajputs, are unwilling to admit strangers to property in their villages. They are closely allied with Rajputs; their possession of parts of Bangar was contemporary with Mandhars, parts of whose conquests, such as *Kohand*, were given to them. In Khadar, they have succeeded Afghans in recent times save in a very few old villages.

**Principal clans: Rawal;** Claims descent from a Rajput beyond Lahore with a Gujar woman of Ghokar Clan; settled in *Rana Khera (now Rajapur)*, but moved to *Kabri & Kohand*. They held 12 villages & Bapauli & eventually settled in 27 villages of Khojgipur Thapa in Khadar. They still hold Khadar villages; but have lost most of those near Kohand. **Chokar;** came from Jewar Thapa, via Bali Qutbpur in Sunipat; hold 24 villages with Namaunda as headquarters. Probably are very old inhabitants and have been mostly displaced by Jats. **Chamain;** Claims descent from a *Tunwar Rajput by a Gujar woman*, came from Delhi, settled *in Nain, Sutana* & neighbouring villages; seems were expelled from neighbourhood of Delhi by Sher Shah. *They have been largely displaced by* **Rors. Kalsan;** Claims descent from *Rana Har Rai*, Chauhan of Jundla by a Gujar wife; had part of his conquests in Doab, still in force here, also hold a little land in Chauhan Nardak. (ibid95 -96)

**(4) Rors:** No satisfactory information as to the origin of the Rors. Most of them tell their origin from Badli, near Jhajjar in Rohtak district; and there are traditions of a *Tunwar Rajput as ancestor.* They hold a *Chaurasi* about Pehowa, and a barah (12) villages beyond the Ganges. They occupy many villages in the Mori Nardak, some in the east of pargana Kaithal, and a few in the south of Kaithal tehsil near the Jind border; *but they have obtained their property in the district almost exclusively by being settled as cultivators by the original owners, generally Rajputs & Gujars, who have since abandoned their village or died out wholly or in part. Ror claims Rajput origin and also Rajputs have been heard to* *admit the origin of the Dopla got of Rors in Amin, from Rana Har Rai by a Rorni wife. Socially-they rank below Jats.*

The Rors, while almost as good cultivators as the Jats, and assisted by their women in the same way, are much more peaceful and less grasping in their habits; and are consequently readily admitted as cultivators where the Jats would be kept at arm's length. They are fine stalwart men, of much the same stamp as the Jats. The number of clans represented in the district is large, almost in every Ror village; and there are not large groups of villages held by a predominant clan, as is the case with other tribes. They are strongest in Indri, Nardak and along the Rohtak canal, where they hold many villages originally possessed by Gujars.

**Principal clans: Jogran/Jaglan;** descended from a Chauhan Rajput called Joga by a Rodni & hold large village Korana, came from Kalayat (Patiala), *via* Pundri (Kaithal). **Ghanter;** came *from* Gurawar in Rohtak, & *Kandol* from Anwali in Rohtak. These two clans hold Alupur & neighbouring villages. **Khichi** or **Khanchi;** came from *Narar Jajru,* in Jaipur, where they are still numerous & hold Ahar, Shera & other villages. **Other clans;** Kulania, Gurak, Maipla, Dumaine, Rojra & Kainwal from Delhi; the Kharangar, Lathar, Jarautia, Dhankar, Khasbar & Chopre, from Rohtak; the Tharrak, Kokra, also Dodan, Turan & Lamra, from Kaithal, & Jind;

the Kultagria from Thanesar; the MuaI from Bikaner; all of which hold considerable areas in the district. (ibid96 to 97)

**Note:** *Intriguing & surprising the largest & the main Ror clan;* **Mehla does** *not find mention in this gazetteer? Or is it Maipla & Mual, came to be called as Mehla later on?*

**Rors of Karnal as in Annals:** The Karnal town was a favourite cold weather resort for retired British officers and their families settled in India (Page-28, Annals of Karnal (1914) by Major C.H. Buck, then Deputy commissioner).

| Principal Ror families; 6 out of 23: Annals of Karnal (1914) by Major C.H. Buck, then Deputy commissioner | | | |
|---|---|---|---|
| Name of Family | The Then Head of Family | Name of Family | The Then Head of Family |
| 1.Gatti family | Tulla | 4.Napaid family | Partapa |
| 2.Dallu family | Khubi and Harnam | 5.Jogi family | Harnam and Aabhe Ram |
| 3.Lachhu family | Hera and Kewal | 6.Jagta family | Nanda, son of Amin Chand |
|  |  |  | Bhagwan Singh, s/o Ganga Ram |
| List of 2 Ror Lambardars out of 15: Annals of Karnal (1914) by Major C.H. Buck, then Deputy commissioner | | | |
| 1.Nand Ram | Ami Chand | Amount of Revenue Rs 875 |  |
| 2.Mangat | Harjas | Amount of Revenue Rs 875 |  |

Chapter IV- Residents of Karnal; Annals states; among Principal Hindu families, Rors with 26 % share were one of the prominent residents with befitting social profile; 23 Principal Hindu families were: 4 Brahmins, 9 Mahajan's, 4 Jats, and 6 Rors as listed, in table below. Similarly, among 15 Lambardars: 2 were Rors; 10 Jats, 3 Arains (Musalman). (ibid29-30)

**(b) Rohtak District Gazetteers** (*Ref; Rohtak district gazetteer-1883-84*) It belonged to Hisar Division until 1894 when 3 districts of that Commissionaire were merged in the then Delhi Division.

**Castes and Tribes distribution;** The figures below in tabular form, show the distribution of population by caste, & area they own in the district as per enumeration made during Settlement.

| Class & Name | Enumeration | | Area | | Class & Name | Enumeration | | Area | |
|---|---|---|---|---|---|---|---|---|---|
| 1. Cultivators | Numbers | % | Acres | % | | Numbers | % | Acres | % |
| Jats-Hindu | 192832 | 35 | 645283 | 67 | Gujar-Musalman | 1930 | | 925 | |
| Jats–Musalman | 1412 | - | 2468 | | Dogars | 246 | | 794 | |
| Brahmin | 60067 | 11 | 78294 | 8 | **Rors** | **396** | | **1261** | |
| Ahir | 15813 | 3 | 25717 | 3 | Shekh | 6965 | 1 | 6091 | |
| Rajput-Hindu | 6072 | 1 | 54641 | 6 | Total | 332626 | 58 | 924215 | 96 |
| Rajput-Musalman | 20563 | 4 | 77012 | 8 | II. Trader & Professionals | 51409 | 9 | 25438 | 3 |
| Afghanis | 5208 | 1 | 22178 | 2 | III. Village Servants | 58478 | 11 | 6126 | -- |
| Malis | 7652 | 1 | 2281 | 3 | IV. Village Menials | 87235 | 16 | 369 | -- |
| Biloches | 3248 | 1 | 2357 | | V. Religious classes | 13145 | 2 | 2102 | -- |
| Gujar- Hindu | 1163 | | 2912 | | VI. Misc. | 20423 | 4 | 3997 | -- |
| | | | | | Grand Total | 563317 | 100 | 962157 | |

**Tribal Settlement;** The distribution of the caste inhabiting Rohtak district having 511 estates (villages), tahsil wise, according to the tribe of the majority of the proprietors are shown in the table below;

| Name of Tribe | No of village held in | | | | Total | Name of Tribe | No of village held in | | | | Total |
|---|---|---|---|---|---|---|---|---|---|---|---|
| | Gohana | Rohtak | Sampla | Jhajjar | | | Gohana | Rohtak | Sampla | Jhajjar | |
| Jat | 64 | 79 | 115 | 108 | 366 | Gujar | -- | 1 | -- | 5 | 6 |
| Ahir | -- | --- | 1 | 25 | 26 | Shekh | -- | 1 | 1 | 1 | 3 |
| Rajput-H | -- | 7 | -- | 19 | 26 | Syeds | -- | -- | 3 | -- | 3 |
| Rajput-M | 7 | 16 | -- | 1 | 24 | Biloch | -- | --- | --- | 4 | 4 |
| Brahmin | 7 | 6 | 6 | 9 | 28 | Kayasth | -- | 2 | -- | 2 | 4 |
| Afghan | 3 | -- | -- | 13 | 16 | **Ror** | 1 | -- | -- | -- | 1 |
| Mahajan | 1 | 1 | 1 | --- | 3 | Dogar | -- | 1 | -- | -- | 1 |
| H; Hindu, M; Musalman | | | | | | Total | 83 | 114 | 127 | 187 | 511 |

The 60% of the existing villages were founded in waste jungle, or on former sites, *whose previous lords have been forgotten.* The remaining 40%, were settled on old Rajput sites; old Jat sites follow next; and then, after a long interval, Brahmins, Afghans, Rangad, Gujars and Biloches. *A few tribes, which are now no longer represented in the district, held estates once Viz, Taga Brahmins, and Meos; the* **Rors** *also formerly held a number of villages.* Of the 511 estates (villages), owners of 223 were from outside the limits of the district, & 288 from villages previously founded inside the district. The pedigree tables show that; 12 villages have existed for 30-35 generations; 48 for 25-30; 70 for 20-25; 128 for 15-20; 140 for 10-15; while 60 only were founded between 5-10 generations ago; & 55 within the last 5 generations; of these last, 33 are in Jhajjar tahsil alone. The pedigree tables are carefully recorded & preserved by the *Bhaat in their pothis,* many of which are of great age: in few parts of the Punjab, perhaps is good written evidence in matters of descent. The above facts go to show that 20% of the villages were probably founded when *Shahab-ud-din* took Delhi, and 20% only are of as recent a date as the British rule in India. (ibid58-59)

**Rors:** The only Ror village, Jwara, was settled from Badli, & they claim to be Rajputs,but can not give definite account of their origin. Rors resemble & have the very same customs as Jats & rank with them including as cultivators; are common in Karnal & bear a good reputation there. Three tribes i.e., Jat, Ahir, & Ror together form the 1st class of cultivators in Rohtak dist. & own nearly 7% of the divided land of the district.

*NB:* **Mohana;** *This most prominent  Ror village inhabited by largest Mehla clan ,that time was part of Sunipat tehsil of Delhi district.(Ref page-102 para-117, gist Sr. no 34,ch-VI statistics of population - final report on settlement of land revenue of Delhi District - 1878-80 by R. Maconachie).* Mohana a canal village had population of 3072, revenue of Rs 5310/- & proprietors were mainly **Rors,** not found anywhere in Delhi District though found in Rohtak dist. & Jamnadas was the most noticeable man.

**(c) Jind as State**: Among 'Phulkian States,'3 native states of Jind, Patiala, & Nabha; Jind though 2nd in area, is smallest in population, containing the sterile Bagad tract of Dadri tahsil with its sparse population ever ready to emigrate in bad seasons. (ibid211) (Ref; Phulkian States Gazetteer of 1904)

**Naming of Villages;** Most of the villages in tehsils Jind & Dadri are ancient settlements of *Jats & Rajputs, immigrants from Rajputana and elsewhere.* In Jind tahsil there are villages named after *Jats, Kumhars,* **Rors,** *Brahmins, Gujars & Ahirs.* Raja of Jind founded several villages & named after various musical nodes; PiluKhera, Bhairon Kheda, Malsari, Sandhoi Kheda, & Bhag Kheda (ibid223to 224)

**Social Position;** Agricultural tribes and other castes like: Hindu *Rajputs, Jats, Hindu Gujars,* **Rors,** *Ahirs, Sonar's & Tarkhan* eat uncooked and cooked food with each other. So, as such are at par in social parlance. Also, they eat both type of food with all Brahmins and Vaisyas, but the latter do not eat uncooked food with them. (ibid245)

**NB:** *Rors inhabit villages like: Dathrat, Ritauli, Morkhi, Anchra etc. Its intriguing & shocking govt authorities, has not included/mentioned* **Ror caste,** *a dominant minor landowning tribe of the state, whereas Khatri & Aroras, who came after 1947, has been described prominently.*

**(d) Saharanpur district Gazetteer** (*ref; District Gazetteer 1901*) The Saharanpur district of Meerut Division, founded in 14th century, & lies in upper Doab of Ganga and Yamuna.

**Principal Communities:** Brahmin, Rajput, Jat, Gujar, who are numerous; Ahir, Lodh **& Ror**, are small in numbers,& are mostly engaged in agriculture & allied occupations like cattle rearing, milk vending, mat & twine making. (ibid83 to 85)

## 5.4 District Gazetteer conspicuously missing Ror caste

Rors, recorded inhabiting in other contemporary govt documents but are found conspicuously omitted in official District Gazetteers while describing its principal community under People heading. Such districts are as below.

**(a) Jind State Gazetteer:** No mention of Rors, except under, "Naming of Villages," & "Social Position; "That they will eat uncooked food with Rajputs, Jats, Gujars, **Rors**, Sonar's & Tarkhan. (Ref Phulkian State Gazetteer Page; 223 to 224)

**(b) Jind District Gazetteer:** No Rors; even though Rors inhabited *Dathrat (Seharda), Morkhi, Anchra, and Ritauli, since 9 to 10 generations.* (Ref; reprint Gazetteer; April 1986; Ch-III People; page- 43)

**(c) Ambala Dist. Gazetteer;** No mention of Rors, whereas census-1881 records 4861 Rors equal *to 4 % of the population of Ambala district* inhabiting Ambala, Jagadhari, Naraingadh, & Pipli etc? (*Ref; Part Abstract; 83; census-1881 Distribution of Minor Dominant Tribe of Eastern Plains, as in para 3.3 of ch-3 of this book*). (ibid57-58)

**(d) Muzaffarnagar & Bijnor District Gazetteer:** No mention of Rors, whereas book, 'Panjab castes' by D Ibbetson (pp178-179) states; "They (**Rors**) also hold 12 villages beyond Yamuna & the Ganges in Uttar Pradesh."

**NB; observation on Omission:** It appears some forces tried to obliviate the Ror caste by such deliberate omission, as authorities have included *Aroras & Khatris*, who migrated to this side after partition in1947, but not the already inhabiting minor dominant landowning Ror caste. Should it not be construed deliberate attempt to obliviate the Ror caste?

## 5.5 Raja Ror: ASI Report 1871-72 Vol-IV

Raja Ror, the ancestors of Ror Vansh, as in Archaeology Survey of India Report 1871-72; Vol IV; by A. Cunningham, Chief Surveyor of India (CSI); (page 210-212), *verbatim* is reproduced below.

**"Kheragarh:** Kheragarh is situated about twenty-four (24) miles to the south of Agra and about eight (8) miles to the west of the Gwalior Road on the banks of the Ban Ganga River. It is a large village or a small town, standing on a large and ancient Khera. About 300 or 400 feet to the north side of Kheragarh there is an old Tila in which ancient sculptures are often found; and there is another Tila, called, "Taisu Tila," about 500 feet to the east side of Kheragarh, in which ancient sculptures have also frequently been found. There are the remains of a mud fort at Kheragarh which is said to have been built on the site of an ancient brick fort, which is the origin of the word, "*Garh*" in the name of, "*Kheragarh.*"

**"Khangar Ror", "Kaga Ror", or "Kagaroll"**: Kagaroll is situated about three (3) Kos (5 mile) this side of Kheragarh, & about eighteen (18) miles from Agra. It is a very ancient place, and the present village stands on an ancient Tila, composed of the debris of an ancient fort. There are the remains of a very strong and thick wall which runs through below the western part of the village of Kagaroll. This wall is composed of huge blocks of red sandstone, some of them beautifully carved. A great portion of this wall lies still buried under the earth of the old Tila on which the village of Kagaroll stands; but another portion of the wall which extended beyond the Tila had been almost entirely dug up by the peasantry. Now there is no wall standing isolated by it. I find, by enquiries made of the inhabitants of the place, that the statement which recently appeared in the *Delhi Gazette* is quite true so far as, that the ancient fort buried under this place was actually founded by a **"Raja Ror,"** said to have been the son of **"Khangar."**

There is a tradition preserved in the neighbourhood about a "White Crow", or "Kag" in consequence of the appearance of which, as an omen of augury, Raja Ror built a fort here and it was called, "Kaga Ror", corrupted to "Kagaroll." But to my mind the name of the fort is evidently derived from the combined names of Raja Khangar & his son Raja Ror, to form the name of Khangar Ror, which in time might easily have been corrupted to Khangar-Roll or Kagarol. It must also be remembered that there is a tribe of Rajputs* called, "Rora." (*RORA, here appears to be a misprint & it is ROR only*) (Legend: * *Or perhaps more correctly, I should say; "there is a division of the Kshatriya race called Rora."*)

It seems there are many remains frequently found, or dug up at Kagaroll, such as sculptures, images, old coins, etc.

Two trustworthy men whom I lately sent there to explore the place brought me the following things, which have been dug up at Kagaroll. (There were numerous other large, heavy images & other sculptures which they were unable to bring away.)

(1)   An image of a warrior in yellowish sandstone; about 18 inches height; but as it has lost the lower part of the right leg from the ankle and the lower part of the left leg from below the knee, its original height was probably about 1 foot 41 inches. It is a very bold sculptured figure, the features of the face are fine & manly, and of the handsomest Hindu type. The warrior has his right knee raised; on his right arm he presents a shield in defence; and in his left hand he brandishes a straight huge sword over his head. In a belt round his waist, he wears a dagger with a cross shaped hilt at his left side. The hairs of the head are full but drawn back in straight lines on the head. The figure is naked, except for a cloth round the loins, a belt round the waist, and a triple necklace round the neck. It is evidently the figure of a warrior of great strength, probably of some ancient hero. I should not wonder if this were figure of **Raja Ror** himself.

(2)   A small female figure, carved in relief, in a kneeling or sitting position. (3) A small figure of a bull, in white sandstone, charging forward in terror, with the forelegs raised, and attacked from behind by either a leopard or a tiger or a lion, which has got hold of the bull's tail in its mouth. Behind the bull's forelegs a man's leg and foot appear, but the upper part of this human figure has been broken and on the top of the back of the bull there are the remains of two human feet of much smaller dimensions than the other. (4) The remains of a small elephant or a bull in steatite. (5) Two very small & curious figures carved in some greyish black stone, one of which is like an Elephant, but with a very long conical shaped human-like face. Underneath its belly there is a young one sucking it. The other a small sitting figure, probably is of some divinity, with a very absurd physiognomy (shape of mouth). (6) A few coins were also found from Kagaroll, all were either defaced or of no importance, except for one which is a thin dice of copper or mixed metal, one side of which is covered with a representation of a circular rayed symbol, resembling a chakra or wheel, and the other side appears to be blank. I hope, however, to obtain more coins from that locality, as the inhabitants of the place say that a great many coins, as well as images and other sculptures in stone, are found there."

## 5.6 Kassaundi or Bawan Garhi

Part of ASI Report 1871-72; Vol IV; by A. Cunningham, Chief Surveyor of India; (pp 208-210), *verbatim* is as below.

The station of Toondla (Tundla), where Agra Branch Railway Line joins Grand Trunk of the East Indian Railway, is well known to most people. The village or small town of Kassaundi is situated about 8-1/2 to 9 miles distant, south-east from Tundla. In fact, this entire tract within about 3 miles of Toondla (or an extent of about 6 miles) is commonly called **Kassaundi Garhi**," as if, it had once been one great capital city defended by a series of forts; and this is by common consent asserted by the natives to have been founded by **"Raja Gaj."**

Leaving Toondla behind on the north-west and proceeding south-east wards on the Kassaundi Road, one first arrives at a village called "Auwara," about 2-1/2 miles distant from Toondla. In the centre of this village, or rather surrounded by the village, there is the site or the remains of the foundations of an ancient fort.

In and around this neighbourhood the remains of the 52 Forts" are said to exist. Some years ago, several of these forts were still standing in a partly entire state, but the villagers gradually demolished the walls; when the Railway was first being constructed, the country people sold a large amount of the materials, of which these forts were constructed, to the Railway authorities & contractors, who probably were utterly unaware as to whence the materials really came from. If, however, the Railway people got any of the materials for use, of which these forts were constructed, they must have been considerably superior to any materials now in use with the Public Works Department! The bricks found may at least be upwards of two feet or more in length and about eight inches in thickness. These are bricks from old foundations. The bricks which belonged to the upper portions of the walls appear to be about the same size as those l found at the Aundha Khera and Surajpur, namely, about I foot 3 inches in length by about 4 inches in thickness. Now bricks of this size as this must be very ancient indeed! As I said before, according to the traditions of that part of the country, Kassaundi Garhi or at least the old, razed fortresses in its neighbourhood, were founded by, 'Raja Gaj!" But which Raja Gaj? Is the question which at once occurs to one? Incidently, there were three or four ancient Rajas of that name. It is a matter of detailed research if it has a corelation with the Raja Ror & Bawan Gadhi etc.

* * * * *

# Chapter-6. Punjab Census and Rors

## 6.1 Census Enumeration

First reliable census was taken on 1Jan 1855, & then next one on 10 Jan1868. Census enumeration method was: 1$^{st}$ step to complete village & district level Areas & Land Revenue details; next step to affix house number in every town & village; then enter house numbers in enumeration list to enable ease in verification by authorities. One enumerator was employed for every 100 houses, one supervisor for 20 Enumerator. Enumerators included govt officials, mostly from among the more intelligent village officers, Town Wardens & private educated inhabitants.

## 6.2 Census 1868 of Punjab and Rors

Census Report of 10$^{th}$ Jan1868; Return no; V-B, tabulates religion wise castes such as Aroras, Khatris, Rajputs, Jats, Gujars, Tagas, Ahirs, Kambohs, etc but **Rors** are not found recorded in it. (pp32 to 40; page-93 to 101/214 -pdf pages)

## 6.3 Census 1881 of Punjab and Rors

It was the 2$^{nd}$ census after Britishers reorganised the entire administrative and political setup of the country. This census manufactured the castes in India for the 1$^{st}$ time to create fission among Indian masses, a social fissure.

**(a) Vol-I; General;** It was done in all possessions of British India, except Kashmir, French & Portuguese areas. Below is the breakup of population of 25, 38, 91,821 enumerated on Feb 17,1881 and Rors are recorded in it;

| Abstract. 1 showing the population for British & Native states as per Feb 17, 1881 Census | | | | | |
|---|---|---|---|---|---|
| **British India Provinces** | Population | Assam | 4881426 | Rajputana | 10268392 |
| Bengal with Feudatory states | 69536861 | Burma | 3736771 | Hyderabad (Nizam's) | 9845594 |
| North-west Provinces & Oudh | 44849619 | Berar | 2672673 | States of Central India | 9261907 |
| Madras with Feudatory states | 31170631 | Coorg | 460722 | Mysore | 4186188 |
| Bombay with Feudatory states | 23395663 | Ajmer | 178302 | Travancore, | 2401158 |
| Punjab with Feudatory states | 22712120 | **Native states** | Population | Baroda | 2185 005 |
| Central Provinces | 11548511 | | | Cochin | 600278 |

Ch-XII Statistics of caste (PP-277); para- 449; Table XVII & its supplement is devoted to the statistics of caste data and herein below *Aroras, Khatris, & Rors* as described in the Census 1881, are extracted as;

**(1) Aroras**: Population; 601440, peculiar to Panjab (Multan & Derajat Division), classed as Mercantile & shop keeping caste. Mr Ibbetson says, "The **Aroras, or Rora(?)**, are the traders par excellence, the Jatki-speaking of south-western portion of the Panjab." They are commonly known as **Kirar** (a coward & contemptuous). But in lower Chenab, they are admirable cultivators, while in west Panjab; he will sew clothes, weave matting & baskets, make vessels of Brass & Copper including goldsmith work. But he is terrible coward: a caste proverb; "*The thieves were four, and we were eighty-four; the thieves came on and we ran away. Damn the thieves! Well, done us!*" Another very terse: "*Trust not a crow, a dog, or a Kirar, even when asleep.*" The Arora is of inferior physique, and his character is thus summed up by Mr Thorburn: '*A cowardly, secretive, acquisitive race, necessary & useful in their places, but has many qualities, both despised and envied by the Musalman tribes of Bannu.*' Few Aroras are returned as Musalman, some 7 % as Sikhs, the rest as Hindu. Aroras claim to be of Khatri origin but Khatris rejects the claim. George Campbell stated, the two belong to same **ethnic stock**. They say that they became outcaste from Kshatriya stock during the persecution of Kshatriyas by Parshu Ram, to avoid which they denied their caste saying it as **Aur or Another**, hence their name Arora. *Aroras are Khatris of Aror, the ancient capital of Sindh, now represented by modern Rori.* (Excerpts; Para:517, ibid287 & 288)

**(2) Khatris**: Population; 419139, claims Rajput origin & 80% are found in Punjab. They do not have one special occupation; many are employed as writers; many in military service. Mr Ibbetson writes; "Khatri is not a mere shopkeeper but occupies a different position among castes; they *are superior in physique, in manliness, & in energy; claims to be direct descendants of Kshatriyas.* George Campbell in his '**Ethnology of India**' describes them as; "Trade is their main occupation; besides monopolising the trade of Punjab & the greater part of Afghanistan, they are chief civil administrators in Punjab, & almost all literate work is in their hands. They are priests or Gurus of the Sikhs; both Nanak & Govind were; Sodis & Bedis of the present day are Khatris. *Even though they don't have military in their character but are quite capable of using the sword when necessary.* Diwan Sawn Mal, governor of Multan, his successor Mulraj, & many chief functionaries of Maharaja Ranjit Singh were Khatris. Todar Mal, famous minister of Akbar, was also a Khatris. Khatris have broader & distinctive features; are very fine, fair, handsome race, and generally are well educated. *There is a large subordinate class of Khatris, somewhat lower, but of equal mercantile energy, called Roras or Rors (**Authors view; a serious error on the part of Campbell; Rors are distinct & of martial nature and are not Arora or Rora**).* Proper Khatris deny all connexions with them, or at least only admit that they are some sort of bastard kindred with Khatris, ethnically same stock & they are certainly mixed up with Khatris in their avocations." (Excerpts; Para 534 ibid289-290)

**(3) Rors:** Mr. Ibbetson devised caste found in Punjab for census-1881 into 17 categories. Rors are part of *Minor Dominant Tribe* & have already been described in Chapter-3; Panjab castes as per above Para of the census. Table below is category wise population (Excerpts from Para 663-64; pp-320-21, page-363-64/518; Ch-XII);

| Category wise population of castes as found in Punjab in census 1881 | | | |
|---|---|---|---|
| 1. Rajputs, Jat, & races | 45,97,725 | 10. Scavenger's caste | 11,58,979 |
| 2. **Minor Dominant Tribes** * | **15,09,218** | 11. Leather workers & Weavers | 20,73, 867 |
| 3. MinorAgricultural & Pastoral | 20,02 509 | 12. Watermen | 6,88,966 |
| 4. Minor Professional castes | 6,70,333 | 13. B'smith, Carpenter, Mason, Potter | 14,15,302 |
| 5. Mercantile & Shopkeeping | 15,99,268 | 14. Metal Workers other than Iron | 1,94,885 |
| 6. Pedlar Castes | 80,960 | 15. Washermen, Dyers, Tailor | 3,36,519 |
| 7. Misc. Castes | 2,18,257 | 16. Misc Artisans | 4,24,506 |
| 8. wandering criminal tribes | 134355 | 17. Menials of Hills | 3,75,686 |
| 9. Gipsy Tribes | 38,485 | Grand Total | 1,75,15,820 |

**Legend:** * Population Breakup for category no; 2, Minor Dominant Tribes, which includes **Rors,** is given below;

| Caste Breakup of the Minor Dominant Tribes as in Punjab Census 1881 | | | | | | | |
|---|---|---|---|---|---|---|---|
| Tribe name | Population | Tribe name | Population | Tribe name | Population | Tribe name | Population |
| Karral | 10,413 | Khokhar | 36,137 | **Ror** | **40,731** | Khanzada | 3,757 |
| Gakkhar | 25,789 | Kharral | 18,845 | Taga | 14305 | Gujar | 6,27,304 |
| Awan | 5,32.895 | Daudpotra | 18,163 | Meo | 1,16,227 | Total | **15,09,218** |
| Khattar | 1,245 | Dogar | 63,437 | | | | |

**(b) Vol-III; Report;** This volume has final tables for the native states (254 pages as Appendix -B). Table no; VIII A, (pp- 4, 7, & 17) lists Aroras, Khatris, & Rors as caste no: 10,16, & 55 respectively.

## 6.4 Census of India-1891: Punjab and Rors

General Report (290 pages) describes *Ethnographic distribution of population* with sketches of the caste, tribe & race,

Chapter-V, (pp-182 to 208, p-183 to 209/290), describes castes enumerated therein & their various statistics.

**(a) Census 1891; Report & Classification of castes on Functional basis:** This classification (pp-188, p-189/290) devised on functional basis (7 nos) & castes groups (60 nos) in each by Mr. Herbert Risley, (as suggested in his paper in Vol-I no; 6 of the Journal of Anthropological Society of Bombay (pp 343-352)), for imperial purposes, is tabulated below.

| Classification on functional basis for group of castes as devised for 1891 census | | | |
|---|---|---|---|
| Classification | Group of castes | Classification | Group of castes |
| A. Agricultural | 1. **Military & Dominant** * | Artisans & | 31. Potters, 32. Glass & Lac workers |
| and Pastoral | 2. Other Agricultural | Village | 33. Salt & Lime workers |
| | 3. Cattle Graziers | Menials | 34. Goldsmith refuse cleaners |
| | 4. Field Labourers, 5. Forest Tribes | Contd. | 35. Goldwashers & Iron Smelters |
| B. Professionals | 6. Priest etc, 7. Devotes & Ascetics | | 36. Fishemen etc, 37. Domestic service etc |
| | 8. Temple's servants | | 38. Distillers & teddy Drawers |
| | 9. Genealogists, 10. Writers | | 39. Butchers, 40. Leather workers |
| | 11. Astrologers & Herbalists | | 41. Village watchmen etc, 42. Scavengers |
| | 12. Musicians & Ballad Reciters | | 43. Grindstone makers, 44. Knife Grinders |
| | 13. Singers & Dancers, 14. Actors & Mimes | E. Vagrants | 45. Earthworkers & Stone Quarriers |
| C. Commercial | 15. Traders | | 46. Mat & Cane workers |
| | 16. Pedlars | | 47. Hunters & Fowlers, 48. Misc Vagrants |
| | 17. Carriers by Pack Animals | | 49. Jugglers & Acrobats etc |
| D. Artisans & | 18. Goldsmith, 19. Blacksmiths | F. Races & | 50. Musalman Foreign Races |
| Village | 20. Barbers, 21. Tailors | Indefinite | 51. Himalayan Mongoloids |
| Menials | 22. Carpenters, Masons etc | Tribes | 52. Burmes & Chinese Mongoloids |
| | 23. Brass & Copper Smiths | | 53. Western Asiatic |
| | 24. Grain Parchers & confectioners | | 54. Mixed races Burmese etc |
| | 25. Perfumers, Betel etc sellers | | 55. Indefinite Indian castes |
| | 26. Weavers & Dyers, 27. Washermen | | 56. Europeans etc, 57. Eurasians |
| | 28. Cotton cleaners, 29. Oil Pressers | | 58. Native Christians, 59. Africans |
| | 30. Shepherds & wool weavers | | 60. Goanese & Portuguese |

Note: *Break up of Military & Dominant group, which includes **Rors**, is shown in abstract no; 84 redrawn on next page.

**(b) Census-1891; Punjab & its Feudatories, Part-I;** This part of census (213 pages) describes social profile of castes that time. Abstract; 32 (part) below shows **Ror** caste; with a figure of 875 females/1000 males; at par with socially similar placed castes Like Rajputs, Jats, Gujars, Ahirs, Aroras, Khatri, Bishnoi & Kambohs. (Page -128/213).

| Part Abstract No: 32 Showing the Sex Ratios; SR (Females/1000 Males) in selected caste | | | | | | | | | |
|---|---|---|---|---|---|---|---|---|---|
| Caste | Sex Ratio | Caste | Sex Ratio | Caste | Sex Ratio | Caste | Sex Ratio | Caste | Sex Ratio |
| Khatri | 797 | Gujar | 848 | Bishnoi | 873 | Ahir | 821 | Kambohs | 887 |
| Jats | 802 | Rajput | 848 | **Ror** | **875** | Arora | 851 | | |

**Abstract 84;** Rors were categorised Class A-Agricultural & Pastoral; Grp 1: Military & Dominant caste. A redrawn abstract showing caste-wise population of this group (20), as in Census 1881 & 1891 is; (pp164 to 167/213 of Appendix: C);

| Redrawn Abstract 84; showing Population of Class A-Agricultural/Group 1 Military & Dominant castes (20 castes) | | | | | | |
|---|---|---|---|---|---|---|
| S. No | Caste | Census 1881 | Census1891 | S. No | Caste | Census 1881 | Census1891 |
| 1 | Awan | 5,32,895 | 6,08,051 | 11 | Karral | 10,413 | 18,122 |
| 2 | Daudpotra | 18,163 | 19,269 | 12 | Khanzada | 3,357 | 3,471 |
| 3 | Dhund | 20,315 | 48415 | 13 | Kharral | 18,845 | 52,029 |
| 4 | Dogar | 63,437 | 69,712 | 14 | Khattar | 1,245 | 9,773 |
| 5 | Dogra | 397 | 2,320 | 15 | Khokhar | 36,137 | 1,39,964 |
| 6 | Gakkhar | 25,789 | 28,771 | 16 | **Maratha** | **242** | **262** |
| 7 | Gorkha | 1,912 | 5,525 | 17 | Meo | 1,16,227 | 1,20,578 |
| 8 | Gujar | 6,27,304 | 7,11,800 | 18 | Mughal | 1,02,979 | 1,30,760 |
| 9 | Jat | 44,32,750 | 46,25,523 | 19 | Rajput | 16,77,569 | 17,90,359 |
| 10 | Kahut | 9,502 | 2,026 | 20 | **Ror** | **40,731** | **43,212** |
| Total Group 1 Military & Dominants | | | | | | **77,40,609** | **84,29,942** |

**Abstract 85;** As per this redrawn abstract showing population of all Agricultural castes as in Punjab census 1891, Tehsil-wise, as below, shows Rors were inhabiting 7 districts & 15 Tehsils. (ibid168 to173/213 Appendix: C).

| Abstract 85; Punjab Census 1891; redrawn Tehsils wise showing selected Agricultural Tribes & castes | | | | | | | |
|---|---|---|---|---|---|---|---|
| District | Tehsil | **Ror** | Saini | Rajput | Ahir | Gujar | Jat | Kamboh |
| 1. Rohtak | **1.Rohtak** | 8 | 25 | 20,123 | 1,102 | 1,369 | 54,629 | 7 |
| | 2.Jhajjar | - | 9 | 5,439 | 14,220 | 1,364 | 34,439 | - |
| | 3.Sampla | - | - | 603 | 1,102 | 124 | 63,697 | - |
| | **4.Gohana** | 399 | - | 6,514 | 563 | 271 | 47,269 | - |

| | | | | | | | | |
|---|---|---|---|---|---|---|---|---|
| | Total | **407** | 34 | 32,714 | 16,987 | 3,128 | 2,00,034 | 7 |
| 2. Delhi | 1.Delhi | - | 1,072 | 3,747 | 9,157 | 2,332 | 35,504 | 43 |
| | 2.Delhi city | - | 289 | 47,336 | 2,352 | 656 | 2,303 | 6 |
| | **3.Sonipat** | 727 | 1 | 1,656 | 700 | 4,325 | 55,636 | 1 |
| | **4.Ballabgarh** | 1 | - | 1,594 | 1,361 | 18,825 | 12,340 | 8 |
| | Total | **728** | 1,362 | 56,905 | 13,570 | 26,138 | 1,05,843 | 58 |
| 3. Karnal | **1.Karnal** | **19,812** | 23 | 28,284 | 389 | 2,204 | 15,969 | 7,883 |
| | **2.Panipat** | **5,610** | - | 11,992 | 508 | 13,424 | 33,034 | 4 |
| | **3.Kaithal** | **14,392** | 38 | 21,564 | 525 | 10,842 | 50,076 | 2,122 |
| | Total | **39,814** | 61 | 61,840 | 1,422 | 26,470 | 99,079 | 10,009 |
| 4. Ambala | **1.Ambala** | 67 | 69 | 15,135 | 1,184 | 2,974 | 24,044 | 2,417 |
| | 2.Kharar | - | 13,327 | 14,260 | 37 | 8,318 | 31,733 | 1,306 |
| | **3.Jagadhari** | 71 | 43 | 10,913 | 58 | 8,500 | 12,832 | 5,229 |
| | **4.Naraingarh** | 12 | 489 | 14,427 | 3 | 14,248 | 11,040 | 19 |
| | 5.Ropar | - | 13,575 | 13,712 | 4 | 13,534 | 42,388 | - |
| | **6.Pipli** | **1,943** | 21 | 19,321 | 611 | 1,542 | 32,357 | 4,105 |
| | Total | **2,093** | 28,024 | 87,763 | 1,897 | 49,125 | 1,54,394 | 13,076 |
| 5. Hosiarpur | 1.Hosiarpur | - | 15,123 | 25,103 | 9 | 17,659 | 43,183 | 10 |
| | **2.Dasuya** | 10 | 13,193 | 23,397 | 2 | 9,676 | 23,734 | 436 |
| | 3.Una | - | 9,397 | 26,827 | 1 | 21,628 | 24,384 | 4 |
| | 4.Garhshankar | - | 8,051 | 28,941 | - | 29,287 | 67,856 | 8 |
| | Total | **10** | 45,764 | 1,04,268 | 12 | 78,250 | 1,59,157 | 458 |
| 6. Montgmery | 1.Montgomery | - | - | 18112 | 12 | 228 | 9767 | 29 |
| | **2.Gugaira** | 25 | - | 14436 | 52 | 18 | 8391 | 4 |
| | 3.Dipalpur | - | - | 20649 | 15 | 74 | 15384 | 9326 |
| | **4.Pakpathan** | 7 | 32 | 13728 | 16 | 142 | 12152 | 7615 |
| | Total | **32** | 32 | 69925 | 95 | 462 | 45694 | 16974 |
| 7. Lahore | 1.Lahore | - | 17 | 11802 | 185 | 4932 | 68199 | 3514 |
| | 2.Lahore city | - | 715 | 14647 | 634 | 1399 | 11099 | 2870 |
| | **3.Chunian** | 2 | - | 5641 | 78 | 877 | 33150 | 9281 |
| | 4.Kasur | - | 3 | 7195 | 25 | 15 | 39129 | 4665 |
| | 5.Sharakpur | - | - | 9475 | 4 | 367 | 20075 | 118 |
| | Total | **2** | 735 | 48760 | 926 | 7590 | 173652 | 20448 |
| | G. Total | **43086** | | | | | | |

**Note:** Population of **Rors of UP in 1891 was 4459**. District wise breakup is indicated in **para 6.10 of this chapter**. (Ref; "The Tribes & Castes of North-western Provinces & Oudh by William Crooke which is based on census-1891).

**(c) Census-1891: Punjab & its Feudatories, Part-III;** It consists of 982 pages & have tables on literacy by caste; redrawn for Ror caste only, as below, shows not very encouraging figures on the literacy of Rors in 1891.: (pp-544-55)

| Table C: literacy of Native territory; redrawn for Ror caste only showing literacy status as per 1891 census | | | | | | | | | |
|---|---|---|---|---|---|---|---|---|---|
| Class | Group | Caste | Total strength | | | | Literate (Males) | | Literate (Females) |
| A | 1 | **Ror** | **Hindu** | **Muslim** | Total | Total | Knowing English | Total | Knowing English |
| Native Territory | | | 98 | 28 | 126 | 1 | 1 | - | - |
| Patiala | | | 98 | 12 | 110 | 1 | 1 | - | - |
| Bahawalpur | | | - | 16 | 16 | - | - | -- | - |

**NB:** It is surprising to note that out of 34 native states, Rors are recorded in 2 states only, whereas should have been recorded in Jind, Nabha, & Kapurthala also. May be Rors have been recorded as *Arora or Rora or Khojah* (?)

**Sub-castes of Rors:** Rors recorded in 7 locations, had 169 Sub-castes (Surnames) as enumerated, recorded & indexed (page-930/982), in 1891 census and reproduced below. Sikhs & Muslim also were recorded among Rors.

| Rors & its sub-castes as recorded in census 1891: Population: 43212 = Hindu 42930 + Sikh 170 + Musalman 112 | | | | | | | | | | | |
|---|---|---|---|---|---|---|---|---|---|---|---|
| Sub-caste | Rl* | Loc** | Sub-caste | Rel* | Loc** | Sub-caste | Rl* | Loc** | Sub-caste | Rl* | Loc** |
| 1. Adbradi | M | 6 | 43.Dateri | H | 5 | 85.Kargra | H | 6 | 127.Naradwal | H | 5 |
| 2.Adif | S | 6 | 44.Dawan | H | 5 | 86. Karhan | H | 6 | 128. Nawali | H | 5 |
| 3.Agranfa | H | 5 | 45.Dehe | H | 6 | 87.Kari | H | 6 | 129. Neli | H | 5 |
| 4. Ardalsi | H | 6 | 46.Dhankar | H | 5 | 88.Karkar | H | 5 | 130. Neorman | H | 5 |
| 5.Badlf | H | 6 | 47.Dohli | H | 5 | 89.Kasir | H | 5 | 131.Nerag | H | 5 |
| 6.Bahandar | H | 6 | 48.Dojan | H | 6 | 90.Kehan | H | 6 | 132. Odana | H | 6 |
| 7. Bajori | H | 5 | 49.Gadaolad | H | 5 | 91. Keharangra | H | 2 | 133.Othai | H | 6 |
| 8.Balasar | H | 6 | 50.Gahonki | H | 5 | 92. Khan | H | 5 | 134.Oudh | M, H | 4,5 |
| 9. Baleri | H | 6 | 51. Galian | H | 5 | 93. Khokhra | H | 2 | 135.Pathan | H | 6 |
| 10.Banfan | H | 6 | 52.Gandal | H | 5 | 94. Lahar | H | 6 | 136.Rajput | H | 5 |
| 11.Banjash | H | 6 | 53.Gargadi | H | 5 | 95. Lahat | H | 2 | 137.Ratai | H | 6 |
| 12.Barag | H | 2 | 54.Garanl | H | 5 | 96. Lani | H | 5 | 138.Redasi | H | 5 |
| 13. Bhagni | H | 6 | 55.Gobadli | H | 5 | 97. Lari | H | 5 | 139.Rehban | H | 5 |
| 14.Bhal | M | 5 | 56. Golan | H | 5 | 98. Larkan | H | 6 | 140.Roheli | H | 2 |
| 15.Bhalan | H | 6 | 57. Goglana | H | 5 | 99. Larwal | H | 6 | 141.Rojli | H | 2,5 |
| 16. Bhanwal | H | 6 | 58.Goli | H | 6 | 100. Lateri | H | 5 | 142.Rora | H | 5, 8 |
| 17. Bhat | H | 6 | 59. Gondli | H | 5 | 101. Machran | H | 2 | 143. Rori | H | 11 |

| 18. Bahtan | H | 6 | 60. Gori | H | 5 | 102. Machhi | H | 5 | 144.Rorian | H | 6 |
|---|---|---|---|---|---|---|---|---|---|---|---|
| 19. Bhogan | H | 2 | 61.Goripal | H, M | 5 | 103. MahaB'man | H | 2 | 145.Sadan | H | 6 |
| 20.Bir | H | 6 | 62. Gwas | H | 5 | 104. Mahela | H | 5 | 146.Sagwal | H | 5 |
| 21.Bodhi | H | 6 | 63.Halu | H | 5 | 105. Mahla | H | 2 | 147.Saigwan | H | 2 |
| 22.Boh | H | 6 | 64.Jagran | H | 5 | 106.Mahrar | H | 2 | 148.Sanwan | H | 5 |
| 23. Chahda | H | 6 | 65.Jahar | H | 5 | 107.Maiwati | H | 5 | 149.Sardak | H | 5 |
| 24.Chand | H | 6 | 66.Janu | H | 5 | 108.Majla | H | 5 | 150.Saradi | H | 5 |
| 25.Chandni | H | 5 | 67.Jhankli | H | 5 | 109.Majli | H | 6 | 151.Saradwal | H | 5 |
| 26.Chandwar | H | 6 | 68.Jod | H | 5 | 110. Majra | H | 5 | 152. Sarmwal | H | 5 |
| 27.Charif | H | 5 | 69.Johri | H | 5 | 111.Malak | H | 2 | 153. Sarsali | H | 6 |
| 28.Chauhan | H | 5 | 70.Joji | H | 5 | 112.Malasar | H | 6 | 154. Sas | H | 5 |
| 29.Chhad | H | 8 | 71.Jokhal | H | 5 | 113.Mangli | H | 6 | 155.S 'man*** | H | 6 |
| 30.Choz | H | 6,4 | 72.Jokran | H | 2,6 | 114.Maniar | H | 5 | 156. Sawari | H | 5 |
| 31.Dadu | H | 5 | 73. Kachna | H | 2 | 115.Marian | H | 6 | 157. Sekhwan | H | 5,6 |
| 32.Dag | H | 5 | 74. Kadan | H | 2 | 116.Matahi | H | 6 | 158. Sewla | H | 6 |
| 33.Dahandal | H | 6 | 75.Kadarian | H | 5 | 117. Matir | H | 5 | 159. Serid | H | 5 |
| 34. Daharigar | H | 5 | 76.Kalaia | H | 5 | 118.Mehgor | H | 6 | 160. Soahri | H | 5 |
| 35.Daia | H | 2 | 77. Kalbakri | H | 6 | 119.Mele | H | 5 | 161. Sothi | H | 5 |
| 36.Daiaban | H | 5 | 78.Kandal | H | 6 | 120. Meli | H | 5 | 162. Taran | H | 2 |
| 37. Dandal | H | 5 | 79.Kangar | H | 5 | 121.Moli | H | 6 | 163. Taoli | H | 6 |
| 38.Dangar | H | 2 | 80.Kanjhan | H | 5 | 122.Morzan | H | 2,1 | 164. Tana | H | 2 |
| 39.Dara | H | 6 | 81.Kansi | H | 6 | 123.Munga | H | 5 | 165. Tanor | H, M | 5 |
| 40.Darab | H | 6 | 82. Kanwal | H | 6,5 | 124.Nahal | H | 6 | 166. Tarlah | H | 6 |
| 41. Darak | H | 6 | 83. Kapur | H | 5 | 125.Nai | H | 5 | 167. Tatar | H | 2 |
| 42.Darhari | H | 6 | 84.Karak | H | 5 | 126.Nangi | H | 6 | 168. Tondan | H | 2 |
| * Rl = Religion | | | **Loc = Locality | | | *** = Satambarman | | | 169. Turki | H | 6 |

**Note**; Many sub-caste or surnames, on close observation appears to be mixed up & common with many other castes. This usually happens when the enumerator/typist/compiler is not familiar with & not knowing the correct name & its spelling.

## 6.5 Census of India 1901; Vol.17, Punjab; its feudatories & the North-West Frontier Province, Part-1

Chapter- II, of Report by H A Rose, (pp-39 to112; total 486pages); deals in the movement of population; Part-1 describes Vital statistics, (pp-39 to 48); Part-II deals in increase & decrease in the population (Ibid48to73),& Part-III; migration of population from Rajputana, UP & other areas (ibid73 to 82).(*But no information on the migration of Rors from Rajasthan etc are found from this report?*). Ch-III, details Age, sexes, & civil conditions of the population (ibid189to262), subsidiary table VII-E, (Ibid 242to251), redrawn as below, for selected castes including **Rors,** indicates population by proportion of sexes.

| Part subsidiary table VII-E, for selected castes showing population as per census 1901 by the proportion of sexes | | | | | |
|---|---|---|---|---|---|
| Caste or Tribe | Religion | Population (1901) | | Females/1000 males | Children under 5 Females/1000 males |
| | | Males | Females | | |
| Gujar | H | 94175 | 75074 | 797 | 868 |
| | S | 1052 | 818 | 778 | 697 |
| | M | 307030 | 261473 | 852 | 940 |
| Jat | H | 889592 | 705669 | 793 | 839 |
| | S | 798128 | 599510 | 751 | 694 |
| | M | 1096215 | 933579 | 854 | 940 |
| Rajput | H | 240032 | 195297 | 814 | 869 |
| | S | 11596 | 8259 | 712 | 869 |
| | M | 723251 | 637258 | 879 | 951 |
| **Ror** | **H & S** | **24415** | **20238** | **829** | **890** |

Note: Population figures are for both Provinces & Native states. Figures in last column are excerpted from sub-table III of Ch- VIII.

Chapter-VIII on Caste, Tribe & Race, details terminologies on the *Ethnology* by Mr Herbert Risley, principal of origin of caste, its organisations, its inter-caste relations, social set up & rituals etc. (Ibid300-57) Excerpts on few castes, *which have some commonality in origin, with* **Rors,** are as below;

**1. Castes of Khatri Type; Khatris, Aroras, and Bhatias**: Khatris are essentially a trading caste, as are Aroras,& Bhatias, only *few engaged in Agriculture*. Khatris stand highest, many as Bankers, & largely employed in civil administration.The link between these three caste is obscure, indeed it is doubtful whether **Bhatias** has any *ethnological connection* (ref para:539; Punjab Census-1883 report) **with Khatri or Arora**. On the other hand, Aroras were described by Sir George Campbell *as a subordinate class of Khatris*, but they themselves claim Khatri origin.

**NB**: For more details refer chapter XII, Para-5 of Punjab census 1901 report pp-303 to 310.

**Khojas**: Para16; Khojas of Jhang, **are mainly Khatris converted to islam**, have hitherto preserved their original Hindu classification into Bari,& Bunjahi.The *converted Aroras also termed Khojas* & their sub-divsions who used not to intermarry with those of Khatri origin, but such marriages now occassinally occur. *Shahpur khojas have*

*10 sub-divisions*; 1. Sahgal; 2.Wohra/Bohra; 3.Sethi; 4.Kapur; 5.Duggal; 6.**Rawar or Ror**; 7.Matoli; 8.Goruwala; 9.Magu; 10. Mahndru. The first six & last three are Khatri section.Khojas of Leiah have the Khatri section-names of Kapur, Puri, Tindan (Tondon) & Gambhir.The term Khoja is a very vague one, as the numbers returned in census as Khojas include many converts to Islam of other castes than the Khatri & Arora. (pp-310; page; 373/486)

**2. Rajputs of Jammu Hills;** Para 27; There exists four hypergamous groups, out of which one group called *Dohri, who exchanges brides & practice widow remarriage as **Rors** do?* (ibid32)

**3. Jats**: Para 32; Jat is simplest in organisation out of four types & they comprise of a vast congeries (disorderly collection) of tribes, which are almost equal, though some of them have a vague & undefined supiriority. Though many Jat tribes have traditions of Rajput origin but neither territorial sovereignty, nor avoidance of widow re-marriage, Karewa, nor refusal of bride price will raise Jat tribe to Rajput status.

This democratic instinct & doctrine of equality among Jats have resulted into equal division of property; no tribal hypergamy & no bar to marriage with women of the *lowest caste*, and issues succeed equally unlike Rajputs where custom gives sons unequal succession & division of property depending on the status of the mother. Only among Jats, there is Bhaichara; tenure, the custom by which there was no division of land, each family cultivating what it could until possessions became the sole measure of its rights. (pp324, p391/486)

**4.Gujars;** Like Jats, Gujars in Gujrat (above Gujranwala, adjoining Sialkot, Shahpur, & below Jhelum in NWF) have 2-1/2 original sub-division; Gorsi, Kasana, & Bargat, the latter being the half sub-division as it descended from a slave mother. In Karnal Dhai-got, are said to be Gorsi, Chechi & half of Kasana. There is, no tribal hypergamy among Gujars, the only instance of hypergamy being in the Dhalak family of Keorak in Karnal as they give daughters only east of Jamuna, but they take wives from Gujars of the dist. (ibid25)

**The Variations in caste population:** Para 51; (ibid341), census of 1901: Variations in the population of certain castes, is sometimes very difficult to explain, especially in case of those caste which are small in numbers, as a change in the name of a small caste/tribe in a single village may largely affect the percentage of variation. One can explain the continued decrease in the number of the Agari's by decay of salt industry in Rohtak & Gurgaon, but not why the Ahirs increased by 13.8% in 1881-91 & only 4% in 1891-1901. Subsidiary table I: (ibid345 to 348): showing variations in numbers, redrawn for few selected castes is as below;

| Subsidiary Table I: Variations in numbers of Persons of caste, Tribe & race since 1881 | | | | | | |
|---|---|---|---|---|---|---|
| Caste | Census year/Population | | | % Percentage variation (+)/(-) | | Net variation (+)/(-) |
| Tribe or Race | 1901 | 1891 | 1881 | 1891-1901 | 1881-1891 | 1881-1901(20 yrs) |
| 1. Agari | 3444 | 4161 | 5122 | -17.2 | -18.8 | -32.7 |
| 2.Ahir | 205739 | 197649 | 173640 | +4.1 | +13.8 | +18.1 |
| 3. Arora | 721571 | 667197 | 601440 | +8.1 | +10.9 | +20 |
| 4. Bishnoi | 17114 | 8213 | 8576 | +108.4 | -4.2 | +99.6 |
| 5.Gujar | 739622 | 711800 | 627304 | +3.9 | +13.5 | + 17.9 |
| 6. Jat | 5022739 | 4625523 | 4432750 | +8.6 | +4.3 | +13.3 |
| 7. Kamboh | 174098 | 151160 | 129589 | +15.2 | +16.6 | +34.3 |
| 8. Khatri | 470976 | 447933 | 419139 | +4.9 | +6.9 | +12.2 |
| 9. Khojah | 102919 | 95887 | 65882 | +7.3 | +45.5 | +56.2 |
| 10.Rajput | 1874620 | 1700359 | 1648700 | +4.7 | +8.6 | +13.7 |
| **11. Ror** | **44771** | **43212** | **40731** | **+3.6** | **+6.1** | **+9.9** |

**Note:** *From the above table it is seen that **Rors** in a span of 20 years increased only by 9.9% whereas castes like; **Bishnoi** increased by almost 100%, Khoja by 56 %, Kamboh by 34%, Aroras by 20%, Ahir & Gujar by 18%, Rajputs by 14%, Jat by 13%. Is it not something intriguing i.e., either Rors have been counted in other castes or Rors might have adopted castes like Jat, Bishnoi, Arora, Ahir, etc.?*

## 6.6 Census of India 1911; Vol.14, Punjab: part 3, Appendices to the Imperial Tables

**Ror**, spelt as 'Rour,' were counted as part of *Arya Samaj Sect*. Pandit Kaul, (superintendent of census), also wrote; "Ror claim a Rajput origin & their social status is same. Rors were largely Hindu (44,511), with only a smaller number being Sikh (142)". (pp57, page; 62/192) **Table IX: Education by caste;** Redrawn as below showing literacy in each case shows literacy of Ror comparable to Rajput, Kambohs but better than Gujar & lower than Jats. (ibid53 to 59).

| A redrawn appendix IX for certain castes in Karnal district by Education: Sect: Arya*; Census-1911 | | | | | | | | | | | | |
|---|---|---|---|---|---|---|---|---|---|---|---|---|
| | Total | | | Literate | | | Illiterate | | | Literate in English | | |
| Caste | Persons | Male | Female | Persons | Male | Female | Persons | Male | Female | persons | Male | Female |
| 1.Gujar | 18 | 9 | 9 | -- | -- | -- | 18 | 9 | 9 | -- | -- | -- |
| 2.Jat | 2110 | 1147 | 963 | 13 | 13 | -- | 2097 | 1134 | 963 | 1 | 1 | -- |
| 3.Kamboh | 117 | 63 | 54 | 5 | 5 | -- | 112 | 58 | 54 | -- | -- | -- |
| 4.Rajput | 114 | 66 | 48 | 4 | 4 | -- | 110 | 62 | 48 | 1 | 1 | -- |
| **5. Rour** | **246** | **144** | **102** | **3** | **3** | **--** | **243** | **141** | **102** | **2** | **2** | **--** |
| Legend *: Among **Rour** (another spelling of **Ror**) none followed Brahmo's or Dev Samaj sect, so table is only for Arya Samaj. | | | | | | | | | | | | |

**Castes having sub-caste name: Ror, Rore, Rode, Chauhan, Mahla, or similar to Ror caste;** Appendix to Imperial table XIII, (ibid61) details the sub-castes of certain selected castes. A redrawn part Table-XIII of castes having sub-caste or surname similar to that of Ror caste etc for reference is as below;

| Part Table –XIII Castes with sub-castes as; Ror, Rore, Rora, Roda, Arora, Chopra, Dahia, Mahla, etc | | | | | |
|---|---|---|---|---|---|
| PP ref | Page ref | caste | Sub-caste | Persons | Locality@ |
| PP-63 | 68/192 | Ahir | Chauhan: H; S; M | 79; 2; 1; | 1,3,12; 12; 26 |
| | | | Chopra: H | 14 | 5 |
| | | | Dahia: H | 265 | 1,2,3,5 |
| | | | Dhabar: H; S | 476; 4 | 1,12; 49 |
| | | | Kandal: H | 125 | 1,2,4 |
| | | | Lamba: H | 536 | 1,2,3,4 |
| | | | Mahla: H | 142 | 2,4,11,32 |
| PP-66 | 71/192 | Awan | Mahla: M | 217 | 19,20,21 |
| PP-85 | 90/192 | Fakir | Bodla: H; S; M | 17; 1; 110 | 1,9,12; 1; 6,12,13,15,17to19,21 |
| PP-86 | 91/192 | | Khichi: M | 162 | 24,26,27,51 |
| | | | Khokhar: H; M | 90; 6,291 | 43; J, L, M |
| 102 | 107/192 | Jat | Jaglan: H; S; M | 3; 286; 32; 25 | 2,4,5,49; 5; 1,5 |
| 104 | 109/192 | | Kadian: H; M | 10; 366; 153 | 2,4,5,6,30, 48; 4,5,6 |
| 106 | 111/192 | | Khokhar: H; S; M | 677; 5764; 25059 | 2,6,16,50,51; 6,10,11,12,1415,17,24,46; 1,12,13,14,17,20,21,23,26,28,51 |
| 109 | 114/192 | | Mahla: H; S; M | 1872; 170; 755 | 1,2to4,10,12,32; 12,25; 1,7,17,18,20,28,51 |
| 115 | 120/192 | | Ror: H; S; M | 39; 1; 31 | 1,12,48; 49; 28 |
| 122 | 127/192 | Khatri | Chopra: H; S | 3,197; 377 | J, L, R, M, 1,4,5,7,39,41,43,44; 28,30,45,47 |
| | | | Dabar: H; S | 22; 1 | 15,25,26; 19 |
| 124 | 129/192 | | Khokhar: H; S | 11940; 427 | 5,11; 12,20 |
| 126 | 131/92 | Minor | Rode | 2 | PP-61, note no; 5, Not specified |
| 139 | 144/192 | Machhi | Mahle: M | 39 | 33,15,17 |
| 148 | 153/192 | Rajput | Khichi: H; S; M | 71; 1; 4963 | 1,2,16,44; 9; 1,12,16,17,19,20,24,26,51 |
| 150 | 155/192 | | Mehla: H; M | 17; 53 | 9; 48 |
| 152 | 157/192 | | Rore: H; S; M | 35; 2; 4 | 1,9,12,25,48; 14,25; 1,10 |
| 155 | 160/192 | Minor | Bodla | 3 | *PP-61, note no; 5, Not specified |
| | | | Dabra | 1 | *PP-61, note no; 5, Not specified |
| 162 | 167/192 | Sunar | Khichi: H; M | 11; 68 | 24,51; 12,44,51 |
| | | | Khokhar: H; S; M | 54; 6; 667 | 4,15; 11,16; 12,13,15,26 to 28 |

**Legend:** 1. Letter after sub-caste denotes the religion i.e., H= Hindu, S=Sikh, J=Jain, B= Buddhist, M= Muhammadan;

2. @: Numbers for localities/areas assigned for entering into census tables (29 Districts; 22 states); 1. Hisar Dist. 2. Rohtak, 3. Gurgaon, 4. Delhi, 5. Karnal, 6. Ambala, 7. Shimla, 8. Kangra, 9. Hoshiarpur, 10. Jalandhar, 11. Ludhiana Dist., 12. Firozpur, 13. Lahore, 14. Amritsar, 15. Gurdaspur, 16. Sialkot, 17. Gujranwala, 18. Gujrat, 19. Shahpur, 20. Jhelum, 21. Rawalpindi Dist., 22. Attuck, 23. Mianwali, 24. Montgomery, 25. Layyalpur, 26. Jhang, 27. Multan, 28. Muzaffargarh, 29. DeraGazi Khan, 30. Loharu State, 31. Dujana State, 32. Pataudi State, 33. Kalsia state, 34. Nahan State, 35. Jubbal State, 36. Bashahr State, 37. Keonthal State, 38. Baghal State, 39. Bilaspur State, 40. Nalgarh state, 41. Simla Minor Hill State, 42. Mandi State, 43. Suket State, 44. Kapurthala State, 45. Malerkotla State, 46. Faridkot State, 47. Chamba State, 48. Patiala State, 49. Jind State, 50. Nabha State, 51. Bahawalpur State;

3. Abbrievation for States; P= Punjab; B=British Territory; S=Native State; D= Delhi Division; J=Jalandhar Division; L=Lahore Division; R=Rawalpindi Div; M=Multan Division;

4. Sub-castes not returning more than 10 have been grouped together under the head, "Minor" with a footnote giving the detail of such sub-castes with the strength of each.

**NB;** The names of sub-castes were carelessly written by the Enumerators, some of whom did not know how to spell the words. The copyist cared equally little about the spellings. The sorting was the third stage at which the names were read anyhow & put down as per opinion of the operator. Tabulation was the 1st operation for rational rendering of the entries. Some mistakes got detected due to the personal knowledge of the compiler staff were corrected. All doubtful sub-castes' entries were sent to the Tahsils of Enumeration & the correct spellings obtained from Tahsildars I, therefore prefix the Table with my apologies for mistakes of spellings as may have crept in.

**Civil conditions of Rors in Karnal District;** Appendix to Imperial Table XIV: shows civil conditions by Age in respect of; unmarried, married, and widows, of Arya *Samaj* followers for certain districts (ref; para 4; ibid167).The detailed table (ref; ibid168 to 183 vol-14) in r.o Arya Samaji sect like; Ror, Rajput, Gujar, Jat, Kamboh, Kayasth, Khatri, Sunar etc of the Karnal dist. shows the civil conditions of Rors for all three (3) marital status related parameters at par with other socially similarly placed castes which were part of Arya Samaj sect.

## 6.7 Census of India 1921; Vol. 15; Punjab & Delhi: part 2, Tables

**Rors** figures only in Table-XIII (a part redrawn below); Caste or Tribe: sex wise at PP-246; p-253/456; Total 456 pages);

| Part Table XIII; Caste & Tribes: sex wise Population of Rors in Punjab census-1921 | | | | | | |
|---|---|---|---|---|---|---|
| State or District | Hindu | | Sikh | | Total | |
| | Male | Female | Male | Female | Male | Female |
| Punjab | **22721** | **18974** | **215** | **135** | **22936** | **19109** |
| 1. British Territory | 22005 | 18414 | 156 | 96 | 22161 | 18510 |
| (a) Ambala Division | 22005 | 18408 | 156 | 96 | 22161 | 18504 |
| (b) Jalandhar Division | -- | 6 | -- | -- | -- | 6 |
| 2. Punjab States | 716 | 560 | 59 | 39 | 775 | 599 |

NB: territory (ref PP-193 to 254; page -200 to 261/486) from original Table- XIII; Total population of Rors; 42045;

No Muslims were recorded among Rors in this above shown table of 1921 census. During the same period, the population of **Arora**, written as **Rora**, were found to have about Musalmans (318= 145 males + 173 females) in all areas except in Rawalpindi Div, Punjab state & Delhi Div, Hindus 5,94,485 (3,20,707 males + 2,73,778 females) & Sikhs 1,23,096 (64,975 + 58,121) State or District were; Punjab; 1.British Territory (a) Ambala Div. (b)Jalandhar Div (c) Lahore Div. (d) Rawalpindi Div. (e) Multan Div. 2.Punjab States,& 3. Delhi. (ref table XIII; at PP-196; page -203/486).

## 6.8 Census of India, 1931, Vol. XVII; Punjab Part- I: Ror caste does not figure in this.

## 6.9 A Glossary of Tribes and castes in Punjab & NWFP

Compiled by HA Rose (3vol) is based on Punjab census-1881 report of Denzil Ibbetson & Census 1891 of E Maclagan. Vol-I deals with socio-political, & other related general subjects about the tribes & castes. Vol-II describes the particular castes alphabetically from A-K & Vol-III from L-Z.

**(a) A Glossary of Tribes and castes in Punjab & NWFP; Volume-I**; It consists of 991 pages & 5 chapters: Ch-I; Description of society & polity; (PP-1 to 730), Ch-II; Rites & Ceremonies of all religions & sects; (PP-731 to 907), Ch-III; Caste & Sectarial marks (PP 908-9), Ch-IV; Superstitions & Ceremonies relating to Dwellings; (PP-910 to 918), and Ch-V; Dances & performing arts (PP- 919 to 991).

**(b) A Glossary of Tribes & castes in Punjab & NWFP; Volume-II; A-K:** It alphabetically describes the clans from A to K alphabet & other ethnographic details of Tribes & castes existing that time in Punjab & NWFP of India. (573 pages) An extract of the castes having *surnames common with Rors,* is as below;

**Ahirs**: Name is derived from Sanskrit *abhira*, a milkman. Ahir's own tradition as to their origin is; that a Brahmin once took a Vaisya girl to wife & her offspring were pronounced *amat-sangya or outcaste*; that again daughter of amat-sangya married a Brahmin, and her offspring were called abhirs i.e., herdsmen, which corrupted to Ahir. Also see para 5(3)(3) on them from the previous chapter. (PP-5 to 7; p-18 to 20/614) They are divided into 3 sub-castes; (1) Nandbansi; consider offspring of Nand; foster-father of Bhagwan Shri Krishna. (2) Jadubansi; claims to be descendants of Yadu, a nomadic race, and (3) Gualbansi; said to be descended from Guala or herdsman dynasty & the Gopis of Gokul & Brindavan. Jadubansi; Mostly found in Ahirwal & Hariana, while Nandbansi & Gualbansi are found in Mathura and Brindavan. Out of 55 gots of Jadubansi Ahirs, **14 gots**, as shown in table **are common** (9 same + 5 almost same) matching with Rors. called abhirs i.e., herdsmen, which corrupted to Ahir. Also see para 5(3)(3) on them from the previous chapter. (P. P-5 to 7; p-18 to 20/614)

| Sno | No | Name | Sno | No | Name | Sno | No | Name | Sno | No | Name | Sno | No | Name |
|---|---|---|---|---|---|---|---|---|---|---|---|---|---|---|
| 1 | 11 | Dabar | 4 | 15 | Dhundala | 7 | 35 | Khosa | 10 | 41 | Mahla | 13 | 54 | Tundak |
| 2 | 12 | Dahiya | 5 | 21 | Jharudhya | 8 | 37 | Kinwal | 11 | 42 | Mandhar | 14 | 55 | Solangia |
| 3 | 14 | Dholiwal | 6 | 33 | Khola | 9 | 39 | Lanba | 12 | 52 | Thokaran |  | or | Solanki |

**Similarities & Social intercourse among Ahirs & Rors;** Both follow Karewa. Birth, marriage & death ceremonies are also same except the dress of the women. Ahirs eat Kachchi & pakki roti with all Brahmin & Vaisyas, but the latter do not eat kachchi from them. *Ahirs eat Kachchi with Rajputs, Jats, Hindu Gujars, Rors, Sunars & Tarkhans*, while the latter eat with formers also & *Rors*. (ibid7; 20/614)

**Arora or Rora:** Further to para 6.3(a)(1); Aroras a Jatki speaking caste dwelling in Multan division & Derajat, is active & enterprising, industrious & thrifty. A Jhang proverb, "when an Arora girds up his loins, he makes it only two miles to Lahore."

Primarily Aroras have 4 territorial groups; 1. Uttaradhi: Northern, 2. Dakhana or Southern, 3. Dahra or Western, and 4. Sindhi of Sindh. Number 2 & 3 inter-marry in some parts, but not in some others like Jhang. Dakhana still take wives from Dahra as earlier. The Uttaradhi are absolutely endogamous east of Indus, except in Bahawalpur where they take wives from the other three groups: in *Hazra they take wives from the Dahra or Dakhana on payments but not exchange; & in Ferozepore they take from Dahras*. Uttaradhi alone seems, have Bari-Bunjahi; 12 sections; Sub-Group (i): 1. Ghumai, 2. Narule, 3. Monge, 4. Bazaz, 5. Shikri; Sub-Group (ii): 6. Manchande, 7. Pasriche; and Sub-Group (iii): 8. Kantor, 9. Manak Tahle, 10. Guruware, 11. Wadhwe, 12. Seth or Sethi.

The names ending in Ja e.g., **Budhraja** (a religious origin) are patronymics. **Narang**- original Raghbansi; (denied it to Parshu Ram, with; **Na rag**). **Narula**- nirala, 'unique'. **Gogia** or Gogas- saying: khat khuh, 'bhar pani, Tan tani parsing Gogiani'. **Dua's**; curing power a sprain or loin. **Chugh,** who cure *chuk,* & **Dhingra** also, by touching their cloth; if non present, their house-wall is as efficacious as a Chugh. (ibid16-19)

Several Arora sections are named after animals; 1. **Babbar;** born feet foremost, 2. **Chutani;** after Bat, 3. **Gaba** after calf, 4. **Ghira;** Dove, 5.**Giddar;** Jackal, 6.**Ghora**/Ghoda; horse, 7.Hans; Goose, 8.Kukar; Kukkar: Cock, 9.Kukreja; Cockrell, 10.Lumar; Fox, 11.Machhar; Mosquito, 12.Makkar; Locust, 13.Menda; Ram or Mindha, 14. Nangial; Snake, 15. Nagpal; Protectors or raisers of snake, 16.Sipra; a serpent. Several sections are named after plants & likely to be Totemistic; 1. **Chaula/Chawla;** after Rice, 2. **Gera;** avoid Geru, 3. **Gheia;** after Ghee, 4. **Jandwani**-Jand tree, 5. **Kasturia;** no use of Kasturi, 6. **Kathpal;** wood, 7. **Kataria;** Dagger-worshiper at marriage, 8.**Khani-jan;** Imley-eater, 9.**Lota;** a vessel- lota, 10. **Manik Tahle** or Shisham tree, 11. **Mehndiratta;** Henna, 13. **Mungi;** a kind of tree, 14.**Pabreja;** a kind of plant, 15.**Rihani;** Basil- a faqir blessed, 16.**Sawi-Buti;** green-herb, 17.**Selani;** pipal tree, 18.**Taneja;** a Grass type, Tiran, 19.**Tareja,** tarri, 20. **Veh Khani,** Viu Khani -poison (arsenic) eater.(ibid19-20) **NB:** 1. Aroras have **192 Gotras.** A group & area-wise list is available at appendix-1 of Vol-III. 2. Region wise number of Aroras gotr; Uttardhe (85) & Dahra (133) in Jhang, and Dakhana (31) in Multan see original Appendix -A; pp-511-13, p-523-25/572. **Marriages;** Women of the Uttaradhi group wears red ivory bracelets, & red petticoats with red border, thus called Lalchudiwala, Dakhana group wears white ivory bracelets & red petticoats with lower part laced with black, whence called Safedchudiwala. Dahra women are said to have red petticoat with a green border. In some places Dahra women wear white, & Dakhana spotted bracelets of both colors. (ibid20)

**Widow remarriage:** In theory it is reprobated (dishonourable), but in practice tolerated among Aroras. The Brahmin recognises the widow remarriage and assist in it, in fact if it is solemnised without a Brahmin, people refrain from eating or drinking with the couple for a short time. In Muzaffargarh, widow re-marriage is not approved, and couples who defy it are called kachchra; mulish/wicked. (ibid20-21)

**Succession Laws:** The customary succession law of the Aroras *differ both from Hindu law & the ordinary Punjab custom.* In its main feature it resembles the Hindus generally in the south-west Punjab, and one of its distinctive features is *Sawai,* i.e., to give an extra quarter share to the eldest son. Many Arora sections allow sons by the wife of another caste provided she was married as a virgin, not as a widow, 1/3rd of their father's property, and 2/3rd going to the sons by the other (Arora) wife. (ibid21)

**The Khatris:** Further to para 6.3.a (2); they occupy a very different position among people of Punjab from other mercantile castes of likes Aroras, being superior to them in physique, in manliness, in energy, not like them; a mere shopkeeper, but direct representative of the Kshatriya of Manu. (PP 506-26; p-545- 565/614)

As in George Campbell's *Ethnology of India*: "They have broader & more distinct facial features, are very fair, fine, handsome race, and educated. Besides monopolizing trade of Punjab & greater part of Afghanistan, they are chief civil administrator & almost all literature work is in their hands. Khatris are staunch Hindus; though they are priests to Sikhs, but they themselves seldom Sikhs."

**Groups of Khatris;** Three main groups; **Group-I; Bari-** consists of 12 exogamous sections; 1. Kapur, 2. Khanna, 3. Malhotra or Mohra, 4. Kakkar or Seth, 5. Chopra, 6. Talwar, 7. Sahgal, 8. Dhawan, 9. Wadhawan, 10. Tannan, 11. Bohra or Vohra, 12, Maindaru: First four; senior group, remaining Junior group. Four sub-groups from marriage point of view; 1. Dhaighar, 2. Charghar, 3. Chheghar, 4. Baraghar (ibid508) **Group-II; Bunjahi-** theoretically consist of 52 sections. **Sub-Group-I**; Khokhran; 8 sections: Section-1; Anand & Basin: Section-2 Chadha, Virbans & Sahni 3. Suri & Sethi, 4. Koli & Sabharwal; **Sub-Group-2**; Bunjahi Khas or Kalan: Asli or Bari Bunjahi comprising of 12 sections; **Sub-Group-3:** Bara or elder Bunjahi, with 40 sections called collectively Dharman or Dahrmain; **Sub-Group-4:** Chhota or younger Bunjahi, with 100 sections called Ansar or sair or Bunjahi Khurd (ibid pp; 509-510). It is mentioned in Ain-e-Akbari Vol-III p-117 (Blochmann's Transcription) **Group-III; Sarin;** *It's not part of Ain-e-Akbari as it originated afterward.* This group is divided into 20 grades, each grade consisting of 6 sections, in fact 128 sections with 2 subgroups. **Sub-group-1**; Bara or elder Sarin; comprises of 13 sections. **Sub-group-2**; Chhota or junior Sarin; comprises of 108 of sections. (ibid510)

**Rules of Marriage:** Normally Khatri avoids 4 *gots*; father, mother, Dadi & Nani. But when the law of hypergamy reduces the circle of alliances, this rule has to give the way. Thus, Dhaighar families of Kapur, Khanna, Malhotra & Seth section are not bound by this rule & avoids only fathers gotr & near relative of mother. Further the rule forbidding intermarriages between the descendants of a common ancestor is not invariably observed, as their 1st three sections are descendant from 3 brothers, yet their descendants are closely intermarried. Khokhran avoid only the gotr of father & mother as they have few sections to marry into. Bari appears to avoid both the parents & relation of their mothers within 7 degrees, but no general rule can be laid down. A common Brahminic gotra is also said to be, as a rule, a bar to intermarriage, but though Khanna & Kapur sections are both Kaushal gotra, but they inter-marry. (ibid512) **Khatri; age of Betrothal & Marriage:** Its group status based. Khatris of Rawalpindi, it is 4-8 yrs & 8-10 among Bunjahi. Marriage follows at 8-12 among former & at 10-12 among latter. Married life in all groups starts at 13-15 year, as there is *no Muklawa.* (ibid513)

**Khatri *Got* name;** (Folk etymology; ancient military name); **Sarin;** Surin-a warrior, **Khokhran;** Karakhan descendant of Krukhak- (one son of Manu). **Bhalla;** spear; **Basin-** Bas-brilliancy, & in-master; Sun. **Bohra;** Buha-a column of military. **Dhawan** messenger of battlefield. **Kakkar**-karkar-strong. **Kapur**-Karpur. **Khanna;** Khaan-mine & also a sapper. **Kochar**- Karach- an armour. **Mahendru**- Mahendra, lord of Earth. **Mehra**- Mihir-the Sun. **Sahi**- bankers/Sahji. **Sahni, Soni** - from Sanokar. **Senani**- head of army. **Seth**-rich. **Tandan**-abbreviation of Martand; Sun. **Beri**- an offshoot of Chopra & born under a Beri tree. **Bhuchar**-originally Talwar. **Chopra** also called Chopra Rajava, Jat, & **Kanungo Chopra;** claim descent from one *Champat Rai.* **Dhir**- brave; from Ajudhia & settled at Kandahar. **Marwaha**-from Marusthal (a sarin group). **Tuli**-saved from a torrent by holding a tula; **Uppal;** a Stone; their guru is in Anandpur, Hoshiarpur. (ibid514-526)

(c) **A Glossary of Tribes and castes in Punjab & North-West Frontier Province; Volume -III; L-Z;** This Vol. (558 pages) describes the clans and other ethnographic details of Tribes & Castes from alphabet L-Z, existing that time in Punjab & NWFP. Rors & Castes with surnames common with Rors are described below.

**Ror:** Punjab Rors, wrote Ibbetson, hold a Chaurasi in the great dhak jungles south of Thanesar in Karnal. Rors have spread down the Western Jumna Canal into the lower parts of Karnal and into Jind in considerable numbers. There is a Ror barah, south of Kaithal, whose *got* is *Turan.* They are said also to hold 12 villages beyond the Ganges. The **Amin** *men (Chauhan-Bachhas by got) say that they came from Sambhal in Muradabad;* but this may only be to connect themselves with their neighbours the Chauhan* Rajput, who certainly, came from there. But almost all the Rors alike seem to point origin through Badli, though some of them say they came from Rajputana. Their social status is identical** with that of Jats; and they practise Karewa or widow-marriage, though only, they say, within the caste. Their subdivisions seem to be exceedingly numerous. A few of the largest are the *Sagwal, Maipla, Khichi and Jogran.* The *Ambala* Rors would appear to be mostly Sagwal. *The Rors of Pipli (Thanesar) are described by Mr. Kensington as having a modified custom of **chundavand:** a system by which brothers succeed their father equally, but only uterine brother, a half-brother sharing same mother but having a different father, inherit from a deceased father, the whole blood excluding the half.* (Ibid334-35)

**Legends:** 1. {* The Chauhan legend admits the descent of the Ror of Amin, etc., from Rana Har Rai. Originally in many cases, if not in all, they held their lands as dependants of the Rajputs, without much doubt.} 2. {** Sir J. M. Douie says they (Rors) rank below Jats and their caste organisation is stronger than that of the other agricultural tribes, the panchayat being still powerful.}

## 6.10 Tribes and Castes of North-Western Provinces & Oudh: Rors

This book in 4 volumes compiled by William Crooke in 1896, based on the report of Census-1891, describes Rors of Uttar Pradesh (which includes Uttarakhand also) in Vol-IV, (pp-243 to 244) and Verbatim is as below;

**Rors**; It is a small caste of cultivators in the western Districts. Of their kinsmen in the Panjab Mr. Ibbetson, (ref section 476 of his book on Panjab Ethnography) write," The real seat of the Panjab Rors is in the great *dhak* jungles south of Thanesar on the borders of the Karnal and Ambala Districts, where they hold a *Chaurasi*; 84 villages, of which the village of Amin, where the Pandavs arranged their forces before their last fight with Kauravs, is their head village (?). But the Rors have spread down the Western Jumna Canal into to the lower parts of Karnal & into Jind in considerable numbers. They are fine stalwart men of very much of the same type as the Jats, whom they almost equal as husbandmen; their women also working in the fields. They are more peaceful & less grasping in their habits than the Jats, and are consequently readily admitted as tenants, where latter would be kept at arm's length. Of their origin I can say nothing certain. They have the *same story as Aroras*, of they *having been Rajputs*, who escaped the fury of Parasuram by stating their caste was **Aur, or 'Another.'** *The Aroras are often called Roras in the east of Panjab; yet I can hardly believe that the frank & stalwart Ror is of same origin as the Arora. The Amin men say that they came from Sambhal in the Moradabad*; but this may be only to connect themselves with their neighbours Chauhan Rajputs, who certainly came from there. But almost all Rors seem alike to point to Badli in the Jhajjar Tahsil of Rohtak district as their immediate place of origin, though some of them say they have come from Rajputana. Their social status is identical with that of Jats; and they practice *Karewa*, 'widow 'marriage', though only, they say, within the caste. Their divisions appear to be exceedingly numerous; some of them are *Sagwal, Maipla* (should be Mehla as even today there is no such surname in Rors?), *Khichi, and Jogran.*

2. Saharanpur Rors are to have been created at Kaithal by Sri Krishna in the war of Mahabharata. *Their marriage ceremonies resemble to those of Jats & Gujars*; they permit widow marriage; the levirate is practically compulsory.

3. From an account of Rors of the Bijnor supplied by the District Officer, it appears that the tribal tradition of their origin is that when Shri Ram Chandra severed his connection with Sita, she was pregnant, and went into the jungle under the protection of the Rishi Valmiki. She bore a son there, who was named Luv, and one day, when she was leaving the house for some work in the jungle, she put the child in charge of the Rishi. The child however followed his mother,

and the Rishi finding him missing, and supposing him to be dead, constructed another child out of a wisp of *Kusa grass*. When Sita returned and saw the other child, she asked the Rishi what is it? The Rishi replied, **"roraphora,"** (apparently meaning, 'this useless thing'), "is also your son." Hence, they were called Rors.

4. They are said to have migrated to Bijnor some 4 century ago (~1491 AD) from a place called Fatehpur Pundri in the Karnal District. Half this village was owned by the Rors, and half by a colony of Sayyids. The Sayyid's quarrelled with the Rors, who were forced to emigrate under their leader Mahi Chand. *By another story they were originally Tomar Rajputs of Delhi, which they were forced to leave after the conquest of their tribe.* By a third account, their *emigration from Delhi took place in the time of Aurangzeb.*

5. They marry & perform their other family ceremonies in the usual manners common to respectable Hindus. Widows can marry again, and the levirate, though permissible, is not compulsory on the widow. There is no regular form of divorce, but a wife detected in adultery is expelled from the tribe by the decree of the tribal council, and cannot subsequently on payment of a penalty be readmitted to caste rights.

6. Their chief occupation is agriculture, to which they add the making of hemp matting & twine. (*Tat, Sutli*; In Haryana side I have never come across such occupation or seen it (?).

7. They eat mutton, fish, fowl, pork(?), and venison (meat of any type of Deer), and drink spirits (?). But do not eat beef, Monkeys, or vermin. It is said that they will eat Kachchi and Pakki cooked by them or any other similar or superior caste, and smoke & drink with Jats & Gujars.

8. Distribution of Rors in North-western province & Oudh (present UP & UK) as tabulated below;

| Distribution of Rors in North-western Province's (present UP & UK) as per Census of 1891 | | | | | |
|---|---|---|---|---|---|
| S. No | Districts | Numbers | S. No | Districts | Numbers |
| 1. | Dehradun | 3 | 5. | Etawah | 5 |
| 2. | Saharanpur | 3,320 | 6. | Bijnor | 614 |
| 3. | Muzaffarnagar | 475 | 7. | Benares | 41 |
| 4. | Mathura | 1 | Total | | 4,459 |

* * * * *

# Chapter-7. People of India and Rors

## 7.1 General

Anthropological Survey of India (AnSI), with the objective to generate descriptive anthropological profile of all the communities residing in India under, "People of India" launched a project on 2 October 1985, & in 1994 produced eleven, People of India; National Series Vol I to XI, and thirty-two series for all states & Union Territories. Present chapter describes the Ror community as in Haryana, & Uttar Pradesh (i/c Uttarakhand). (PP 424-29) & (PP1220-23) (This chapter is an extract from People of India: Haryana, Vol-XXIII, and Uttar Pradesh (includes Uttarakhand) Vol-XLII part-III, series)

## 7.2 A Note on the series (Abridged version of; General Editor & Former DG, AnSI; Mr K.S Singh)

The identification & listing of communities have a long history, starting from the early period of Indian history, with Manu. Regional list of communities figured in Sanskrit works. Medieval chronicles had a description of communities of entire India. Listing of communities in the colonial period, was done in the census of India 1881 & 1891.

This group starting with 6748 communities & finalised 4635. Treating each state & UT a unit, study was conducted starting with least-known, then lesser-known, & better-known communities. Scholars interviewed large numbers but recorded only 24951 (i/c 4981 women) key informants i.e., 5 per community. On an average a community was studied at 2 places, but smaller ones were studied at one place only, being not located in more than one area. The study was conducted in 3581 villages, & 1011 towns in 421 dist. of states & UTs. Five scholars collected information from about 25000 informants in 26510 days (5.5 day/community), over a period of 7 years from 1985 to 1992.

## 7.3 Haryana: An Overview of Ethnic Profile (from forward by K.S. Singh, abridged from the original pp- XIII to XIX)

Present communities of Haryana were studied through ethnographic survey from November, 1985 to June, 1988, by Anthropologists from AnSI, Sociologists from HAU, Hisar & MDU, Rohtak. The results of survey were discussed at the workshop held at Hisar in August, 1989, & "People of India: Haryana," series was published in 1994.

In folk perception Haryana, defined by ethnicity, dialects, and ecology, have five eco-cultural zones. Ahirwal region of Mahendergarh dist. & part of Gurugram, is dominated by Ahirs, Mewat region of Gurgaon & Faridabad dist. by Meos. Bagad, dist. of Sirsa, Hisar, & Bhiwani derives its identity from the Bagadi dialect of Rajasthan & shares its ecology also. Nardak region, of dist. of Ambala, Kurukshetra, Kaithal, & Karnal bordering Punjab, is marked by the influence of Punjabi, and areas adjoining Himachal Pradesh have some influence of Pahari dialect also. The heartland of Haryana; Bangar; part of Karnal, Rohtak, Sonipat, & Jind speaks Khadiboli, and shares with Nardak features such as; fertile soil, irrigated land, the green revolution. Haryana lying between Yamuna & NH-1 consisting of Yamunanagar, part of dist. of Karnal, Panipat & Sonipat touching Delhi border, called Khadar, has influence of western UP having dialect of western UP (towards Yamuna) & Khadiboli (towards Highway).

Most of the 82 communities are widely distributed, but few like Megh, Bangali; Chidimaar etc lived in small pockets. There is no ST in Haryana, but it has a high proportion of SC (24%). Among agricultural castes like *Rajputs, Gujars, Rors* etc, Jats are the most dominant. About 54 communities, identify themselves regionally with NW region of India in r.o. biological structure & social organisation. *Ethnographic account exists for 45 & historical for 29 communities. About 52 communities have migrated to their present habitat, migration is recalled & remembered in oral tradition by about 37 communities.* People of Haryana are *above medium to tall, have a long head, and a narrow nose.* Few groups only have been studied in Haryana for blood group & other genetic traits.

Though a small state, but, sixteen (16) Dialect are spoken in Haryana. These are Bagadi, Bangri, Bazigar Boli, Dogri, Gujjari, Haryanvi, Hindi, Khadiboli, Marwari, Mewari, Nepali, Pahari, Punjabi, Rajasthani, Sansi, & Urdu. Haryanvi is spoken by largest number of communities (38), followed by Hindi (18), Punjabi (11); & Urdu is spoken by (3) communities. The Bazigari & Sansi Boli are spoken by Bazigar and Sansi communities.

People of India are identified with 776 cultural traits of ecology & settlements, cropping patterns & food habits, identification markers & dress, social organisation, economy & occupation linkage, and impact of change & development. Some of the traits; unique to Haryana; which relatively standout w.r.t the rest of the country are; wearing turban; wearing of Ornaments both by females & males, and tattooing.

Haryana has a very high level of Vegetarianism (74%), due to pastoral cult & influence of Vaishnavism/Arya Samaj. However, now there is a marked change to non-vegetarian. As to consuming pattern, wheat and gram are consumed by all. The intake of Rice (91%), Bajra (57%), and Jowar (32%), is also higher than national average. The intake of Moong and Urad is most common. There is high consumption of Maize (86%), & Mustard oil (93%).

As traditional milk producing state-Haryana is a center of the white revolution-report high production & consumption of milk and its products. However, Haryana also reports high consumption of Alcohol, particularly among men (80%). Smoking of Hukka as a symbol of status & sharing among equals is embedded in cultural traditions. The incidence of smoking Bidi & Cigarette has also increased, at a faster rate than elsewhere.

As elsewhere, social divisions exist in majority of the communities, and as per hierarchy it regulates marriage in large number of communities (93.9%). In marriage gotra exogamy is observed, even gotras of mother, step mothers, grandmothers as well as maternal grandmothers are also avoided. All communities follow negotiation as the common mode of marriage by observing endogamy & monogamy norms. Marriage symbols are wearing bangles & bindi. Incidence of Kanyadaan & dowry is reported higher.

There is strikingly a high incidence of levirate (the custom of marrying brother's widow-Karewa) 84% Vs national avg.14%; Junior levirate is practised by 44 and senior levirate by 13 communities. There is slightly higher proportion of junior sororate (opposite of levirate; in this a husband engages in marriage or sexual relations with wife's sister, usually after death or proven infertility of his wife) practised by 50 communities, and senior sororate is practised by 12 communities.

An important trait in Haryana is village *exogamy* (69% Vs 9% of India). Marriage within same village is prohibited as all living in a village are considered of same descent-*a survival of uni-gotra settlement*. It is true, even if a village have different gotras, as children of same village are considered bother–sisters & it is sin to marry the girls of same village (even of different caste). Only a few communities (10%), accept inter-community marriages.

Land the main resource, is controlled by individual upper-class proprietors. Paradoxically about 2/3rd of the communities is landless. Animal husbandry, a dominant traditional occupation, is practised by 70% communities, & is more widespread than settled cultivation which is pursued by 44% of communities Vs national avg. of 54%.

Pastoralism, is by 3.66 % of communities; it is almost double of the national average. As landlessness is rampant, 56% communities work as labourers. While bonded labour is non-existent, there is a significant proportion of child labour. Due to landlessness, there are large numbers of both skilled & un-skilled labourers.

With the spread of Arya Samaj movement, many traditional kinds of worship have declined. Worship of family deities is confined to only 17% Vs national avg. of 61%. Deities of wider pantheon are worshipped by a large number of communities (79%). The Priests from other communities perform the life cycle ceremonies like marriage & death. The patron-client relationship is on the decline.

Haryana has a vibrant folk culture. Oral traditions are reported from all communities (95%) in all forms; folksongs (95), folklore (90), and folktales (94%). Women participate in folk dance (41 Vs national avg.10%). Significantly both men & women participate in folk dance (37 % Vs national avg. 27%), showing popularity of folk culture.

A small but dynamic state, Haryana shows ubiquitous impact of various developmental programmes. Education is favoured for both boys and girls even at PG level. Family planning is favoured by 91% communities with 2 or 3 children's norms. Hand pumps & taps are the main source of drinking water. Irrigation by tube-wells & canal is widespread. Haryana has been a dynamic region of agriculture development. The green & white revolution have made their contribution to the central pool of food grains, besides developing the best breed of cows & buffaloes.

## 7.4 Introduction; Haryana series (By A.K. Bhatia; abridged from original ibid pp-1 to12)

The origin of the name Haryana emanates from *Hari-ka-ana*. It appears in Mahabharata as well as on ancient coins, especially of Yaudheyas. In *Rigved*, *Hariana is* used as a qualifying adjective to King Varu Raja who is said to have ruled it (Ref; Singh 1989). This region was a cradle of Vedic culture, a place of greatest battle of history, Mahabharat. The legendary Saraswati holy river is believed to have flowed past Ambala, Pipli, Kurukshetra, Pehowa, and Sirsa before vanishing in the Bhatner (Bikaner) desert (Ref; Datta and Phadke1985). It was on the banks of this river that the Vedic hymns were composed & recited, and the roots of Indian culture were planted. An inscription of 1327 AD, refers to this region as heaven on earth & includes Delhi (Dhillika) founded by Tomars in it.

Haryana was tagged to Punjab as "political punishment" after 1857 war of Independence by Britishers. It always got step-motherly treatment & suffered on all fronts. So, in 1927 Lala Deshbandu Gupta of Panipat asserted that this Hindi speaking region had never been part of Punjab, and demand it to be a separate state. So, as per 23 September 1966 resolution of parliament, Haryana came into existence on 1 Nov, 1966 as 17th State of India comprising of 7 districts; Gurugram, Mahendergarh, Rohtak, Hisar, Karnal, Jind, & Ambala.

**People of Haryana:** Pre-British ethnographic profile of people of Haryana, can be gleaned from the description given for earlier Punjab Province. *Yasastilikachampu* (a 10th century work) of Somadeva, stated this region as: *"The Yaudheyas country*, which included parts of Kurukshetra, was like an ornament of the earth, replete with all requisites of good and happy life. Its people having all objects necessary for pursuit of *dharma, artha*, lived as it were in heaven. They lead a peaceful and quite life without social frictions; caste remained intact, and people respected the *Varna ashram dharma*. As per Somadeva, the metropolis of Rajpura, near Ambala, as 2nd capital of the Yaudheyas other than Rohitaka (Rohtak) is mentioned in Mahabharat". (Ref; Datta and Phadke, 1985)

The rural Haryana was described by Charles Metcalfe as: *"The village communities are little republics having nearly everything within themselves; independent of any foreign relations. They seem to last where nothing else lasts. Dynasties tumble down; revolutions succeed; Hindu, Pathan, Mogul, Maratha, Sikh, English all are masters in turn; but the village communities remain the same. In times of trouble, they arm & fortify themselves; a hostile army passes through the area; the village communities collect their cattle within their walls, let the enemy pass unprovoked. (My village: Gudha, was a fortified village). If the country remains scene of continued pillage for years leaving villages uninhabitable, they return whenever the peaceful possession revived. A generation may pass away but the next generation will return. The sons will take the place of their fathers at the same site, same position for the houses, & same land in the village will be re-occupied."*

Mr Denzil Ibbetson's *Punjab Ethnography* 1883, and *Punjab Castes* 1916 details remarkably religion, languages, castes, race, & tribes of the people. Settlement Report of Karnal (1893) by Ibbetson, details marriage customs of the people & social intercourse among castes. The 2nd important document on the *People of Haryana* is found in Rose's three volumes titled, "*A Glossary of Tribes and Castes of Punjab and NW Frontier Province*".

During the present study, it is observed *that most of the communities lack a definite account of origin. There is a tendency to claim descent from Rajputs by lower rank like; Jhinwars, Bharbhujas, Bazigars, Bairagis, Banjara, Sansi etc.*

They also use clan names of Jats, & Rajputs to have higher social status. Some lower categories of Brahmins viz., Bura-Brahmin, Dakaut, Taga, and Bhaat are adopting life style and surnames of Vedic Brahmins to enhance their social status. Some like Jogi, Khaati, and Kumhar also claim Brahmanical origin.

No community have any specific identification mark, except all Hindu keep shikha. In dietary habits, vegetarianism is more prevalent, though non-vegetarianism is also being adopted. Avoiding liquor & meat on Tuesday is almost norm even among habitual meat-eaters. Milk consumption is directly related to the socio-economic status of the community. Monogamous, adult and negotiated marriages are the rule. Nuclear families are replacing the joint families.

## 7.5 Communities of Haryana

All the 82 communities of Haryana as included in the compilation by ANSI, along with the name of the scholar, who contributed for that particular caste with page index is tabulated as below:

| Alphabetically comprehensive list of Communities of Haryana along with Scholar and page ref | | | | | | | |
|---|---|---|---|---|---|---|---|
| S. No | Community | Scholar | Page ref | S. No | Community | Scholar | Page ref |
| 1 | Ahir | K.S. Sangwan | 13-21 | 2 | Arora | A.K. Bhatia | 22-27 |
| 3 | Bairagi | A.K. Bhatia | 28-32 | 4 | Balmiki | S.K. Garg | 33-37 |
| 5 | Bangali | A.K. Bhatia | 38-42 | 6 | Bania | S.K. Garg | 43-49 |
| 7 | Banjara | S.K. Garg | 50-55 | 8 | Bawaria | Raj Singh | 56-62 |
| 9 | Bazigars | A.K. Bhatia | 63-67 | 10 | Behrupia | A.K. Bhatia | 68-72 |
| 11 | Bharbhujas | A.K. Bhatia | 7375 | 12 | Bhat | S.K. Garg | 76-80 |
| 13 | Bhatia | A.K. Bhatia | 81-86 | 14 | Bhubalai Lohar | S.K. Garg | 87-91 |
| 15 | Bias | S.K. Garg | 92-96 | 16 | Bishnoi | R.K. Poonia | 97-103 |
| 17 | Bura Brahman | S.K. Garg | 104-109 | 18 | Chamar | S.K. Garg | 110-116 |
| 19 | Chhippi | S.K. Garg | 117-121 | 20 | Chirimaar | A.K. Bhatia | 122-125 |
| 21 | Christian | B.K. Nagla | 121-131 | 22 | Dakaut | B. Joardar | 132-136 |
| 23 | Deha | A.K. Bhatia | 137-141 | 24 | Dhanak | S.K. Garg | 142-148 |
| 25 | Dhobi (Hindu) | S.K. Garg | 149-153 | 26 | Dhobi(M) | S.K. Garg | 154-158 |
| 27 | Dum/Dom | S.K. Garg | 159-161 | 28 | Gadaria | A.K. Bhatia | 162-165 |
| 29 | Gandhila | A.K. Bhatia | 166-170 | 30 | Gaur-Brahman | S.K. Garg | 171-177 |
| 31 | Gawaria | Jagmati Singh | 178-184 | 32 | Ghasiara | A.K. Bhatia | 185-188 |
| 33 | Gorkha | A.K. Bhatia | 189-192 | 34 | Gujar | Sheela Nagar | 193-198 |
| 35 | Gosain/Gusain | T.M. Dak | 199-208 | 36 | Heri | S.K. Garg | 209-215 |

| 37 | Jain | Manjusha Jain | 216-224 | 38 | Jat | Hukam Singh | 225-259 |
|----|------|---------------|---------|----|-----|-------------|---------|
| 39 | Jat Sikh | Malkit Kaur | 260-264 | 40 | Jhinwar | A.K. Bhatia | 265-268 |
| 41 | Jogi | S.K. Garg | 269-275 | 42 | Julaha | B.D. Yadav | 274-283 |
| 43 | Kamboj | A.K. Bhatia | 284-287 | 44 | Khaati | Jitender Prasad | 288-293 |
| 45 | Khatik | S.K. Garg | 294-299 | 46 | Khatri | A.K. Bhatia | 300-304 |
| 47 | Koli | S.K. Garg | 305-309 | 48 | Kuchband | A.K. Bhatia | 310-312 |
| 49 | Kumhar | S.K. Garg | 313-318 | 50 | Labana | A.K. Bhatia | 319-323 |
| 51 | Lakhera | S.K. Garg | 324-328 | 52 | Lohar | S.K. Garg | 329-333 |
| 53 | Madari | B. Joardar | 334-337 | 54 | Mazbi | Malkit Kaur | 338-341 |
| 55 | Meena | G.S. Somawat | 342-354 | 56 | Megh | A.K. Bhatia | 355-359 |
| 57 | Meo | B. Joardar | 360-364 | 58 | Mochi | A.K. Bhatia | 365-369 |
| 59 | Nai | S.K. Garg | 370-374 | 60 | Nalband | Raj Singh | 375-379 |
| 61 | Nat | S.K. Garg | 380-384 | 62 | Nungar | S.K. Garg | 385-389 |
| 63 | Od/Beldars | S.K. Garg | 390-395 | 64 | Pasi | A.K. Bhatia | 396-399 |
| 65 | Perna | S.K. Garg | 400-403 | 66 | Rahbari | S.K. Garg | 404-409 |
| 67 | Rain/Arians | S.K. Garg | 410-415 | 68 | Raisikh | Satnam Kaur | 416-418 |
| 69 | Rajput | B. Joardar | 419-423 | 70 | **Ror** | **K.S. Sangwan** | 424-429 |
| 71 | Saini | T.M. Dak | 430-439 | 72 | Sansi | S.K. Garg | 440-444 |
| 73 | Sapera | S.K. Garg | 445-448 | 74 | Shorgir | A.K. Bhatia | 449-452 |
| 75 | Sikligar | S.K. Garg | 453-459 | 76 | Singikat | S.K. Garg | 460-463 |
| 77 | Sirkiband | Snehlata Rathi | 464-468 | 78 | Sood | B.D. Yadav | 469-474 |
| 79 | Sunar | A.K. Bhatia | 475-479 | 80 | Taga | A.K. Bhatia | 480-483 |
| 81 | Teli | S.K. Garg | 484-489 | 82 | Thathera | Raj Singh | 490-493 |

## 7.6 Ror Community of Haryana

The Rors are mainly settled in Karnal, Kurukshetra, Jind, and Ambala districts of the state. Some of their villages are found in Saharanpur, Muzaffarnagar, and Bijnor districts of Uttar Pradesh and also in Haridwar a district of Uttarakhand. In all there are *about 350 villages* inhabited by Rors in Haryana, and UP & UK. In Haryana Rors constitute about 2% of the total population of the state. Almost all Ror trace their origin from Badli Village near Jhajjar in Rohtak district. According to Ibbetson (1916), the people living in Amin village have reported to have come from Sambhal in Moradabad district (UP). But he adds further this may be only to connect them with their neighbour Chauhan Rajputs, who certainly came from there (?).

Usually, whole village of Rors is dominated by a single gotra, but there are lot of cases, where people of multiple gotra due to reasons like shifting of sons-in-law to their father-in-law's village due to no male successor or no live male member. The people of this community speak Hindi & Haryanvi. The dress pattern is similar to that of Jats, i.e., they wear *dhoti & Kurta*. Males, in old times used to wear white or colored Pagdi, also called Safa sometimes. Young boys wear Kurta Pyjama or Pant, shirt, and coat. Ladies used to wear Ghaghara and Kurta in old times.

Rors are pure vegetarians, even the egg is considered part of non-vegetarian diet. But Crooke (1896) states that the Rors eat mutton, goat's flesh & fowls, but not eat beef, monkeys or vermin. The practice of eating meat might have existed in the past, but now under the influence of *Arya Samaj*, the people have confined themselves strictly to a vegetarian diet. The use of Alcoholic drinks is also not a common practice, but on certain occasions like marriages etc. A person having frequent use of alcohol is looked down upon.

All Rors enjoy equal status and there is no hierarchical division within the caste. Social division exist on the basis of gotra, but all gotra are considered equal irrespective of their strength. *Mehla is the largest & Ghartan is the smallest.* Many of their gotras such as Mehla, Kadiyan, Sangwan, Dahiya, Malik, and Lather etc, are also found in Jats etc. From an economic point of view, the Rors living in Karnal and Kurukshetra districts consider themselves better off than their counterparts in Jind & Sonipat districts. With increase in education & political consciousness now the Rors have begun to use their surnames which were not a common practice in the past. Ror community is at par with Jat, Ahir, & Gujar, but inferior to Brahmin, Rajput but superior to castes like the carpenter, barber, potter, etc. With Jat, Ahir, and Gujar, they share hookah, water and food on equal terms. They claim themselves as kshatriyas in the *Varna* system. The Jat, Ahir, and Gujar, also treat Ror as equal to them in status. Some of the Rors are Sikh also with inter-religious marriages. Most of the Sikh Rors are concentrated in Kurukshetra and Karnal district of Haryana.

Marriages take place within their own caste except in few cases, now a days, educated Ror go for inter-caste marriages. But no Ror girl has been married outside her own caste. Rors exclude four gotras, i.e., self, mother, grandmother, & mother's mother. But now the gotra of latter is being ignored in some cases. Previously among the Rors the common practice of marriage was through exchange (known as *satta*), but outside their own gotra by excluding four gots. This practice of exchange of girls was very common among Rors, (but now it is steadily declining among educated & well settled families). The rulers started marrying beautiful girls from other religion in the name of *Dola*. The Ror caste saved their girls by introducing this system of marriage. Another advantage of this practice was that it put a check on the dowry and that's why the practice of dowry is almost non-existent even today among Rors. It also has proved helpful in having better status for the women in this community.

Earlier the marriages were fixed by Brahmins and Nais, but now the practice of middlemen is disappearing. It is only through the parents and in accordance with the satisfaction of the boy that the final decision is taken. The common practice of marriage is monogamy except in cases where the wife dies or the wife fails to bear a child. There was a provision of widow remarriage and mainly levirate, though it was not compulsory for the widow. This practice is called *Chadar Udhaana* or Karewa. Some cases of Sati have also been reported in this caste e.g., a girl from Amin married in Basdhara (Bastada; Gharaunda) village in Karnal district performed *sati* in the 19th century. They erected a worship-place which can still be seen (being worshipped every year on the eve of Diwali), from the GT Road passing nearby this village. The married girls are usually identified by their ornaments like *Pendle aka Mangal-sutra*. After marriage; girls go to the boy's parent's house. The practice of divorce is negligible except in cases of adultery. The age at marriage is now increasing (even well past 25 years), mainly among educated Rors including for girls.

There is emphasis on joint family system and it is still considered good for increasing the economic condition of the family. Within family, the sons and daughters are guided by the rules of respect, fear and avoidance. Joking relation is common with the elder brother's wife. But with the elder brother the relationship is guided by the rule of respect. On the other hand, the parents and elder brothers have obligations towards the younger ones. The property is inherited mainly by the males. Though under the existing rules, sisters have a share in the property of their father but generally they do not claim their share. It is the eldest son who takes the position of responsibility after the death of his father. Inter-family linkages are guided by the feeling of the commonness and there are close ties with other families who had common ancestors some three to five generation ago. However, among the educated Rors, a tendency is growing to stay in nuclear families, residing in towns, & cities.

Ror women though have a subordinate status, but they enjoy a better status in the family. Agriculture being the main occupation of this caste, the women also work in the fields, but they confine mainly to domestic activities e.g., managing household, and tending to domestic live stocks. Their role in the economic activities cannot be denied, and also, they play an important role at the time of marriage and on other important social occasions.

There is not much emphasis on life-cycle rituals, as Rors are an agricultural community and people do not have much time and money to spend on various rituals (*perhaps it's due to effect of Arya Samaj*). But on important occasions like birth of a male-baby, a feast called 'dashutan' is organised to celebrate it. The name-giving ceremony takes place six days after the birth of a child; it is performed by a Brahmin or by some Arya Samaji. Other major ceremony takes place only at the time of marriage.

After *sagai* (betrothal) Nai brings the lagan to the boy's family wherein day, date and time of marriage are indicated with the numbers of *Baraatis*. On the fixed day, the marriage party leaves for the bride's place and is received by her father & other relatives. The marriage rituals are completed & at the time of *bidai*, the father of the girl declares the gift given to his daughter and to the boy, & other relatives, by him. Consummation of marriage usually takes place after one year of marriage. If couple is still young, then the period may be extended from two to five years. But these days one year is considered the maximum period for, even, rural background couples.

Rors are mainly an agriculturist community and majority own medium-size land holding. The main source of income is agriculture, & in addition animal husbandry is given importance. The main livestock are buffalos & cows for getting milk and butter whereas bullocks & camels are kept for agricultural activities. The main crop is wheat, sugarcane & paddy, & market situation does not affect their pattern of crops much. Some, who are poor takes land on lease (written or oral contract) or rent and cultivate the land of others, however belonging usually to same community. The child begins to contribute in various activities to the family from the age of about 10 years. Educated Rors have begun to migrate to urban areas where they work & have also begun to take up occupations like business, service in secondary & tertiary sectors etc. With each generation due to the division among siblings, the size of the land holdings is declining.

Traditionally, there are no Khap, caste or Jati councils of Rors. At the village level, the councils were made up of influential persons of the village from different caste which used to decide the issues of the village. The problems related to a particular caste were decided by its own peoples, but if they failed to do so, the Ror community (if it is dominant in that village) played an important role in deciding the issues. On major issues concerning the Ror community as a whole, the people from different villages used to gather at a *chabutra* (raised platform) in Amin village, (*Incorrect & I never heard so?*), in Kurukshetra district to take decision, but now no such panchayat exists. With the increase in political awakening among the Rors, a caste organisation by name, *Ror Mahasabha* was constituted in 1958, with its head office at Karnal. The main purpose of this *Mahasabha* is to bring social reforms among its community members, lay emphasis on the education of girls, and to reduce expenditure on marriages and other social ceremonies. Though the meeting of this organisation is called once a year, but its members are active throughout the year for implementing its decisions. The form of punishment by the traditional council was fine or social boycott. The punishment by the *Ror Mahasabha* varies from a fine up to Rs 11000/- to social boycott (?). The role of the *statutory panchayat* has not been found encouraging. It has led to the growth of factions in the village and between and within caste. During the past 61 years, the council/Mahasabha has not been found very effective and fulfilling the purpose of its establishing.

Most of the Rors are Hindus & some are Sikhs also. Their religious deities at village level are same as those of Jats. The religious deities are significant only at the time of birth, marriage, and death. The places of pilgrimage are Haridwar, Kurukshetra & Pehowa, which are considered holy places among the members of this community.

Holi and Diwali are the major festivals among Rors. They believe that Mughal* attacked them on this particular festival day and they had to leave Badli & shifted to present areas in Karnal and Kurukshetra districts. But educated Rors have started celebrating the festival. It may further be added that during Muslim regime no case of conversion* to Islam were reported from this community. (**Not true; ref ch-6 Panjab census & ch-9; Paradoxes & Rors*).

The Arya Samaj has played a very important role in bringing social reforms like widow marriage, education of girls, opposition to idol-worship. Swami Brahmanand Saraswati (1908-1973) of Ror caste from Chuhad Majra village emphasized on the girl's education, vegetarianism, and Gurukul type of education. Being agriculturalists Rors do not have any interest in special arts and crafts. The oral traditions are maintained through folksongs and folktales. Only in the month of *Phagun*, the women, after completing their house chores, dance and sings for their enjoyment.

Rors, traditionally being agriculturalist community, enjoy *relations of equality with other peasant castes such as Jats, Gujars, Ahir etc. As the Rajputs claim to be superior to Rors, the exchange of water and Hookah with them is somewhat restricted.* Regarding food, a Ror can have food in the house of Rajput caste and vice versa. With Jats and Gujars the exchange of water, food and hookah is at an equal level. At the time of marriage, Jats, Gujars, and Rors invite each other. But inter-community marriages, (in same or the neighbouring village) are strictly prohibited as, '*Simjor Biradari*'. The system of *Dharm bhai* exists, but incidents are few. There is a change in patron-client relationship because of urbanisation and impact of outside forces. The traditional *jajmani* system is fast weakening. The inter-community linkages are undergoing swift changes. Except endogamy caste rigidity is fast disappearing.

The Rors with inroad in education and exposure to outside world are becoming political conscious. Though the basic purpose of Ror Mahasabha is to bring about social and cultural reforms among the Rors, it also acts as a political instrument mainly at the time of elections (Not so true?). A magazine named *Ror Drashta** is published monthly from Delhi which highlights the socio-cultural, economic, and political aspects of the *Rors*. (*Not true, ref Rors & social life Ch-11)

The Rors being a landowning and self-cultivating community engages agricultural labourers in the form of share-croppers, tenants, and workers from other lower vagrant castes. In the past, relationship between the cultivator-labourer or landlord-tenant or share-cropper has been very harmonious but now there is bargaining from both sides and therefore some sort of contract is emerging between the two groups.

The educated Rors have a positive attitude towards development works. The uneducated Ror now realise the importance of education but still few have some reservation regarding girl's education, family planning, modern health, and medical care. Traditionally, Rors are interested in military or police services but, now they are serving in various departments of Government, semi-government, or even private organisations.

Rors are fairly exposed to the outside world through Radio and TV which are found in most of the families. They also use electricity for their tube-wells and other purposes like grass cutting machines, sugarcane crushing, wheat grinding and rice impeller, wheat thrasher etc and other purposes including in homes.

Rors are concentrated in the areas where irrigation facilities exist. In their area both underground as well as canal water is available for irrigation. Hence paddy, sugarcane and wheat are the main crops and the use of chemical fertilizers and insecticides is very frequent. The educated and well-to-do families make use of banking facilities. Saving is also found to be higher among the affluent families. The major source of expenditure or investments is purchase of land, marriages, and organizing feast at the time of the death of an elderly person, in the family, whose next generation is well settled. By K S Sangwan (Verbatim *&
abridged also from People of India: Haryana series: Rors: pp 424 to 429*)

## 7.7 Ror Community of Uttar Pradesh & Uttarakhand; (Abridged from People of India: Uttar Pradesh i/c Uttarakhand series)

The Ror spelled as Rod, by scholar J.K. Pundir, are described from pp; 1220 to 1223 at s.no; 240. The Vol-XLII part-3 series of UP contains the anthropological profile of 307 communities. The survey of UP were discussed at the workshop held at Meerut University in March 1990, and at regional workshop held at Dehradun in October, 1987 and April-May 1991. (Sh. K.S. Singh; former DG, Mr. J.C Das; an Asst Anthropologist, AnSI regional center Dehradun & scholar J.K. Pundir)

**About Uttar Pradesh & Uttarakhand Series:** Uttar Pradesh, the northern province which derives its identity from its unique geographical, and historical situation, constitutes most of what was known as Madhya Desh or the middle country of Aryavart and as Hindustan in the medieval period. Hindi is the official language widely spoken and there are 36 other dialects/languages, mostly belonging to the Indo-Aryan language family. The most populous state of India, UP is the second largest state in terms of the number of communities (307) of whom Schedule Caste & Minorities form a high proportion. The traits that stand out are higher incidence of vegetarianism, junior & senior sororate and levirate, textual & folk components of life cycle rituals, patriarchal norms, syncretism, or a blending of religious traditions, etc.

Uttaranchal known as Uttarakhand in the ancient texts was formed as a separate state on 8 Nov.,2000. The hill people are marked by the presence of Mongoloid's traits, relative absence of untouchability, freedom for women in choice of mates & recognition of their property rights, hypergamy, and hypogamy, fraternal polyandry, bride price, etc.

**Rod of UP & UK;** As per Crooke (1896) Rors of Saharanpur claim to be created at Kaithal by Krishna during Mahabharat war. From an account by the district officer in 1891 census, Rors of Bijnor claim their origin is related to Shri Ram Chandra who severed his connection with his wife Sita, who was pregnant and went into the jungle under the protection of Rishi Valmiki. She bore a son there, who was named as Lav and one day, while going out of the house, she left the child in the charge of Rishi. The child however followed his mother, and the Rishi, who find him missing, supposing him to be dead, derived another child from Kusha grass; when Sita returned and saw other child, and she asked what it all meant? The Rishi said rora- phora (useless thing) is also your son. Hence, they were called Ror after his Kusha name. Some Rod traces their origin from Bhagwan Krishan while others (not Rajputs) from 'Aur' to escape from wrath of Parshu Ram. Some also trace their origin from Rohit- the son of Raja

Harishchandra. They speak Khadi Boli and Hindi, and use Devanagari script. Their dress is not different from the neighbouring communities. They consider themselves to be of high status but others place them at par with agricultural Jat.

They are vegetarian, eat seasonal vegetables & fruits. Staple diet is wheat & rice but they eat gram, tur, urad, moong, peas & beans but males have started taking eggs & meat. Mustard & groundnut oil are the medium of cooking. Men take alcoholic drinks purchased from the market. Smoking Hookah, Bidi, & Cigarette is common.

The Rod community is divided into several exogamous clans, namely Laharwan, Mahela, Ghiyad, Goochley, Maniyale, Tahen, Thoule, Kahalwan, Rayatan, Badsar, and Khokhar. The clan's names & Arya as surnames are used. They practice endogamy at community level & exogamy at clan & village level. Junior sororate & Junior Levirate are preferential marriages. Now adult marriages are in vogue. Earlier marriage by exchange of sister or niece was also practised. Symbols of marriage are bangles, rings, and tika. Kanyadaan & dowry are essential features of marriage (?). Divorce is allowed(?). Divorcee & widow remarriages are also permitted.

Mixed extended family pattern is common among Rods. Avoidance (*purdah*) is observed with father-in-law & husband's elder brother. Joking relations exist between elder brother's wife & wife's sisters. The point of conflict arises on property (mainly land), check on the freedom of youngsters, and challenge to the authority of elders. Inheritance is male equigeniture & daughters are not entitled to parental property unless nominated. Women contribute to family income and attend to agricultural husbandry & household chores, and educated one's are doing services. They participate in all rituals & control family expenditure. Their social status is somewhat lower to men.

Post-delivery pollution is observed upto five weeks in the community. Naming ceremony is observed for both sexes but that of the male child is with elaborate ritual. Mundan is not observed unless promised to be performed before some deity. Janeu ceremony is observed & is conducted by a Brahmin or Jogi priest. Pre-and post-marriage rituals also take place at the bride's place & feasts are arranged on both occasions. The dead are cremated & bones (asthi; mortal remains) are immersed in the Ganga at Haridwar. Death pollution is observed and ancestor worship is not obligatory. The rituals are now becoming more elaborate & expensive.

They are an agricultural community. Land is the main source, augmented by animal husbandry & different type of services in pvt & govt organizations both technical & non-technical and skilled & non-skilled. They are self-employed in dairy farming, sale of automobile parts, workshops & transport.

Rod professes Hinduism & worship all deities of the pantheon. They celebrate Holi, Diwali, Raksha Bandhan. Haridwar, Kashi, Ayodhya are teerathsthans for them. Traditional caste council at village level exists to decide marriage disputes, property, dowry, divorce cases etc. (?), and has a right to accord punishment of social boycott. Besides, the president of the council looks after socio-religious welfare of the community.

Floral & mural paintings and designs during festivals & marriages are common. Craft of making mats of different sizes for different purposes along with embroidery over pillows & bedsheets, etc., is in vogue in the community. Folk-tales, folk-songs, dance, music, and musical instruments of the region are shared by the community.

Water is taken from the village wells, and Handpumps as pvt source are installed as drinking water etc. They share the village crematorium with similar status castes. Rod community visits the religious shrines of the village & the region. Dussehra & Holi are the festivals when their participation is elaborate with other communities.

Modern education is favored as it improves the quality of life, particularly cleanliness, urban way of life etc. Boys & girls both study upto secondary & higher level, but girls drop out if there is no facility of a college nearby. Being a well -to- do agricultural community, lesser number of boys take interest in studies. Therefore, many stagnate in classes, or failure in a class result in leaving the school or college. After getting education in the towns & cities, a few have become teachers, research scientists, transport entrepreneurs, white-collar & skilled workers, administrators, defence personnel & political leaders etc.

The community makes use of the facilities of modern Medicare. Traditional Herbal & Ayurvedic medicines are also used. The community has very favourable attitude towards family planning. One or two children is becoming almost the norm in the villages. The reason suggested very revealing. Methods other than sterilization are usually followed by menfolk & the ladies get sterilized. Radio, television, cinema is used. The planned development program has improved communication. Electricity has reached most of their villages & is used by the majority. Kerosene, firewood & dung cakes are mostly used in cooking. Organic manure is used same way as it was used earlier.

* * * * *

# Chapter-8. Rors; Overview of Origin Theories

## 8.1 Literature available on Ror caste

There is a huge information gap about Rors in all respects, as nothing substantial has been written about them. It may not be an exaggeration to say, Ror caste is an enigma & unresolved nightmare, even for a historian. So, this chapter will seek three W about them i.e. Who are Rors, When, & from Where they came, by providing brief overview of origin from all available; written or by words of mouth material about Rors from various writ-ups.

Pre-British Period: Whatever information exists, it is oral words of mouth, or in Bhaat's Pothis and unsubstantiated. The information on its origin is quite obscure & sketchy and needs to be researched methodically for factual data. It does not find place in 16th century Ain-e-Akbari, the book having the details of castes existing that time in north India.

British Period: Description about Rors exists in; "Panjab Castes", by Sir Denzil Ibbetson, an authentic source, Census of Punjab in particular of 1881 &1891, A Glossary of caste & Tribes of Punjab & NWFP, District Gazetteers, settlement report of districts, and Archaeological Survey of India report 1871-72 Vol-IV.

Post-Independence: "People of India: Haryana & UP, series under AnSI project having the anthropological profile of all the communities of India, have a fair description of Ror community albeit with some inaccuracies (may be resource person or informant might have lack of access of correct information?). Lot of individual publications by some self-financed individual Rors or sponsored by some Ror group came between 1987 to 2012.

Documents on the history of any race or caste normally are; Govt documents Chronicles & books by historians, annals on the caste, folk tales, ballads, Raso's, People's History or words of mouth from the elders, archaeology reports documenting artefacts etc. For Ror caste each type of available documents is briefly stated below.

(a) **Govt Documents**; Documents on social structure & other ethnical details on the Ror caste, are as below.

1. District gazetteers written by British East India Company from 1872 onwards.

2.  Archaeology Survey of India Report of 1871-72, Vol IV; by Chief Surveyor of India A. Cunningham; (pp 210- 212).

3.  Census reports of 1881 & 1891; has substantial description about Rors, their population & areas inhabited by them.

4.  A Glossary of Tribes & Castes of Punjab & NWFP Vol-1, Vol-II, & Vol-III, based on census report 1883 of Denzil Ibbetson & 1892 of E. D. Maclagan, compiled by H.A. Rose, have good description of socio-economic profile of Rors.

5.  Book "Panjab Castes", by Sir Denzil Ibbetson, published in 1916, based on his census report of 1881, which describes all the castes including **Rors**, inhabiting the northern part of India, the then British territory.

6.  AnSI, "People of India: Haryana", series published in 1994, documenting the anthropological profile of all the eighty-two (82) communities residing in Haryana. Abridged version about Rors, already given in chapter-7.

**(b) Old Write-ups;** The prevalent theories of origin, stage acts (swangs), & writeups based on Folk tales, ballads, words of mouth from elders etc, which can be classified as 'People's History', & given as below.

1.  Ror Etihas; By Sh Sultan Singh & Sh Desh Raj based upon Prithvi Raj Raso & Pothis of Bhaats.

2.  Sauram Khap Panchayat records of Jaats in Muzaffarnagar UP; states that Rors have sprung from them?

3.  Ror Jati ka Etihas, by Ram Lal Maniyal and Bhaat; states that Rors have sprung from Rajputs?

4.  Bhartiya Etihas ki Ruprekha, by Master Ratan Singh Shastri; states that Rors have sprung from Rajputs?

5.  Puratatva Nibandhavali, by Rahul Sankrityayan; It states that Ror have sprung from Rajanya Gan?

6.  Haryana ke Prachin Mundrank; Swami Omanand Saraswati; Marshal Races i/c Ror have sprung from Yodhaygan?

7.  Rohad Jati ka Etihas; Baljit Singh (Ravli-Bijnor); states that Rohad yodhas of Mahabharat times are Rors of today?

**(c) Recent Writeups;** Recent formal documents by few individuals, based upon various resources by few independent writers, either from the Ror community or having been commissioned by community groups are as below;

1.  Ror Etihas ki Jhalak: Dr Rajpal Singh; 1987: It states that Rors are a branch of warrior Rajput race only. In the 2$^{nd}$ century BC, they ruled from their seat of power at Kagarol near Agra (present UP).

2.  Ror Maratha-Etihas; Ek Jhalak; 2002: By Prof. Om Prakash, and Mahender Singh Arya; It states Rors, now they call as Ror-Maratha, sprang from the left-over Maratha soldiers of third battle of Panipat. It has Part-2 also.

3.  Ror-Udhbav and Vikas; Dr Surender Singh Kadiyan; 2003: It refutes Maratha theory & surprises everyone stating that Rors have sprung from Aroras of Aror-Sindh.

4.  Ror Maratha History; Dr. Vasant More; 2009: States Rors have sprung from the left-over Maratha soldiers of third battle of Panipat-1761. Foreword; Ror Maratha Spirit in Haryana by: Uday Mahurkar (Ex India Today).

5.  Ror Vansh Ka 5000 Varsh ka Etihas: Shri Ram Das Rode; 2009; It states Ror, Rora, Aror, Rore, Arore, Rohad, Jat, Gujar, Rajput, Ahir, Bishnoi, etc, long back, all were one tribe only & later on separated as distinct caste (?).

6.  Clarification to unification: Major M S Keshwar (Retd); 2011: Citing Migration theory of Mr Denzil Ibbetson; states that Ror have sprung from Rajput only after many migrations from Mewar, Malwa and Gujarat, after various incidents.

7.  DNA based study; 2012; by Anurag Kadian & others: This DNA based research study published in American journal of Human Genetics, states Ror came to Sindh area from Eurasia during Indus valley civilization?

## 8.2 Why the name of the caste 'Ror'?

A Caste is named after an 'eponymous', or name of the place, or on the name of profession of the caste. The postulations on the evolution of the caste name as Ror are described below.

**(a) Ror: Etymology of word**: "Ror", appears to be the corruption of word; "Rashtra Kula-Rathor", (ref pp-34, p-48/680, Udaipur Gazetteer); sounds similar. Rathor migrated to their present locations in Marwad area of Rajasthan and established their capital at Mandore from Malwa -Chitore & Rors also, originally are said to be from Malwa area.

**(b) Ror: A Territorial name;** There are many places in Rajasthan with Ror as subscript to their name, such as; Behror, Bhainsror, Kahror, Khichror, Rorwas, etc. To continue the legacy, the Rors at migrated places in Haryana, constructed Chaupal at elevated level, & passer-by used to call, "Jai Ho Raja Ror ki". Rana Amar Singh also was known as *Ror*, because he was Rana of

Chitore, which is situated at high elevation. Similarly, the name '*Raja Ror*', in swang "*Raja Ror & Saurath banjaran*", was Raja of Deshu, (or was he Raja of Kagarol?) & Known as 'Ror Raja' because he was Raja of Gir Nagar (Saurashtra); situated on the top of hills. (PP-35 Clarification to Unification; by Major M S Keshwar*).*

**(c) Ror: of Aror:** Another version, is Ror were inhabiting **Aror**, the capital of Sindh Province (now in Pakistan). A social media twitter handle: @pid_gov of Govt of Pakistan also states," Aror was the ancient capital of Sindh originally ruled by *Ror Dynasty*. After capturing Debal in 711AD, Aror was captured by Muhammad bin Kasim in 712 AD. Aroras & Khatris also claims to be Arora or Rora of Aror. Many who's who Ror, also confirms, that in 1932 they were invited for reunion with Aroras in their 11th Akhil Bhartiya Arora Maha Panchayat held in Amritsar. (Ref; Dr Kadiyan Book pp-69 & 70).

**(d) Ror: Guhile of Chitore:** As described in the Annals of Rajasthan by Col Tod, Guhile /Guhilas/ Guhilot or slang Gula, Rajputs of Mewad had adopted, "Bappa Rawal", the 1st ancestor, as their *Baap (father)* & they never called their biological father as "Baap". There is a similar tradition prevalent among Rors also wherein no Ror, like other caste; Jats, Gujars etc, would call their biological father as *"Baap"* but, would call *"Chacha"* only. This tradition among Rors, to address their biological father as "Chacha" & not "Baap", was prevalent even upto the latter part of 20th century. Interestingly Bappa is Prakrit form of word for 'Baap'.

**(e) Ror or Rode from Rashtrakutas;** As per 'Rashtrod Vansh Mahakavya', (by court poet Rudra of king Narayan Shah of Mayurgiri in 1596), Rashtrod was a valiant son of king Narayan Shah. It is said that after Rashtrod name, a branch of Rashtrakutas was called Rod. Synonymous of Rashtrakutas is, 'Rashtrik', 'Rathik', 'Rathak', & Rathor or Rathod etc. As per *'Rohad Jati ka Etihas'* (part 1) by Chaudhary Baljit Singh of Ravli, Rod or Ror word is corrupted form of Rashtrod or Rathod or Rathore. (Ref; Ror-Udhbav and Vikas; Dr Surender Singh Kadiyan pp- 8)

**(f) Ror or Rode of Rodvansh;** Sh Ram Das in his book ('Rodvansh ka 5000 Varsh ka Etihas', pp-13), states that Punjabi Aroras, & Khatri of western UP also believe their origin, like Rodvansh (Rors) from Prayagraj king Yayati of lunar race. In Yayati clan, as per the material expounded by Bhaats, King Dushyant & his son Bharat were 24th & 25th generation, & the 26th generation king Pratip had 3 sons viz; 1. Shantanu; who had a son by name; *Bhishm*; the famous patriarch; Bhishm Pitamah of Mahabharat; 2. Devapi Mahabahu;

*whose eldest son Ruru; is said to have established Ror or Rode Vansh*; 3. Balhik or Balika; whose son by name *Arut*, is said to have established *Arore or Arode* Vansh.

**(g) Ror; an old Categorization of Kshatriyas;** Mr A. Cunningham in his Archaeological Survey report (1871-72), Vol-IV, states; the old categorization of Kshtriyas[1] itself is 'Ror'. (Ref foot note pp-210). From the family tree of Ror Vansh (as recorded by genealogist/Bhaats), it can be seen that if Ror did not establish from Ruru (S No.28), then it must have been from Ruruk, the grandson of Raja Dhaj (S No. 60). As per ASI report the name of the fort built by Raja Khangan of this Vansh is called Khangan-Ror, ruins of which can be seen in Kagarol. Thus, it can be said that Ror Vansh may have started from the time of Ruruk as present Ror caste comprises of not only Ror Rajvanshi from the past but people from other Varnas/castes, perhaps due to marriages with similar castes due to relaxed marriage rules. (Ror Etihas ki Jhalak: ASI report also corroborates it pp 11-13). {[1]: Ksha +triya= Ksha; means land, & triya means Ruler; so, a kshatriya is ruler of the land).

**(h) Rors: Yodhaygans;** As stated in the write-up of Sultan Singh & Desh Raj Jagge Bhaat; (ref appendix, 'A', pp- 35 to 37) part of: Dr Rajpal Singh's book Ch-3 and Rodvansh ka 5000 Varsh ka Etihas by Ram Das Rode (pp193-195) part-5, Yodhaygan race were warriors during Mahabharat time & Raja Ruru, the ancestor of Rors; a 5th generation ahead of Talandev & Devapi, fought in Mahabharat war. This Ruru is said to be later corrupted to Ror.

## 8.3 Overview of various theories of the Origin of Rors

From the latter part of 20th Century, there had been an urge among the Rors to know the origin & history of their caste. This generated an impetuous in few individuals, & some assigned parties, for writing on the history & origin of Rors. An overview from such write-ups, is given below.

**(a) Ror Etihas ki Jhalak (Glimpses of Ror History):** Dr Rajpal Singh; Edition1987: 6 Chapters; 103 pages

Referring ASI report 1871-72 Vol-IV, he says Rors have not originated from Rajputs but they themselves are a warrior race, & they ruled over Kheragarh or Kagarol, near Agra around 2nd century BC. Excerpts from its 6 Chapters are;

Ch-1; Describes; (1) Literary material like; Raso, folk literature, Swang (folk art) like 'Bija Saurath' the love story of Raja Ror & Saurath (from a Rajasthani book 'Anushil'), and; (2) The ASI report-1871-72 vol-IV of Raja Ror. (ibid1-5)

Ch-2; Describes few postulations on the origin of Bijnor & Saharanpur Rors; as per Pothis of Bhaats, by Ibbotson's description as in 'Panjab Castes', and Parshuram's version of Ror caste, (which Aroras, & many more castes also quote). But in case of Rors, he says, Parshu Ram's version can't be true as due to fear *Ruru, a powerful king, (considered to be ancestor of Rors?),* will not change caste. In old times all rulers were called 'Rajputs'. The word, 'Rajput' became a caste during Muslim rule (Historian Mr Pramatma Saran also corroborates). (ibid7-10)

Ch-3; As per ASI report 1871-72, Rors had power centres around Agra. The ruins of forts, palaces & other artefacts, coins etc, related to Rodvanshi Raja Tisman, Dhaj, & Khangan Ror have been found from the places around Agra. Also, Ror Raja had close relationships with rulers of Indraprastha, Mathura, Virat Nagar indicates; Rors were important regional power in this region. (ibid14-18)

History of Rorvansh takes a turn when *'Raja Dhaj' most famous of the race, abducts Saurath*; a damsel from Saurashtra, & had to desert his capital after losing fight with kins of Saurath. *Karewa* among Rors perhaps started after this as lot of young women became widow. (ibid19-20)

As per ASI report, the ruins of about 52 forts (Gadhi) are found in Kasaundi Gadhi of Agra region. So, it can be inferred that someone from Rorvansh must have established these Baavan (52) Gadhis as this area that time was ruled by Rorvanshi Raja Dhaj (S. No 60). (ibid21-24)

The position on the existence of *Badli*, said to been established by Baalandev, as described in traditional version of Bhaats, is mysteriously same as that of *Khatka Nagari*, but no ruins. In the description of Bhaats, after Dadror (S. No 101) of Badli, there is a huge gap of facts lacking in clarity & exactness. Details of seven (7) sons of Dadror by Bhaats also, is ambiguous. One of the Raja among these was *Mahalsi*, who ruled over Umpal towards Lucknow. The family of these brothers, perhaps, after losing battle over giving 'Dola', to 'Qutbuddin', fled towards Haryana to Badli in Jhajjar by deserting Badalgadh (Khatka Nagari) in the end of 12th century.

To remove the ambiguity about the location / position of **Khatka Nagari of Raja Ror**, as per book - **Settlements in The Yamuna-Hindon Doab**, An Archaeological Perspective; By Rewant Vikram Singh it is stated that, presently it is a village called **Katha** - near Baghpat in Meerut dist of UP north of Delhi & its description as per above book verbatim is; "The villagers informed that Katha was once a fort from where a king called **Raja Ror** ruled. He was a cruel ruler therefore the God turned the village upside down hence they called it palta-hua-khera. In fact all mounds are referred by the same name in the entire region where the exploration was under taken. According to villagers the present border of the village is relatively new."

Raja Mahalsi, said to be responsible for the death of 2 sons of Prithvi Raj of Mahoba, had a bloody duel with him and Ror might have been forced to desert the *Badalgadh or Badli* (?), even before the battle between Qutbuddin Aibak and Rors of Badli. Also, this may be the reason of non-availability of descendants of Dadror after Mahalsi left the Badli. From here Rors are said to have gone into 3 directions Viz; towards Lucknow, Bundelkhand, and Haryana to *Badli in Jhajjar tehsil where still a Ror Kuan (water well) and Gate (Darwaja) exists.* (ibid24-26)

Now Yaksh question where is Badalgadh, ruled by the founder Baalandev (SNo.48) & his 54 descendants up to Dadror (SNo.101)? One such fort known by Badalgadh is Agra fort, also known as Lodhi Khan Ka Tilla. *Incidentally Agra fort is called Badalgadh fort also.* Perhaps the story of founding, & fall of this fort can reveal the obscure & silent history of Ror rulers of this region. (ibid26-34)

Dr Rajpal Singh further says, to understand the history of origin of Ror caste, a hand written manuscript of Ror Etihas, based upon *Prithvi Raj Raso & Old Bahis of Bhaats*, by Sh Sultan Singh & Sh Desh Raj; appendix, 'A' (pp-35to37), has also, lot of information on the history of various Ror Gotras viz; the founder of Dopla Chauhans clan; Sh Deep Chand Chauhan was given Jagirs of Amin & nearby 84 villages in AD 967 by his father Rana Har Rai Chauhan. Similarly, Balda gotra Ror had Jagirs of Ramrai-Bhain-Mori etc in1078 AD. Also, there is a mention of Jagirs by Prithaviraj Chauhan to Kanyan gotra Ror Jeet Singh in 1187 AD in Haryana. Similarly in 1207 AD & around, there is mention of settling of *Rors of gotra Mehla, Thaula, Kalyaniya, Khasbar, Ghadtan, Bhukna, Kandhol, Kanyra, Ruhlyan, Kadian, Khokhra, Sagwal, Lather, Beniwal, & Jaglan* in various villages of Haryana. Also, it has a mention of Vir Singh Mehla & his brothers under the patronage of Sarva Khap Haryana, as part of Prithaviraj Chauhan's forces, commanding a troop against Md Gauri at Taraodi in 1192 AD. It means Rors had settled in Haryana before capture of Delhi by Muslims. But the traditions of Rors & Pothis of Bhaats, have different versions on it, as given below.

**People's History or Ror Traditions:** Ror strongly believe that their ancestors deserted Badli over quarrel on giving 'Dola' with Qutbuddin & their consequent defeat due to treachery of a priest & only 84 people could escape, who settled around Kurukshetra. (ibid35-36)

**Bhaat's versions:** It is bit different from above & states; descendants of seven sons of Dadror in 1207-8 AD had a quarrel with Qutbuddin over giving Dola of their fairs. To help Rors, the Kachhwaha Rajput Raja Malyasi (Mahalsi) of Aamer sent his 31 sons. However, Ror lost the battle & 84 people could escape who settled around Kurukshetra. *Hence 84 are said to be principle gotra. The 31 sons of Kachhwaha Rajput Raja Malyasi of Aamer, also settled with Rors only and gave further 31 gotras.* But, immediate earlier para states that Rors had already settled in various villages in Haryana before the Mehla gotra Rors of Badli had a quarrel with Aibek in 1207-8 AD. (ibid37-38)

Ch-4, Describes arrival of Rors in Haryana as they ceased to be a political power after the death of their last *Raja Dadror* & settled in Mohana after deserting Badli; Jhajjar. Then they spread to *Ambala, Kurukshetra, Karnal & Jind* districts and settled in the villages and made social relations with similarly placed castes *like Rajputs, Jats, Gujar, Ahirs* etc. Also, Dr Rajpal says when Ror joined Sarva Khap Sauram panchayat, they spread to Saharanpur, Muzaffarnagar, & Bijnor dist. of UP. (*Not true see ibid-56, 2nd para?).* (ibid39-41)

Chapter-5, Describes the history & social life of all castes in r.o. village life from 1803 when British entered North India. On participation in 1857 war of Independence, he says that Rors also participated but he could not give any names. Haryana was part of Delhi, under East India Co, but consequent to role of its public in 1857 revolt as per Act 38 of 1858, it was merged in Panjab & all its developments became a casualty. (ibid61-65)

As per him few Rors like; *Shri Naurang Singh of Ahar, Singh Ram of Kurana, Bhagat Maan Singh of Sutana, Tulsi Ram Pradhan of Kaul, & Ram Lal of Kutail,* took part in the awakening of Hindu Samaj undertaken by Swami Dayanand Saraswati, who established Arya Samaj. Rors were not given the chance to participate in Vidhan Parishad election between1920-36 as part of home rule governance. But in 1937 out of 33 seats earmarked for Haryana part, Babu Anant Ram Ji, (*1st Ror legislator*), contested from Karnal (south) seat for combined Panjab Parishad & won. (ibid66-68).

Ch-6; Is the epilogue & Appendix1; Excerpts; on Ror caste; 1. by Ibbotson, 'Panjab Castes', 2. by William Crooks, 3. from ASI report 1871-72, vol-IV; 4; Old Ror Vanshavali, 5; Hand Written Ror Etihas by Sh. Sultan Singh & Desh Raj Jagge Bhaat, & 6; Ror clans/Gotras & Villages.

**(b) Ror Maratha Etihas;** Prof Om Prakash, & Mahender Singh Arya; ed 2002; part I pages; 24; ed2005, Part -2, pages; 28.

The basic premise is; Rors are Marathas; have sprung from the left-over Maratha soldiers of 3$^{rd}$ battle of Panipat; 14 Jan 1761, who did not go back due to shame and guilt of defeat, but settled in south side of Kurukshetra.

**(1) Pre-beliefs or Precursor of Maratha theory:**1.Demand of Dola by Sultan; 2.Refusal,& flight from Badli; 3.No celebration of Raksha Bandhan among Rors; 4 Ritual of, 'Jayroya', 'Bad Maratha' & 'Chhatrapati ki Jay'; 5.Celebrates Govardhan Puja instead of Diwali; 6. Marriage by direct exchange called,'Satta'; 7.Pride of caste; purity of blood; 8.Availability of Genealogy of 7 to 9 generations only with Jagge Bhaats as obtained in 1970; and 9.System of giving annual share (laag) to Jagge Bhaats as caste bards. (Part-1 ibid9)

**(2) Present ground realities/proofs:** 1. No Rors beyond Pipli towards North side but only in South side; 2. Matching of physical features and nature of Rors with Marathas; 3. Similar festivals & rituals of Rors & Marathas; 4. Similar Gotras of Rors & Marathas. (Part -1, ibid10)

Further, based on Hypothesis of Dr Rajpal's book that, '*Rors are not Rajputs but themselves were a ruling class*,' they say that rule of *Raja Ror s/o of Raja Khangad,* around

Agra through 52 Gadhis from the central fort of Khagrol sometimes in 1206-08 (?), came to end on the day of Paunchi, when Raja Ror being less powerful preferred to desert Kagarol & 52 Gadhis lock stock & barrel & settled in Western Ghats Maharashtra further west away from Qutbuddin Aibek on his demand of 'Dola' and to accept his authority. (Part-1, ibid11-12)

Herein, cunningly the writers link the above incident with the flight of the ancestors of the Shivaji, who migrated somewhere from Rajputana to Western Ghats, due to conflict with Muslim rulers sometime in 13th Century. With this they want to prove that ancestor *was Raja Ror* only as Agra etc at that time were part of Rajasthan and the cause, time, and place of desertion is same in both cases. Being from the ruling class, they enrolled in the army and other court jobs of different kings there & established themselves by 16th century in ruling arena due to their deeds of valour and prowess. They define Maratha as Mar + hatha, persons of diehard/obstinate nature in the battle. (Part-1, ibid12-13)

On Ror-Maratha hypothesis further, they say defeated Maratha warriors, who already had their family stationed at Kurukshetra for pilgrimage after the war, reached their family stealthily and crying for victory, their wives taunted them with the phrase prevalent in present Rors, 'the 'Jayroya'(?). Initially when people asked them as to who they are, they replied that they are; Aur ~ Aur and after sometime, remembering their *ancestor Raja Ror*, they started calling themselves, '*Ror*' (too weird, bizarre & illogical justification?). (Part -1, ibid13 -15)

Next, they dismiss exodus of Rors from Badli, on the ground like; were Rors inhabiting Badli only, how is it possible that so many Rors living in one place, how they were marrying, were there no other Rors near Badli, how & since when Rors were living in Badli? (ibid15-18 part-1).

Hereafter, they establish that Rors are Marathas only by citing similarities like; same physical, social, lot of common words in language, same type of marriage rituals, tradition of Satta, same food habits, same way of celebrating festivals, similar cultural traits etc. (Part-1ibid19-24)

**(3) Part-2; Ror Maratha Etihas:** It states, after the defeat of Prithaviraj Chauhan in 1192 at Taraodi, Md Gauri appointed his slave Aibek ruler of Delhi, who in order to expand Muslim rule further, told Hindu rulers either accept defeat & offer 'Dola' of your fairs or fight war. Options with Hindus were either; 1) Give Dola & have Treaty; 2) Fight & perish; & 3) Flee to safer place. Raja Ror of Kagarol perhaps chose the 3rd option; further story & sequence of 3rd battle of Panipat between Abdali & Marathas is same as explained in earlier paras and then hiding of left-over defeated Maratha soldiers around Kurukshetra & their transforming into Rors. (Refer Part-2 ibid7-9). (For more ref page 9-28).

**(b-1) Rod Maratha History:** By Dr Vasant More: Maratha Spirit in Haryana: Uday Mahurkar (Ex-India Today) pages-89

"For over two centuries, a question that has defied an answer, was: what became of the Maratha soldiers who disappeared on 14 January 1761, after the third battle of Panipat? On 250th anniversary, now there is finally an answer", writes Uday Mahurkar. Research of Vasant Rao More (a historian of Kolhapur University), & Virendra Varma, (a former Haryana bureaucrat & president of Maratha Jagruti Manch), have evidences to prove that the six lakh-strong Rod community, spread across *230 villages around Panipat, (in part-1, they said Kurukshetra)*, has descended from the *500-odd* Maratha soldiers *who hid in the jungles around Panipat*. Varma, who 1st started investigation into the origin of the Rods a decade ago says, "Right from the Marathi words in our Hindi dialect, the style of our old havelis, our love of horses, our surnames & typical customs-all prove; we are descendants of the lost Maratha soldiers of Panipat.

Mr More, author of The History of Rod Marathas of Panipat Battle, (published by Shivsangram Prakashan, Kolhapur) adds that, *"Research to locate the lost Maratha soldiers of Panipat by the Peshwas and later by scholars of Punjab University failed because none came across the Rod community (why?)*. Over 80% of Rods surnames match those of Marathas (uncanny?). As do many customs and words in their dialect." They call Puran Poli, a Maharashtrian sweet roti, polt (?). They refer to a rupee as han (not true?), same what Shivaji's currency was called. They stand out in Haryana for eating dal and rice at night, a common practice among villagers in Maharashtra even today.

As many of the soldiers in Maratha army were from the Konkan region that explains as to why Rod marriage songs have mention of the sea, unheard of in Haryana. And, also, Rods assign a prominent role to maternal uncle in wedding, similar to the practice in Maharashtra. Though the Rod women dress like other Haryanvi, their style of covering their heads before elders is also akin to women in rural Maharashtra.

As per him, conclusive proof of Maratha heritage of Rods is the practice of saying *"Chhatrapati ki Jai"* at the drop of hat. Indraj Singh Dudhane, 81 of Dadupur village Says, "when a child sneezed, a mothers would say 'Chhatrapati ki Jai'." Adds Aabhe Ram Dudhane, 86, sitting beside him, "As in Maharashtra, Bhai Dooj after Diwali, is more important to Rods compared to Raksha Bandhan."

The book has 7 Chapters detailing; Ch-1: Mard Marathon Ka Gauravshali Etihas, Ch-2: Panipat Ka Tisra Yudh aur Rod Maratha (But It's all about Maratha history up to1760), Ch-3: Rod Maratha Vichardhara Ka Parichay: Rod Biradari Ka Etihas (an abridged version of Ror Maratha as in book part-1&2 of Prof Om Prakash & M S Arya), Ch-4: Rod Maratha Vichardhara: Justifications/significance of Proofs, Ch-5: Marathon Ki Badnami Kyon?

(a para wise rebuttal of Chapter-4 of Dr Surinder Singh Kadian's book), Ch-6: Rod Maratha Vichardhara Ke Virodh Ka Khandan, Ch-7: Haryana Ke Rod Maratha Ke hi Vanshaj Hein: comparison of surnames etc of Marathas (Note; comparison of similarity in spoken word/ language, surnames & marriage rituals are ill-conceived, & illogical), Epilogue: About study tours & interactions.

**(c) Ror: Udhbav and Vikas**; Dr Surender Singh Kadiyan; ed 2003:124 pages

He rejects all theories & sprang a new surprise; *"Rors are Aroras of Arore"*. His book has 14 chapters & excerpts are;

In Chapter-1, Dr Kadiyan states five (5) beliefs/postulations on the origin of Rors, excerpted as;

(1) **Panini Kalin Bharatvarsh**; By Vasudev Sharan Agarwal, Publisher; Moti Lal Banarasi Das ed 2092 VS, 31 pages; clearly indicates that Rors inhabited Haryana since old times. 'Ashtadhyayi', grammar book of Acharya Panini (500BC), which has history of that time, in a vartika (4/1/80) related to Krodyadi Gana, has a description of Rohdyadi Gana also. As per Acharya Patanjali Vyakarana (200BC), Krodyadi & Rohdyadi are name of same Gana. It proves Rors inhabited Kuru Pradesh (Kurukshetra), Karnal, Kaithal & Panipat, the same places where Rors are inhabiting presently, in BC era also. (ibid1)

(2) **Bharat ke Prachin Ganrajya**; Book by Bhagirathi Dube Publisher; Tulsi Sahitya Sadan Indore, ed 1955; states that Rajanya Gana of Mahabharat times, later on came to be known as Rohityan, Rorwal or Rodwal, or Ror. Rajanya Gana Pradesh which included Rohtak, Mahesh (probably Maham) & Sirsa, came into light during the period of Maurya rulers in 200-100 BC on the basis of their coins. The Rorwal Pradesh of Rajanya Gana ruled from Hoshiarpur to Mathura. These independent Gana were merged into a single national entity in 400 BC under Magadha Ganrajya by Chandragupta Maurya. Perhaps during these merger time Rajanya Gana changed to Rohityan, Rorwal or Rodwal, or Ror and fled to Sindh due to some mishaps (?). (ibid2)

(3) **Arorvansiy Etihas**; Dr Harnam Singh Monga, in his book, (page 83-84) referring a, 'Prachin Khandani Etihas', says, that when Aurangzeb was in Deccan to settle the matter with Chhatrapati Shivaji, the *Rajputs of Hindan & Karnal areas revolted & refused to pay revenue*. To suppress them, he called Mirdad Khan, the military commander of Baluchistan & Yangistan, who on his way; recruited *'Arodvansiy' from Multan in his army*. He was successful in suppressing the revolt. To stop reoccurrence & as a permanent solution; Mughal ruler assigned Jagirs and land to these Biloch & Arodvansiy. (ibid2-5)

(4) **Rors from Badli**; His next belief of origin of Rors from Badli is after the **defeat of Tanval Brahm s/o Binjal Dev** in 1208 after fight with Aibak in place of belief of majority of Rors that their ancestors fled from Badli on Raksha Bandhan day to various parts of Haryana & UP after Ror ruler of Badli **Mahil Bagh lost the fight** with Aibak.

This premise he evolved from the fact that between Binjal Dev, one of the allies of Chauhan, who had captured Gauri in the battle of 1191, a mistrust had grown. So Chauhan apprehending Binjal Dev may not connive with Gauri & defeat him in future, got killed Binjal Dev at Hansi & his all commanders by calling them to Delhi. So, to avenge this, Rani Zalim of Binjal Dev despatched his son in 1192, who camped at Badli, but he fought in 1208 (Quite intriguing as to what he did for 16 yrs).

After this queen of slain Binjal Dev with her son Mandu fled to Kurukshetra camouflaged as **Mahad Ror** (why Ror?), remained under secrecy, and later came to be known as **'Ror'** and thus the beginning of Ror Caste.

(5) **Rors from Rashtrakutas;** Dr Kadiyan's 5th view - Rors have sprung from Rashtrakutas.(ref; details in para 8.2.(e))

In Ch.2, Ror Maratha context: Purpose & justification; he describes few opinions making events, publishing of material & conferences & asserting influence on Ror Mahasabha functionaries, even calling some Marathas leaders from Maharashtra for certifying that Rors are left- over Marathas soldiers who could not return to their land. Also, he cites the efforts of 'Ror Sadbhavna Dal' & 'Ror Chetna Manch' to counter & nullify the agenda of Ror Marathas theory propagators to save community from disintegration, disrepute & split. (ibid11-14)

In Ch.3 Justification of eight proofs: part-1, that Rors are Marathas, he refutes the postulation with justifications, & most of his points are logical except the 6th one, which is partially true as couple of Ror *gots* matches with Marathas. But that way these also matches with other castes e.g., Rajputs, Jat, Gujar, and Ahirs etc. (ibid 15-28)

In Ch.4 Who are Marathas? I agree with his views, that no anthropological reports, physicals, or pothis of Jagge Bhaats, etc have never recorded any lineage connection between Rors & Marathas (except the sinister campaign of 2002). *But I do not agree with his views that Marathas are low-life, ethicless, robbers, cheaters, crafty, cunning, deceitful, traitors, trickish, mendacious.* I totally disagree with his views & that of Dr K C Yadav wherein he states that Marathas are Shudras & not kshatriya. His views, that Marathas have a natural tendency & traits of plundering & despoilment, are malicious, bad in taste & reflects some personal enmity or some axe to grind). (ibid28-36)

In Ch.5 How the Shivaji was crowned, Dr Surender Kadian continues his disdain, towards this Hindu warrior Shivaji Maharaj, who taught most tyrant Muslim ruler Aurangzeb, a lesson of life in his own style of treachery & deceit, and revived Hindavi pride. (ibid37-43)

Ch.6 Lineage of Shivaji, Dr Kadiyan finds the answer to his three questions as to; did Rajputs & historians accepted Shivaji as Sisodias & also did Shivaji and his clan changed their Bhonsle surname to Sisodias, as negative? *So, he sticking to his belief of, Shivaji as a Shudra and not kshatriya, is disgusting, malicious & condemnable.* (ibid44-47)

In Ch.7 Which side defeated Maratha escaped, he writes that the proponent of Ror Maratha theory says, the leftover Maratha hid in the Jungles south of Kurukshetra & later on resurfaced & announced them as Ror. But the Marathas who hid in the Jungle were slain by the Abdali soldiers in hot pursuits. The one who hid in Villages are recoded. (Ref; Dr Hari Ram Gupta's book, 'Panipat and Marathas', page 274-300. Also book by Shankar Purshotam Joshi in Marathi does not support any leftover Maratha family in Haryana as Ror). Further he puts forth seventeen (17) very convincing points, to establish that defeated Maratha soldiers did not hid in the Jungles but headed towards Maharashtra only through Sonepat, Bahadurgarh, Rohtak, Hisar, Jind, Bharatpur, Mathura & Gwalior etc, which are agreeable. (Ibid 48-57)

Ch.8 Overview on Ror Maratha Etihas: Part- II; Out of 13 points (page 9-10); which claims that *'Rors are Maratha'* only, the 4 points he scrutinizes, in this chapter are; Rors like Maratha (1) Don't celebrate Paunchi; (2) Celebrate Govardhan Puja only instead of Diwali; (3) Pay annual laag to Jagge Bhaats; & (4) Matching of about 20 Gotras.

He cites two incidents in r.o of point no1. Though both incidents appear to be unconvincing, but it is true Rors were not celebrating Raksha Bandhan earlier; reason has been discussed already. For no 2 he states that all agrarian caste like Jat, Gujar, Ahir celebrate Govardhan Puja only instead of Diwali. So, no logic that Rors are Marathas since both does not celebrate Diwali but Govardhan Puja. Point no 3 annual laag given to Bhaats is in lieu of their services for keeping & updating lineage of Rors. Rajputs also pay laag to Bhaats, can it be construed that Rors are Rajputs? In r.o of point no 4, it can be said that gotras of Rors matches with Rajputs, Jats, Gujars, Ahirs, etc also. So, it cannot be considered a valid reason for Rors & Marathas being the same. (ibid59-63)

In Ch.9; Dr Kadiyan says Rors have not originated from Rajputs, and to prove it, he puts forward lot of inconsistent & illogical views. Simultaneously, he says, as per Bhaats some Rors are Suryavanshi, some Chadervanshi, and it is believed Rodvansh is one of the Vansh of Rajputs (rulers) only, (ref ASI report 1871-72, vol-IV, pp-210-12), and later on Ror caste originated from this Vansh only. *Mehla Rors have mainly originated from this Rodvansh. First, they were called Mahror, thereafter Mad Ror & later Ror only as Mehla are in majority in the caste.* He also describes some *Ravadvansh* (page-80) and says may be Ror or Arora are descendant of this Ravadvansh. (ibid74-81)

In Ch.10 Are Rors part of Jat tribes? he puts forward the records of Sauram Khap Panchayat (page 82-83) and also clarifies that record nowhere have clear cut reference as to when and from where Ror nomenclature came into use. On page 87-88, he lists *45 surnames matching between Rors & Jats (a good numbers seems to have been spelled to match. On page 89-90, contrary to this, in case of Marathas, he himself says matching of surnames does not mean that a caste has originated from another caste).* As gotras are not on the name of ancestor only but after Kul purohit, Rishi, Place, or on mother's gotra in case of inter caste marriage, so merely similar gotra does not construe to be of same caste. *In the end, he does not accept Khap records as authentic & rejects that Ror are part of Jats Jathas.*

In Ch.11 Blood relations of Rors and Aroras; *though he himself admits that no Ror would agree that Aroras & Rors is same caste but he tries hard;* all his points have no substance & even a novice would not believe his point of views. (In fact, this postulations of his is another disaster like, "Ror are Marathas") His comparison of 34 surnames of Rors & sub-caste of Aroras (page104-105), to be similar is illogical, & absurd. Same is the case wherein he compares names of another 23-sub caste of Aroras with the name of Ror villages. (Ref; A Glossary of tribes & castes of Punjab & NWFP Vol-II, pp-506 to512 (p-544-60/614); surnames of Aroras, & Khatris are on the name of plants, animals, event, & action etc). Every significant statement appears to be prejudiced & ill-conceived for proving his pre-decided notion that Rors & Aroras have blood relations, without any evolutionary medical DNA or physical features. (ibid92-110)

Ch.12 Epilogue; He concludes the origin of Rors as Vikas of Rajnya > Rohityan > Rodwal > Ror >Rore (Arore)Panjab; Rohtak>Mahesh> Sirsa called Rodwal; then arrival of Aroras in Bloch army in UP & Haryana. He summarily rejects Ror- Maratha theory, & Rajput origin theory (of Master Ratan Singh Shastri ji) & Bhaat pothis theory, & Sarva Khap theory. In the end he closes the subject by establishing that; Ror came to the present area some 300 years back only (w.e.f from which time; not stated by Dr Surinder Kadiyan? May be 17th century.).

Finally, without malice to any group/view; Dr Kadiyan concludes the subject requesting elite & elders of the community to deliberate on all the matters & come out with a consensus final & permanent decision to put to rest all the conflicting theories on the origin of the Ror caste, to avoid further disintegration of the caste. (ibid111 to 124)

Ch.13 Appendix in r.o. transcribed version of Ror Drashta (March-April1991) on Rajnyagan (p-125 to127), meaning of Rodwal & its scrutiny, (p-128 to133). Ch.14 List of references (p136 to 141)

**(d) Ror Vansh Ka 5000 Varsh Ka Etihas:** Sh Ram Das Rode, ed 2009, pages-368, This 6th book of his, has seven Bhag / chapters which are in the form of 55 question-Answers, which are on various matters related to Ror Caste.

His main premise is that Ror, Aror, Rode, Arore, Rohad, Jat, Gurjar, Rajput, Ahir, Bishnoi, etc earlier were part of one tribe only and they had very important role in the 36 vansh of Aryans. His book delves on the proud history of 5000 years of Ror Vansh. This book on page-18 & 19, starting with the king Ruru, a 28th generation descendant of Yayati Vansh & ending with Dadrod(r) have recorded names of 101 generations Raja of Ror Vansh. Few most famous of Ror vansh are Baalan Dev (who established Badli) at sr no 48, Tisman at 58, Indraman at 59 & Samrat Dhaj or Raja Ror at sr no 60.

**(e) Clarification to Unification:** Tracing of Ror caste history–by Major M.S. Keshwar (Retd); ed. 3/2011, 128 pages

The book in the form of questions & answers incidentally has 37 questions, perhaps author has in mind that Rors are 37th caste (36 Royal Races +1 Ror Race). He says, Rors were Rajputs only & some compelling circumstances forced them to migrate from Malwa & Mewar and convert themselves from Rajput to Ror (?). He says, Ror were known as *Rajput or Guhila or Chaudhary* before migration from Mewar. (Ref; section 8.3.(4)).

Major Keshwar, quoting Migration theory, of Herbert Risley, 'People of India', (pp-88; ref para 2.5.(6) Ch-2 also) states that, "it appears Ror instead of name of a caste, is a *territorial name & might have got attached at the time of migration.* Mr Risley said, 'a group of people who decides to shift permanently (various reasons), from one place to another selects their original old territorial name for their caste.' But owing to the loss of identity, the number of instances of formation of a caste by migration, however, is comparatively small. (Appears to be true & relevant in the case of Rors also, as they are still struggling for their identity). He says that Ror caste was residing in Mewar, even before 14th century, where many territorial names such as Behror, Bhainsror, Khichror, Chitore, Rorji-ka-Kheda, Rorwas, etc were in existence. Further he cites names of many villages in Mewar are similar to those occupied by Rors in the present locations such as *Ahar, Gudha, Shamgadh, Mathana, Picholia, Raipur, Umari, Lohari, Jwara, Untla,* etc. But at this point of time, the caste was in initial stage of its formation & preferred to associate with their kulas (such as Guhila, Rathore, Chauhan, Solanki, Parmar, Khenchi etc.). (ibid23-25)

A brief on the migration as sequenced by Maj. Keshwar (pp-31 to 35 of his book) is; 1st **Migration;** 1303, when Allauddin Khilji demanded the *"Dola"* of queen Padmini; 2nd **Migration;** After Rana Sanga's death by his own nobles, post the loss of Bayana (Khanua)

battle; **3rd Migration;** Due to Earth Scorch Policy of Maharana Pratap, before the battle of Haldi Ghati.(Thousands of Chaudhry farmers deserted their villages in Mewar, to find a place of safety and survival somewhere else); **4th Migration;** after the battle of Haldi Ghati on 18 June 1576; **5th Migration;** People felt cheated and deserted Mewar when Rana Amar Singh, on the insistent of his nobles entered into agreement with Jahangir at Gogunda on 5, Feb.1615, against the promise made by him to his late father Maharana Partap at the time of his death.(Ref; Udaipur Dist. Gazetteer page 49); **6th Migration;** It relates to rescue operation of Infant Raja Ajeet Singh of Marwad and his mother Dowager Rani from the Delhi Darbar of Aurangzeb; **7th Migration;** Famine of 1630 in Gujarat & Khandesh etc forced thousands of people to migrate; **8th Migration;** Took place after severe famine of 1661 during the reign of Rana Raj Singh; **9th Migration;** A civil strife in 1762 between Rana Uri Singh & other chiefs of Udaipur, lots of Mewar subjects deserted & migrated to safer places. (Rors of Bhaini Khurd are said to have migrated to present location due to this civil war); **10th Migration;** Believed to have taken place after the poisoning of Rana Bhim Singh's daughter Princess Krishna Kumari, as subjects of the kingdom lost faith in Rajput Royals; **11th Migration;** Final migration after the battle of Tunga (battle of Lalsot) in 1789; all Rajput took part in it.

Maj. Keshwar concludes his book with, "Since it is revealed that Ror caste is an amalgamation of seventeen (17) Royal Races consisting of Rajputs & Jat clans, it has now become uphill task to trace the real history of Rors."

**(f) Rors: Eurasia roots: DNA Theory**: By Sydney based Sh. Anurag Kadiyan of Karnal

As per Tribune News Services item from American Journal of Human Genetics, pasted below, Saliva & blood samples of 154 Rors from 11 villages including from Amin, Katlahedi, Staundi & Dathrat were collected in 2012. The ancestral lineage of the Rors, by a group of researchers has been traced to western Eurasia. Gyaneshwar Chaubey, a prof of Banaras Hindu University, a member of research group says that *Rors do not have any genetic ancestry with Marathas.* The study based on DNA profiling of about 200 persons in Haryana & Pakistan revealed that *Rors have strong genetic similarities with the Pathan & Kalash communities in Pakistan.* The study indicates that Rors might have moved from the swat valley, a peripheral region of Indus valley, about 1500 yrs ago. (*This corroborate the rule of Ror Dynasty between 450BC to 489 CE*), The study was conducted at Institute of Genomics, University of Tartu, Estonia by an international group of Inter-disciplinary researchers under Prof Dubey & Dr Ajay Kumar Pathak.

**NB:** 1) Eurasia roots of Rors need to be reconfirmed from Hyderabad based firm Mapmygenome's, to know ethnicity composition for cultural, ethnic, & geographical diversity to establish genetic legacy.

2) An Instagram post; In Post Mauryan period **Satavahana & Ror Sakas, known as Western Satraps** contested for the control of city of **Ujjain.** After end of Satavahana dynasty, **Rors** retained **Ujjain** 78-130 CE. Raja Tisman ruled vast part of western India (Rajasthan, Haryana Gujarat MP, UP).

3) **A correction;** Baghpat, is not in Meerut dist but it itself is a district.

# Rors have roots in Eurasia: Research

## DNA-based study published in American Journal of Human Genetics

VISHAL JOSHI
TRIBUNE NEWS SERVICE

KURUKSHETRA, DECEMBER 10

Working on the desire of Sydney-based IIT graduate Anurag Kadian to know the ancestral lineage of Rors in Haryana, a group of researchers has traced the community to western Eurasia. The DNA-based study was published in the American Journal of Human Genetics last week.

Gyaneshwer Chaubey, a professor at Banaras Hindu University and member of the research team, said the Rors did not have any genetic ancestry with the Marathas.

He said it was the first comprehensive genetic study of the modern Harappan region. He said the movement of people of the Indus Valley towards the Gangetic plains was likely to have taken place after the collapse of this civilisation.

"Our study, based on DNA profiling of over 200 persons in Haryana and Pakistan, reveals that Rors have strong genetic similarities with the

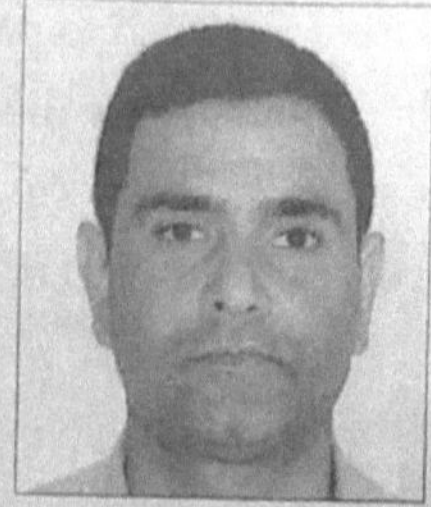

Sydney-based Anurag Kadian

The team of researchers who studied the ancestral lineage of Ror community in Haryana through DNA profiling.

Pathan and Kalash communities in Pakistan. The study indicates that Rors may have moved from the Swat Valley, a peripheral region of the Indus Valley region, about 1,500 years ago," said Chaubey, senior author of the report.

Light skin colour and average height of 6 feet were distinct characteristics of Rors, he said. "Saliva and blood samples of 154 Rors from 11 villages, including Amin, Katalheri, Sataundi and Dhatrath, were collected in 2012. Later, more samples were taken from Pakistan by our collaborators and the analysis were conducted in a state-of-the-art laboratory in Estonia," he added.

Rors were predominantly an agrarian community in Haryana. They were present in various parts of the state and had a dominant presence in several villages of Kurukshetra, Kaithal and Karnal. Kadian, a native of Karnal, said he wanted to end widespread confusion about the Ror ancestry.

"As I floated the idea to identify Rors scientifically, Dubey and Dr Ajai K Pathak of the Institute of Genomics, University of Tartu, Estonia, formed an international group of inter-disciplinary researchers. The research has given a new dimension to the background of the community," said Kadian.

The claim of Rors' genetic connection with Marathas was first floated more than 10 years ago by Virender Verma, a bureaucrat-turned-politician in Karnal district. Quoting a few historians, he had claimed that Rors had their lineage to Maratha soldiers who survived the third battle of Panipat in 1761.

Kadian said the Maratha theory was questioned within the community and it was important to end the confusion.

* * * * *

# Chapter-9. Paradoxes and Rors

## 9.1 Definitions

A Paradox is a statement seemingly absurd or contradictory which despite being sound or apparently of sound reasoning from acceptable premise, leads to a conclusion that seems self-contradictory. Myth is; a widely held but false belief or a traditional story concerning history etc. Legend is; a traditional story popularly regarded as historical but not authenticated. History of origin of Ror community if analysed critically, then one would come across numerous paradoxes, myths, and intriguing tales, which of course, also is true for similar social standing communities.

## 9.2 Various Paradoxes and Myths about Rors

There are plenty of paradoxes about Ror community which are quite contradicting & intriguing, and when put to authentication they don't have any supporting facts to substantiate their claim or are found completely opposite to what is being said or was believed otherwise. Some of such paradoxes are described as below.

(a) **That there were no Muslims among Rors?**

**The Prevalent Belief;** Every Ror, assertively state that there were no Muslims among Rors. This belief is permanently ingrained in their mind & psyche and none accepts that there ever were Muslims among Rors.

**Facts;** British time census records Muslims among Rors; Data from census reports of British Punjab, which are authenticated official documents are stated herein as below to establish the truth.

(i) Census-1891; Punjab & it's Feudatories-part-III; Total population of Rors was 43212 with the break-up; Hindu 42930, Sikh 170, and Musalman 112 (Ref; page-930/982 of the census-1891 report).

(ii) Census-1891; Punjab & its Feudatories, Part-III; Refer section 6.4(c), Ch-6, Literacy Table-C redrawn for Ror caste only, shows 28 Muslims among literate Rors out of total 126 Rors (ref; census 1891; pp-544-55).

(iii) Census1901; Vol.17, Punjab; its feudatories & NWFP-Part-1; Para 16: (pp-310, Ch-VIII on Caste, Tribe & Races), khojas of Shahpur has a sub-division called **Rawar or Ror**. If these were not Aroras, then they may be Ror only. (Sec-6 (5)ch-6)

(iv) Subsidiary Table-III of census-1901; Part table-III; proportion of sexes in selected castes, tribes & races; (pp-350 to 357); redrawn for Rors & Jat only as below, shows Jats & Rors, both comprised of *Hindu, Sikh & Muslims.*

| Part Subsidiary Table III: Proportion of sexes in selected castes, tribes, races; census 1901 (pp- 350 to 357) | | | | | | | | |
|---|---|---|---|---|---|---|---|---|
| **Caste, Tribe, Race** | | Numbers of Females per 1000 males | | | | | | |
| | Religion | All ages | 0-5 | 5-12 | 12-15 | 15-20 | 20-40 | 40 - above |
| Ror | H, S | 827 | 890 | 789 | 730 | 654 | 882 | 881 |
| | M | 639 | 667 | 643 | 1200 | 167 | 524 | 818 |
| Jat | H | 795 | 839 | 754 | 686 | 682 | 812 | 871 |
| | S | 740 | 694 | 650 | 581 | 643 | 828 | 811 |
| | M | 859 | 940 | 848 | 709 | 795 | 899 | 842 |

(v) Major M S Kheswar in his book (pp-37); Clarification to Unification, also states that after the formation of Ror caste, there appears to be no incidence wherein Rors have converted to Islam, means before that there were.

**Conclusion;** The facts stated above establishes that there were Muslims among Rors also. Perhaps it is not possible also not to be so, as policy of all Muslim invaders was to convert Hindus on capturing their territory. But this may be an error also by the enumerator writing Ror in place of Arora/Rora, as has happened at number of places between these two castes. (Ref; page-930/982; 1891; census; Mr Risley, census commissioner accepted it). But it is fact that post partition of India in 1947, there are no Muslims among Rors. So, the matter needs research to clear the air of Arora or Ror as Muslims?

**(b) Rors preferred to be ruined but No Dola of their Fairs to Muslims?**

**The Prevalent Belief;** Another deeply ingrained belief in the memory of every Ror and pride runs in their veins that their ancestors preferred to be ruined rather than offering Dola of their Fairs to Muslim rulers. *This belief connects them with the Rajputs of Mewar, who also never gave Dola of their Fairs to Muslim ruler come what may?*

**Facts;** Book, 'Clarification to Unification,' (pp-27 to 30); Major Keshwar; states that Mewar was the only protector of Hindus who never compromised with its honour (Tod's Annals of Rajasthan vol-I pp-210). Rors also are known for their purity of blood & to maintain it they adopted *Satta System of marriage.* Rors abandoned Badli in a rift with Qutbuddin on the question of Dola only? Few Dolas demanded by Muslim rulers but declined by Mewar;

1. Dola of Padmini queen of Rana Ratan Singh, demanded by Allaudin Khilji but declined, perished in battle & Jauhar.

2. It is said that when Uda (the parricide) s/o Rana Kumba, in 1473, offered Dola of his daughter to Delhi sultan to obtain the sanction of his authority, but as a manifestation of vengeance from Heaven, he was struck by lightning, as soon as he left the diwankhana on taking leave of sultan of Delhi?

3. That Dola will not be given, was the precondition in the agreement between Rana Amar Singh (also known as Rana Amar Singh Ror) & Jahangir in 1615.

These facts of Dola not given are true and written all over in Mewar documents, inscriptions/Shilalekhs and in the memory of people. About Dola not given by Rors, may also be true, as they also have same traits as Rajputs of Mewar. But census of Panjab as stated in previous para, has recorded there were Muslims among Rors, which means, some Rors might have been converted by force but some, who gave Dolas, might have avoided the conversion?

**Conclusion;** So, the belief that ancestors of Rors preferred to be ruined rather than offering Dola of their Fairs to Muslim rulers, need further detailed research for all the facts of that times to prove it otherwise. Till research of the true facts, Rors can retain this belief & feel proud of their ancestors & remain in high esteem?

**(c) That there were/are no Rors beyond Pipli?**

**The Present Position;** As of today, and perhaps since the last quarter of 19th century, there were/are no Ror villages beyond Pipli on northern side. It seems as if, there is some, "Lakshman Rekha", with Pipli as the boundary.

**Facts;** (1) Maharaja Ranjit Singh in 1803 was offered boundary of his territory up to Sutlej River, (Ref 'Sikhs' by Patwant Singh), but Viceroy Wellesley remained undecided which suited Maharaja. In 1806, Maharaja Ranjit Singh on invitation to mediate a dispute between Royals of Patiala, crossed Sutlej River thrice (1806,07, & 08). During this trans-Sutlej campaign, he annexed Faridkot, Ambala, Shahbad, imposed levies on Malerkotla, & Thanesar, and there was wide spread looting, killings, & annexation of areas. Many Rors villages in Ambala dist. like; Panjokhara, Khanpur, Dhoolkot etc were deserted &, had to face evacuation. (Ref; clarification to Unification', pp-26-27)

(2) The area between Ambala, Pipli (Thanesar) & extending to Karnal, after the third battle of Panipat in1761, was a sort of, *'No man Land'*, having unstable rulers, & chaotic political situation & it was constantly being raided by Marathas & Sikhs alternatively, known as *Singha Shahi ka Ram Raula*. Karnal which was

under Raja Gaj Singh of Patiala in 1763, was recaptured by Marathas & given to George Thomas on Chauth (1/4$^{th}$ revenue share). British occupied Karnal on 5$^{th}$ April, 1805 and this ended the Sikh invasions towards south & east of Ambala. These constant raids of this area by Sikhs resulted into either deserting of Villages by Rors or conversion of Rors to Sikhism to end their woes. Hence no Ror villages, beyond Pipli in Ambala dist.

(3) Punjab Castes: based on census-1881, Abstract:83 (pp166 to167), shows Rors as part of Minor land-owning & Agricultural tribes or castes like Rajputs & Jats, dominant in parts of Panjab, not so numerous or so widely spread as to rank with those great races. (Also see section 3.3; Ch-3). A part abstracts 83, reduced only for Rors, shows that Rors were inhabiting Ambala, Ludhiana, & Patiala state also, in addition to Delhi, Karnal, & Jind, which clearly establishes that there were Rors or their villages beyond Pipli on its northern side.

| Part Abstract; 83; Showing Distribution of Minor Dominant Tribe in Districts and states; Ror (Caste no 55)-census1881 | | | | | | | | | |
|---|---|---|---|---|---|---|---|---|---|
| Delhi | Gurgaon | Karnal | Ambala | Ludhiana | British Terriroty-1 | Patiala | Jind | East Plains -2 | Total |
| 666 | ---- | 34094 | 4861 | 26 | 39467 | 36 | 1048 | 1084 | 40371 |
| 1% | -- | 55% | 4% | - | 2% | - | 4% | - | 2% |
| The percentage of population Per 1000 & Rors were found to be 2% of the total | | | | | | | | | |

Further Ibbetson in tabulation of sub-divisions of Rors (also see section 3.3.(1) Ch-3), writes that, "Ambala Rors appears to be mostly Sagwal", which confirms Rors were inhabiting Ambala district, which is beyond Pipli.

(4) Part Abstract 85; Census 1891 Punjab by Tehsils, as redrawn here only for Rors shows they were residing in 7 districts & 15 Tehsils of Punjab, not only in Ambala & Hosiarpur districts but even in Lahore & Mongomery etc. (Ref; section 6.4(b) Ch-6 for other castes and page-168 to173/213 Appendix; C of census report for main abstract);

| Part Abstract; 85; redrawn for Showing Distribution of Minor Dominant Tribe in Districts and states; Rors (Caste no 55)-census1891 | | | | | | | | |
|---|---|---|---|---|---|---|---|---|
| District | Tehsil | Population | District | Tehsil | Population | District | Tehsil | Population |
| 1. Rohtak | 1. Rohtak | 8 | | 3. Kaithal | 14392 | 5. Hosiarpur | 1. Dasuya | 10 |
| | 2. Gohana | 399 | | Total | **39814** | | Total | **10** |
| | Total | **407** | 4.Ambala | 1. Ambala | 67 | 6. Montgomery | 1. Gugaira | 25 |
| 2. Delhi | 1. Sonipat | 727 | | 2. Jagadhari | 71 | | 2. Pakpathan | 7 |
| | 2. Ballabgarh | 1 | | 3. Narayangadh | 10 | | Total | **32** |
| | Total | **728** | | 4. Pipli | 1943 | 7. Lahore | 1. Chunian | 2 |
| 3. Karnal | 1. Karnal | 19812 | | Total | **2093** | | Total | **2** |
| | 2. Panipat | 5610 | | | | | G Toal | **43086** |

**Conclusion;** So, the statement that there were no Rors beyond Pipli, is not fully true. However, now why there are no Ror villages beyond Pipli is a matter of research for the facts of that times to prove it otherwise. It means during political instability between1761-1805, all Rors, to avoid the wrath of Sikh armies, might have either become Sikhs or might have migrated to safer places in Haryana or UP.

**(d) If Rors are Kshatriyas, then why they are not registered with All India Kshatriya Mahasabha?**

**The Present Position;** Kshatriyas are rulers, warriors, & landowners. So, Rors being land owners & rulers in old times are Kshatriyas but their caste is not registered with any Kshatriya Mahasabha. (Ref; clarification to Unification' pp; 36-37)

**Facts;** (1) Mr A. Cunningham says; *"old categorization of Kshtriyas[1] itself is 'Ror', which appears to be quite logical."* (Refer section 8.3.(7); & foot note page-210 of ASI report 1871-72, Vol-IV)

(2) Rors are Minor Land-Owning Dominant caste, like Rajputs, Jats, & are dominant in parts of the Panjab, but are not so numerous & so widely spread as to rank with those great races. *They claim to be of Kshatriya origin.*

(3) Ror caste is one out of 20 castes classified as Agricultural Military & Dominant tribes' classification as adopted for Punjab Census 1881 & 1891 (Abstract 84 part-1; page-164-167/213; Appendix: C); which establishes that Rors are Kshatriya. *Mr Denzil Ibbetson in the census 1881 report* speaks high of Rors & he classify them in Kshatriyas category only.

(4) The Amin Ror says they came from Sambhal in Muradabad; (*notwithstanding the quote of Ibbetson; this may be to connect themselves with their neighbours*), the Chauhan Rajputs came from there only. Almost all Rors point to Badli in Jhajjar Tehsil as place of origin, though some of them say; they came from Rajputana.

(5) By physical features Rors are fine stalwart men, body stamp, demeanours, & other traits fully match Kshatriya race but in public parlance they seem to be in no man's land.

**Conclusion;** The facts above establishes that Rors, a Minor Land-Owning Dominant Tribe are Kshatriya, notwithstanding the ambiguity in origin & lack of documents but supported by all circumstantial evidences, and people's history. *Further, as on date, and as to why the Ror caste is not registered with All India Kshatriya Mahasabha, is irrelevant, as present day All India Kshatriya Mahasabha is a body of Rajput caste only, but the people of Ror Dynasty, who were earlier a distinct Rajput tribe, are now a distinct & separate Ror caste.*

### Or Are Ror Outcastes from Kshatriya stock, like Aroras?

Aroras, say they became outcaste from Kshatriya stock during the persecution of kshatriyas by Parshu Ram, & to avoid killing they denied their caste, and described it as *Aur or Another,* hence the name. Similarly, are the **Rors** also outcaste Kshatriyas? Here, it is said that Rors & Aroras does not belongs to same ethnic group and of their origin also, Mr Denzil Ibbetson says, "They (Rors) have the same story as the Aroras of they having been Rajputs who escaped the fury of Prashu Ram by stating that their caste was Aur or Another." The Aroras are often called Roras in the east of Panjab; yet I (Mr. Denzil) can hardly believe that the frank and stalwart Ror is of the same origin & ethnic stock as the Aroras. (Ref; Punjab Castes; Ibbetson; pp178 to179). *So, as examined above, Rors are not outcaste from Kshatriya stock like Aroras.*

### (e) That Rors do not celebrate Raksha Bandhan?

**Belief/Past Events;** Three version behind not celebrating Raksha Badhan by Rors narrated by words of mouth are; (1) Battle of Badli; This is the main version which every Ror strongly and convincingly believe that their ancestors had to desert Badli (Jhajjar-Haryana) over a quarrel on giving, 'Dola', with Qutbuddin, after defeat due to treachery by the priest, who had taken all arms of Ror warriors on Raksha Bandhan Day, on the pretext of Puja.

(2) Raja Khangar Ror of Bhawangadhi; Prof Om Prakash, proponent of Maratha theory, says that the rule of Ror Raja s/o of Raja Khangad, ruling the area around Agra through 52 Gadhis from the central fort of Kagarol sometimes in 1206-08, came to end on the day of Paunchi (Raksha Bandhan), when Aibek sultan of Delhi, demanded 'Dola' & accept his authority. Raja Ror being less powerful chose to desert Kagarol & 52 Gadhis lock stock & barrel, and settled in Western Ghats Maharashtra further west away from Aibek. (Refer section 8.4.(2) (b))

(3) Rors if of Rajput origin; Major Keshwar (ref his book 'Clarification to Unification', pp.61-62), says; (a)The Demand of Dola by Alaudin Khilji, consequent battle between Rajputs, their supreme sacrifice including of Rana Ratan Singh followed by Jauhar by Padmini along with Royal Fairs, which culminated on the day of Raksha Badhan on 26th August 1303.

Also, he says Ror became13-03(Tehra-teen) i.e., fled from Mewar; (b)The Rakhi by Maharani Karnavati to Humayun, when Bahadur Shah of Gujrat attacked Chitore, but the help did not come & battle was lost; Maharani & other perished by Jauhar. So, the very purpose of Raksha attached with Rakhi was forfeited.

**Facts;** It is true, in the past, even up to the last quarter of 20<sup>th</sup> century, Rors were not celebrating Raksha Bandhan enthusiastically. However, Rors, who were in services and living in cities were celebrating it seeing other Hindus doing so. It's also true that Paadha (Kul Brahmin) on Paunchi/Rakhadi/Saluman day used to send, Kalawa to tie on the wrist of all males to all Jajman's houses. The purpose though is not clear, may be to seek the protection from kshatriyas or for their well-being while going to some proverbial battle as they used to go earlier.

**Conclusion;** The Shastra puja as stated in (a) (1) above is not logical as it is done on Vijay Dashami day only. Further why no Ror do it on Raksha Bandhan now & also why don't they keep ceremonial arms like swords etc as other Kshatriyas sports even now-a-days during marriages etc. So, it needs to be authenticated by research. Description at (a)(2) & (3), however are true as these are well recorded in history of Mewar in Annals by Col Tod.

**(f) If Rors are kshatriyas then why; no records of Battle fought by them & not in the army in large numbers?**

**Belief/Past Events;** Rors claim them to be Kshatriyas and believes they have fought many battles. All informal books on their history (ref Ch-8), except govt documents like; dist. Gazetteers, Census, People of India; ANSI book etc., speaks Rors fought battles starting from Arore (Sindh), but no formal records.

**Facts;** (1) Major Keshwar says, "Rors evolved out of 17 royal races viz; Chauhan, Khichi, Dabiya, Bala, Parmar, Solanki, Rathore, Gohil, Jat, Dhaiya, Sengar, Tunwar, Budgujar, Mohila, Kushwaha, Attri, & Bhatti. These Kulas fought battles, so, the Rors can be presumed to have fought the battles. (Ref; his book pp-64)

(2) Next, he cites, Rawal Samar Singh Guhila (all Rors collectively are called Guhilas), brother-in-law of Prithvi Raj Chauhan of Delhi & Ajmer (ref; Annals by Tod), fought with him in the Battle of Taraodi in 1192 against Md Ghori. Also, the Guhilas of Chitore; ancestors of Rors fought battle of Mahoba, Haldi Ghati, Bayana, Hansi, Gagraun (waterloo of Khichi/Khanchi Rajputs; & Khanchi's are Ror also) & Tunga (battle of Lalsonth). So, the Rors fought battles. (ibid65)

(3) ASI report 1871-72 Vol-IV by CSI, A Cunningham speaks of Rors as a warrior race, and a branch/clan of Rajputs only. He mentions a figurine of Ror Raja as artefact as a proof to this from his excavations. And this Ror dynasty fought many battles & had relations with all neighbouring rulers of Indraprastha, Mathura etc.

(4) Since the time of Harshavardhan (rule 606 – 647 CE), Sarva Khap sauram Panchayat, have records of Ror yodhas, who in association with warriors of other castes, participated in various battles against invaders & even in 1857 British period. Rode Vans ka 5000 Varsh ka Itihas by Sh Ram Das Rode also mentions the names of these Ror Yodhas who fought various battles (ref; page 216 to 217, & 241 to 253 of his book).)

(5) As per Karnal dist. Gazetteer 1883-84 (pp-90 to 91) Nardak used to supply maximum numbers of soldiers to army, but Rors, who occupied Nardak after Rajputs, did not contributed much to the army. So, the disheartening matter about Rors as a community, pre-or post-independence, is that they did not prove any martial character in the military except few individual Rors who proved par excellence in some caste regiments only. Maybe they left or changed their martial character for some very serious reasons or maybe they have a narrow easy going tribal mentality who are not very keen to expand beyond reasonable means or might have fallen below redemption level in some unknown battle or social mishap which shook their soul & still buried deep in their psyche & DNA.

(6) Mr. Douie's Karnal settlement report, also states that, "except Powadh circle of Kaithal tahsil & few scattered villages, the people do not generally take up military services." Even as of now (2025) as a rough estimate there are about 1850 Rors (100 officers, 250 JCOs, & 1500 ORs) in Military services, about 5.5% officers. And highest rank achieved till date is **Major General** by **Mr Devender Kumar VSM of RVC who retired** in 2025. (Para; 29 pp-21)

(7) Even the efforts by the stalwarts of the community (like; Ch ShivRam Verma ji, Ch Ram Singh ji, Babu Anant Ram Ji etc), of having a Ror Regiment by meeting the then defence minister of India (Sh Y B Chavan) in 1962-65, could not fructify as the proposal was turned down due to less population of the caste. However, Ch Shiv Ram Verma ji was appointed as Honorary Recruiting Officer & also was confirmed a Commendation Card by the Adjutant General of Indian Army for his services as he could get enrolled 200 plus soldiers from the Community in the Army. Another mass recruitment of about 50 plus Ror Youth took place when Col Sunehara Singh was Recruiting Officer.

**Conclusion;** So, the statements at f (1), (2), (3), except at f (4) above, with indirect inferences saying Rors have fought many battles, in the absence of direct records, need to be backed by authenticated research, though traits, stamp, physique, & features of Rors have all the necessary ingredients of Kshatriyas. Keeping in view matter in the statements at f (5), (6), & (7) above who's who of the community need to brainstorm on the subject to increase their strength in the Army.

**(g) Why are Rors known as 37ᵗʰ caste?**

**Belief/Past Events;** Ror elders have been passing down their generation's mind that Rors are 37ᵗʰ caste, as if there are only 36 castes? Even people of other castes from rural background also say so. It is not understood how the belief originated? May be just to cover their ignorance of realities & confused theories of the origin of the caste, or Ror elders in a zeal to equate it with Kshatriya Rajputs invented this 37ᵗʰ caste nomenclature?

**Facts;** (1) Major Keshwar in his book (pp-38, based on The History of India, by Herman Kulke & Dietmar Rodurmund pp-116 &117) states that the list of 36 Royal Races was prepared by Rishi Vashishta. In 747AD to purify the various warrior races/tribes, a sacrificial Yagna was conducted by Rishis & 36 warrior clans were given the status of Rajputs Kshatriyas.

(2) In 17~18ᵗʰ century it was machoism to have followers, besides own offspring, to present a sword force for capturing territories. Ror Raja of Banera, who had come to Kurukshetra for pilgrimage & to get dug the Brahm Sarovar, might had been working on these lines to create a 'Ror Raja' sword force. The concept of 37ᵗʰ Royal Race/Caste might have lured, Rajput soldiers & Chaudhary; workers, to remain behind Ror Raja because he was closer to the rulers of Delhi. If this bait of remaining closer to the king of Delhi by being followers of Ror Raja had not been there, people who had come from Rajasthan would have returned to their home states/territories.

**Conclusion;** The story that Rors are 37ᵗʰ caste appears to be a myth only. But yes, it is true some Rors clan have evolved from 36 Royal Races. Ror elders might have fact (2) above in view or might have concocted the concept of 37ᵗʰ caste just to hide ambiguous theory of origin or some old guilt? However, the story of Ror Raja of Banera, who came along with his subjects for the Kurukshetra pilgrimage tour of widow Rajputni wife of Aurangzeb (who was from Banera), needs detailed study & research, as it appears, he wanted to create a new 37ᵗʰ Royal Race after him with his followers, who are said to have settled in Haryana, instead of returning to Rajasthan?

**(h) That Rors were allotted Land as Dependants of Rajputs?**

**Belief/Past Events;** It is said, & propagated that Rors were allotted lands being the descendants of Rajputs. But few says that Rors got landed property as dependents of Rajputs & Gujars. It is also said, Rors were not allotted lands initially during land settlement but they got the landed property as dependants of Rajputs only after a Bania from Gharaunda, a Rajput from Jundla and a Ror from Amin, met the settlement officer Mr Douie.

**Facts;** (1) Para-25 (page-34/84 pp-20) of Mr. Douie's settlement revision report (1882-1889); on Transfers & cultivated area sold, states: The Skinner Estates have passed to some extent into the hands of agriculturists. Mortgages to the agriculturists are chiefly to Banias and Brahmins. Jats and Rors of the Panipat and Karnal tahsils have added to their holdings from this sale, but they have lost ground in Kaithal.

(2) Para–26 Grazing lands; Mr. Douie's report: A large part of district was pre-eminently grazing country. Digging of canal brought a change, and the interests of Karnal farmers shifted to agricultural than pastoral. But still the nos of cattle especially in Nardak, were large & the provision of grazing was considered essential. So, some Government estates were reserved exclusively for grazing, & cultivation of same was prohibited. Mr. Douie in granting proprietary rights to lessees of Government lands in last settlement set apart from an area for *Charand* which was not to be broken up even under penalty or a fine. (Ref; Karnal dist. Gazetteer1883-84 pp-20)

(3) Settled Cultivator's Right: It was, and is still, a common practice to settle cultivators in a small outlying hamlet *(called Gadhi* or *Majra* or *Khedi)* to cultivate surrounding land; old maps & papers show that it was very much a matter of chance whether, when survey was done and in the record of rights on land, these were marked out as separate villages or not? Such areas were confused as cultivating possession and consequent liability for revenue with proprietary right; and when these small hamlets were held by cultivators of a caste different from that of the parent village, they were generally marked and declared to be their property.

*This is particularly the case with Rors, many small villages of whom are dotted around the Rajputs of Nardak. These were originally small communities settled by the Rajputs as cultivators in their land to assist them, to bear the burden of the Government demand; and even in Panipat, where the Ror are far stronger than in Karnal, they have, almost in every instance, been similarly settled by former Gujar inhabitants, of whom a few families still remain in many villages as the sole representatives of the old owners.* (ibid85-86)

**Conclusion;** So, the statement that, "Rors were allotted land as Dependents of Rajputs", is factually incorrect as it was allotted on the basis of, **"Settled Cultivator's Right"**, and also partly due to the facts at (1) & (2) above.

**(i) Theory of 2002; The Rors are left over Maratha soldiers from the 3rd battle of Panipat?**

**Belief/past events;** (1) The flight by Raja Khangar from Kagarol to Western Ghats & his descendants inhabiting in Konkan & Marathwada were called Marathas. Later after defeat in 3rd Battle of Panipat, the left-over Maratha soldiers are said to have resurfaced as Rors in the memory of their ancestor Raja Khangan Ror? (2) See section 8.3 (b-1) - Ror-Maratha Etihas - Prof Om Prakash, & MS Arya, (3) See section 8.3 (b-2) - Panipat Yudh ke-Ror Maratha Ka Etihas- by Dr. Vasant More, have same basic premise postulated in 2002.

**Facts;** (1) Refer section 8.3 (c) of this book having extract of ch 8 of Dr. Surender Kadiyan's book,which details similarities & dis-similarities between Marathas & Rors, & Ch-7, which analyses the question of leftover Marathas hiding in the Jungles & their resurfacing as Rors ; says that as per historians, Abdali had sent his soldiers all around in the hot pursuits of Marathas with the order to slain them, wherever they find them. *The one who had hidden in the Villages are recorded on page 274-300 of the book 'Panipat and Marathas' by Dr Hari Ram Gupta, but none of them were Rors. Another book by Sh Shankar Purshotam Joshi in Marathi also does not support any leftover Maratha families in Haryana as Ror.* All defeated Marathas through Sonepat, Rohtak, Jind, Bharatpur etc, had headed towards Maharashtra only. (ibid48-57)

So, as described in section 8.3 (c) & refuted in sec-14.8 ch-14 of this book & elsewhere in more details there is no basis & substance to prove that Rors are left over Marathas.

(2) Ref ch-6 Census & Rors; of this book; Abstract 84, *sec 6.4(b) which records 242 & 262 Marathas under caste serial no; 16, whereas it records 40371 & 43212 Rors under serial no; 20 in 1881 & 1891 census respectively.*

(3) As already stated in the forgone para f(1)(4) of this chapter, Sauram Khap Panchayat records state that Rors were already inhabiting the south-west Haryana from the time of King Harshvardhan.

(4) A hand written manuscript of Ror Etihas by Sh Sultan Singh & Sh Desh Raj, based on Prithviraj Raso & old pothis of Bhaats also states that the founder of Dopla Chauhans clan; Sh Deep Chand Chauhan had Jagirs of Amin & nearby 84 villages in AD 967 by his father Rana Har Rai Chauhan. Similarly, Balda gotra Ror had Jagirs of Ramrai-Bhain-Mori etc in 1078 AD. Also, there is a mention of Jagirs by Prithaviraj Chauhan to Kanyan gotra Ror Jeet Singh in 1187 AD in Haryana. Similarly in 1207 AD & around, there is mention of settling of *Mehla, Thaula, Kalyaniya, Khasbar, Ghadtan, Bhukna, Kandhol, Kanyra, Ruhlyan, Kadian, Khokhra, Sagwal, Lather, Beniwal, & Jaglan got Rors* in various villages of Haryana. Also, it has a mention of Vir Singh Mehla & his brothers under the patronage of Sarva Khap Haryana, as part of Prithaviraj Chauhan's forces, commanding a troop against Md Gauri at Taraodi in 1192 AD. It means that Rors were well settled in Haryana in 10th century onwards also. Hence it

corroborates the Sauram Khap records of Ror inhabitation in Haryana from 7th century onwards. (ibid pp-107, para 8.3(a) abstracting ch-3 pages 35 to 37 of Dr Rajpal's book)

**Conclusion**; Writers & Historians of repute, & majority (about 90%) of the Rors, except Maratha theory proponent writers, do not subscribe to the Maratha theory. Fact is, that it was a political ploy to gain the political space in the Ror belt by winning the confidence of Ror masses, who are hungry for a befitting identity of their caste since long time, but are ignorant of their legacy & history that they were inhabitant of this area of Haryana since the times of King Harshvardhan of 7th century as per sarva Khap panchayat & various other old records.

### (j) Are Rors Aroras of Arore/Aror?

**Belief/past events**; Sometimes pre-independence; Aroras had proposed Rors to merge in them being one of their lost branches from Arore of Sindh. Dr Kadiyan in Ch.11; Blood relations of Rors & Aroras, of his book, brings this to the center stage, though he himself *admits that no one from the Ror community would agree that Aroras & Rors are same.*

**Facts**; (1) Mr Denzil on the origin of Rors in his report of Census-1881 says that, "Rors have the same story as the Aroras, of them having been Rajputs who escaped fury of Prashu Ram by stating that their caste was *Aur or Another*." The Aroras are often called Roras in the east of Panjab; yet I (Denzil) can hardly believe that the frank & stalwart Ror is of the same origin as the Arora. (ibid178 to 179)

(2) Sir George Campbell's "*Ethnology of India*", describes another position of *Rors Vis-a-Vis Aroras*; "There is a large subordinate class of Khatris, somewhat lower but of equal mercantile energy, called *Roras or Rors*. The proper Khatris of higher grade often deny all connection with them, or at least only admit that they have some sort of bastard kindred with Khatris; but, *I think, there can be no doubt that they are ethnologically the same, and they are certainly mixed up with Khatris in their avocations.* I shall treat the whole kindred as genetically Khatris." *As has been admitted by census commissioners also, this perhaps suffers from the confusion on the part of the enumerator who due to poor knowledge have clubbed together Roras & Rors.*

(3) Rohtak Dist. Gazetteer 1883-84 on Rors: "Rors have the very same customs as Jats. *The only Ror village, Jwara, was settled from Badli.* Rors claim to be Rajputs, but they can give no very definite account even of their traditional origin. *Rors rank with Jats whom they closely resemble.* Rors, as cultivators, rank with Jats; they are common in Karnal, and bear a good

reputation there. These three tribes i.e., *Jats, Ahirs, Rors* together form the first class of cultivators in Rohtak, and own nearly 70 % of the divided lands of the district.

**Conclusion;** So, from the above it can be construed that Rors might have come from Aror, but are not Arora of Aror. Even they do not match ethnically. Also, their features, traits, stamps & ways of conducting socially & day to day life practices are at vast variance.

**(k) Are Rors Ods?**

**Belief/past events;** Some historians like Shyam Sharan Agarwal, as Dr Kadian, has also written in his book, states that; Ods only are Rors. Rors, however always refuted this canard of the prejudiced historian.

**Facts;** As enumerated in Census of India, 1931, vol. XVII; Punjab, Part-I, PP-343, Para 297; Ods, are found in the districts where canals are under construction, as Ods both male & female are considered very useful for excavation and earth work. The population figures of Hindu & Muslims Ods, as a testimony that they are different from Rors and much less in population, of the Punjab from census 1881-1931 are given below.

| Caste | 1881 | 1891 | 1901 | 1911 | 1921 | 1931 |
|---|---|---|---|---|---|---|
| Ods Hindu | 11,540 | 12,316 | 17,911 | 20,375 | 18,282 | 19,583 |
| Ods Muslim | 4,065 | 10,082 | 8,174 | 11,170 | 10,192 | 13,041 |

Ods a nomadic tribe might be enumerated in one district at one census & in another at the next, whereas in r.o. Rors it is not so. Ods have been returned in good numbers from Gujranwala since1891 to the time of the construction of lower Chenab canal, Montgomery since 1911 to that of the lower Bari Doab canal, & Karnal since 1921 for digging of WJC (western Jamuna canal) etc. As many as 2486 Ods have returned their caste as Rajput, but have been included among Ods.

**Conclusion;** So, the statements of the historians who says that, 'Ods' may be Rors is absurd, malicious, defamatory, & factually incorrect. Rors are kshatriya having befitting stature & standing in society. Rors, as cultivators, rank with the Jats; they are common in Karnal, and bear a good reputation there.

* * * * *

## 10.1 Inhabited Areas

Rors, presently inhabit 11 districts in all in Haryana, Uttar Pradesh, & Uttarakhand at 331 locations (i/c urban locations): with break-up; 143 locations/villages in Karnal dist.,47 in Kaithal, 36 Kurukshetra, 24 in Panipat dist. of Haryana, 21 in Muzaffarnagar, 20 Saharanpur dist. of Uttar Pradesh, 13 in Haridwar dist. of Uttarakhand, 10 in Jind dist., 6 in Yamunanagar, 5 in Sonipat dist. of Haryana, and 6 in Bijnor dist. of Uttar Pradesh. The villages earlier in Rohtak dist. are now in Sonipat dist. By including metro & other big cities (14) total locations comes out to be 345.

## 10.2 Rors: In British and Princely states

As per Punjab Census 1901, Rors were found in Rohtak, Delhi & Karnal Districts under British; Ambala, & Ludhiana under Sikhs, and in Princely state of Jind. In addition, they were found in United Province also. Their approx. nos in British, Sikh & Princely states are tabulated below. (* NB; The figure of 47866 seems to be incorrect as even in 1891 census, Ror population put together in Panjab, Native states & NW United Province was 48863)

| Punjab & Delhi-1901 census | | United Province (UP+UK) | |
|---|---|---|---|
| District | Population | District | Population |
| Karnal | 42187 | Saharanpur | 1,020 |
| Jind | 1290 | Bulandshahr | 1,100 |
| Delhi | 651 | Muzaffarnagar | 754 |
| Rohtak | 450 | Mathura | 148 |
| Misc. Dist. | 193 | Other Districts | 73 |
| Total | 44771 | Total | 3,095 |
| Grand Total | 47866* | | |

Pandit Harkishan Kaul Census Commissioner of Punjab in 1911 wrote; Rors (44511) were largely Hindu, & only a smaller number are Sikh (142). *"They claim Rajput origin and their social status is the same as that of Jats.* Their chief occupation is agriculture & are declared an agricultural tribe in the dist. of Rohtak, Delhi & Karnal. (**NB;** The above figures include 214 males & 204 females recorded under Aroras in Rohtak in Imperial Table XIII, who were actually Rors, mostly from village Jwara in Gohana Tahsil of Rohtak Dist." Figures of 1911 census also seems to be incorrect as even figures of 1891 were higher than this.)

## 10.3 Presently State & District-wise Rors

In late 20th century, Rors in services shifted to urban areas or settled at their place of posting. So, now, in addition to inhabiting in original villages, huge numbers are residing in cities, & good numbers in Delhi-NCR etc.

**(a). Haryana State:** Ror inhabits about 269 locations (villages & towns) in Haryana in 7 districts & 16 tehsils.

**(1) District Karnal:** It has maximum numbers of villages (142) inhabited by Ror community. in its 5 tehsils viz; Asandh, Gharaunda, Indri, Karnal, & Nilokheri. This city, headquarter of the district, have large numbers of Rors residing in "Kot Mohalla" the old walled township and in addition, plenty of Ror employees of all sorts, after retirement as well even from neighbouring villages for the sake of the education of their wards, are residing in urban estate. Karnal was a favourite cold weather resort for retired British officers also and their families settled in India even in old times as it was a cantonment then. (More details about Karnal city, named after Karan of Mahabharat fame, can be had from the book Annals of Karnal; 1914; by Major C H Buck, the then DC).

**(2) District Kurukshetra:** It was part of Karnal dist. till it was separated as a dist. on January 23, 1973, with 3 tehsils; Thanesar, Kaithal & Guhla. Major changes took place on November 1, 1989 with the formation of Kaithal as a district, taking out Kaithal & Guhla Sub-divisions from Kurukshetra District. Presently, it comprises of 3 tehsils; Thanesar, Shahabad, & Pehowa. Ror inhabit at 36 locations.

**(3) District Kaithal:** It was founded by Emperor Yudhishthir, & historically its known as "Kapisthal;" "Abode of Kapi". It has a temple dedicated to Anjani, the mother of Hanuman ji known as "Anjani Tilla." Kaithal with many temples is an important landmark in 48 Kos pilgrimage Parikrama with its rich cultural & historical heritage and is surrounded by 7 ponds & 8 gates. It came into existence on November 1,1989 by taking out Kaithal & Guhla from Kurukshetra district. It consists of 3 tehsils; Kaithal, Guhla, & Pundri. Ror inhabit 46 villages & towns.

**(4) District Panipat:** It is one of the *Prasath* which ShriKrishna demanded from Duryodhan for Pandav as their share of ancestral kingdom. It is famous for its three Battles of 1526, 1556, & 1761, which changed the course of the history of Bharatvarsh. Panipat as a district was formed by including the areas of Panipat & Asandh tehsils on 1 November 1989. It was abolished from 24 July 1991 to 31 December 1991, but revived again on 1 January 1992. Rors inhabit 24 villages/locations; Korana is the largest Ror village followed by Ahar.

**(5) District Sonipat:** It is also one of the five *Pats or Prasath* (Indrapat, Panipat, Talpat, Bhagpat & Sonipat), demanded by ShriKrishna from Duryodhan for Pandav in the Mahabharat period. Another tradition ascribes it to Raja Soni, a 13th descent from Arjun. Sonipat area remained attached to Delhi district from 1861 to 1912. After separation of Delhi territory from Punjab in 1912, it was added to Rohtak district. Sonipat as district came into existence on December 22, 1972, after separation from Rohtak district. It has 4 tehsils; Ganaur, Gohana, Kharkhoda, & Sonipat. Rors inhabit at 5 locations 3 villages; Jwara, Mohana, & Tihad plus 2 urbans.

**(6) District Yamunanagar:** It was created as a new district on 16 October, 1989, by carving it out of Ambala district. Yamunanagar town has many large industries in plywood, paper, sugar, and utensils sector. Yamunanagar district have 3 tehsils e.g., Bilaspur, Chhachhrauli, and Jagadhri. Rors inhabit only at six (6) locations.

**(7) District Jind:** Jind town is said to have been founded during Mahabharat times by Pandavs, who built a temple in the honour of Jainti (victory) Devi. The town Jaintapuri later got corrupted to Jind. Before 1947, it was part of Phulkian state; Jind & Safidon tahsils were part of Jind State. Jind dist. has 4 tehsils; Jind, Julana, Narwana & Safidon. Rors inhabit 8 locations (6villages +2 urban) in Safidon tehsil. Morkhi & Dhathrat are the oldest villages.

**(b). Uttarakhand State:** Ror inhabits about 13 locations in Haridwar district & 2 tehsils of Uttarakhand. It became a separate state after carving it out of Uttar Pradesh, on 9 November, 2000. There are 13 districts in the state & as per census 2011, it has population of about 1 crore.

**(8) Haridwar district:** Haridwar is a kaleidoscope of Sanatan culture & civilization; a 'Gateway to Swarg', and known as Mayapuri, Kapila, Gangadwar as well. The followers of Bhagwan Shiv (Mahadev) and Bhagwan Vishnu (Hari) pronounce this place Hardwar and Haridwar respectively. It has 3 tehsils viz; Haridwar, Laskar & Roorkee. Rors are in 13 locations/villages in Haridwar & Roorkee Tehsil.

**(c). Uttar Pradesh State:** Rors inhabits 47 locations in Uttar Pradesh in 3 districts & 10 tehsils e.g., Bijnor (6 no), Muzaffarnagar (21 no) and Saharanpur (20 no).

**(9) Bijnor District:** Legend ascribes it to Raja Ben (Vena), of Mahabharat times, who never realised any tax from his subjects & raised revenue by the sale of *Bijana* (hand fans). So, name is corruption of Bijana or Vijaya (victory) Nagar. Out of its 4 tehsils of Bijnor, Chandpur, Dhampur & Nagina, Ror inhabit at 6 locations; 3 in Bijnor & 3 in Chandpur.

**(10) Muzaffarnagar District:** It was founded during Shahjahan's time at the site of an old town known as Sarot or Sarwat, & is situated in the doab of Yamuna & Ganga. The district has 5 tehsils namely; Budhana, Jansath, Kairana, Khatauli, Muzaffarnagar, and Shamli. Ror inhabit at 21 places in Muzaffarnagar district.

**(11) Saharanpur District:** It has 5 tehsils namely; Behat, Deoband, Nakur, Rampur Maniharan, & Saharanpur. Ror inhabit 20 villages/locations tehsil wise; 2 in Deoband, 7 in Nakur, 6 in Rampur Maniharan, and 5 in Saharanpur.

## 10.4 Political standing of Rors

Stature of a caste is judged by the political space it occupies in the politics of the state where it dwells. Rors for that purpose though not very strong politically but it is said they had been playing the role of arbitrators in their own & nearby villages since long. Nothing is written, except as specified in section 8.3 (a) sub para describing ch-5 of Dr Rajpal Singh's book, about their participation in freedom struggle, political standing as their political arena is completely blank up to the 1st quarter of the 20th century till the arrival of Shri Babu Anant Ram ji of Kaul/Mirzapur on the political scenario, who became 1st MLC from the Ror community in 1937, from Karnal (south) General Dehati seat of combined Panjab Haryana Parishad. He remained so till 1946, as part of the home rule governance scheme in pre-independence era.

From 1937 to 2022 there had been 15 MLAs; one MLC from 1937 to 1946 & 14 MLAs from 1957 to 2022 from Ror community. There had been a cabinet minister, a Speaker of Vidhan Sabha, two as minister of state & a Deputy Speaker once only. There is no substantial space of this community on the state political stage, as stalwarts of the community who were MLA 3~4 times were limited to regional political canvass only & had no state-wide role, leave aside the role in the centre. Also, few insignificant ministries in the state were insufficient to catapult the community to a respectable political & socio-economic stage. This limited the stature, & standing of the community. Though Rors have wherewithal to have their own legislators elected from 7 seats, but lack inter-community repo & public popularity.

Post-independence, 3 political stalwarts from the community were on centre stage; 1st Ch Multan Singh; 3 times MLA, 10 years period between 1957 to 1962 & 1962 to 1966 in Punjab state, when Haryana was part of it wherein he was Dy. speaker of Punjab Vidhan Sabha, and 1967 to 1968 MLA Haryana assembly as Minister of State after creation of Haryana state; 2nd Ch. Shiv Ram Verma; 3 times 11 years as MLA, 3 Years as Cabinet minister, and Ch. Ishwar Singh; 4 times, 19 years as MLA, 1991 to 1996 as Speaker Vidhan Sabha Haryana.

| List of Ror Legislators w.e.f. 1937 till 2019 (Sources: Ror Mahasabha website but format redrawn by the author) | | | | | | |
|---|---|---|---|---|---|---|
| S. No. | Name S/Shri Haryana only | Village | Assembly | Period | | Type of legislator/Description |
| | | | | From | To | |
| 1 | Babu Anant Ram | Kaul | Pundri | 1937 | 1946 | 2 times, 9 years as MLC, Punjab state |
| 2 | Multan Singh | Kutail | Gharaunda | 1957 | 1962 | 3 times, 10 years as MLA, Punjab state |
| | | | Nilokheri | 1962 | 1966 | MLA, Dy. Speaker Vidhan Sabha, Punjab state |
| | | | Naultha | 1967 | 1968 | Minister of State, Haryana |
| 3 | Bhag Singh | Rasina | Pundri | 1957 | 1962 | MLA, Punjab state |
| 4 | Chambel Singh | Amin | Nilokheri | 1957 | 1962 | MLA, Punjab state |
| 5 | Hukam Singh | Kunjpura | Karnal | 1962 | 1967 | MLC Punjab state and Haryana state, the only |
| 6 | Ch. Shiv Ram Verma | Jhanjhadi | Nilokheri | 1967 | 1968 | 3 times, 11 years as MLA, and 1979 to 1982 Cabinet Minister– Dept of Animal Husbandry Govt. of Haryana. |
| | | | | 1972 | 1977 | |
| | | | | 1977 | 1982 | |
| 7 | Ishwar Singh | Staundi | Pundri | 1968 | 1972 | 4 times, 19 years as MLA 1968-72; 1972-77; 1982-87; and 1991 to 1996 Speaker Vidhan Sabha Govt of Haryana |
| | | | | 1972 | 1977 | |
| | | | | 1982 | 1987 | |
| | | | | 1991 | 1996 | |
| 8 | Chanda Singh | Butana | Nilokheri | 1968 | 1972 | 2 times, 9 years as MLA, and 1982 to 1987 State Minister, Govt of Haryana |
| | | | | 1982 | 1987 | |
| 9 | Makkhan Singh | Kaul | Pundri | 1987 | 1991 | MLA |
| 10 | Tejbir Singh | Staundi | Pundri | 2000 | 2005 | MLA |
| 11 | Dharmpal | Sidpur | Nilokheri | 2000 | 2005 | MLA |
| 12 | Kali Ram Patwari | Morkhi | Safidon | 2010 | 2014 | MLA |
| 13 | Sultan Singh | Jadaula | Pundri | 2010 | 2014 | MLA |
| 14 | Harvinder Kalyan | Kutail | Gharaunda | 2014 | 2019 | 2 times MLA |
| | | | | 2019 | Cont. | |
| 15 | Randhir Gollen | Pundri | Pundri | 2019 | Cont. | MLA |

The political standing of the Ror community can be inferred from the above data that from 2000 to 2022, a period of 22 years, though there were six (6) MLAs from this community but, none had a ministerial berth. Further frustrating reality is that there was not even a single MLA from the community;

between1946-1956,1996-2000, & 2005-10. Another frustrating fact is; there is No MP, till date, neither elected nor nominated; though; Ch. Ranjit Singh, Ch. Rajinder Verma, Ch. Raghubir Singh & Sh Virender Varma had contested election from Karnal constituency.

The politicians of this caste subscribe to all major national & regional political parties but have not been given much space worth stating by any party, in spite of the caste having sufficient electoral strength to get elected at least 7 MLAs & 2 MPs from Haryana. May be an MLA each from UP & Uttarakhand, also?

(NB: There is no MLA or MLC in UP assembly till date from the Ror community. However, there is a legislator in Uttarakhand from Haridwar rural assembly seat (2017-22), by name Swami Yatishwaranand, who belongs to Ror caste, though he has renounced the caste & works for all Samaj welfare, and is a minister of state also. He originally belongs to Kaimla village of Karnal district Haryana.)

## 10.5 National and International Sports Persons

Rors being an agrarian community & a martial race are strong, & well-built fine stalwart men. So, it is very natural that they take to sports easily like a duck take to water. Games like Kabaddi, Volley ball, Football, Basketball and Hockey etc were the obvious choices. But now they excel in athletics like Boxing, Javelin throw, weight lifting, etc at all levels including in Olympics. Now many Ror girls also have come up exceptionally well in individual athletic events in addition to conventional games including in U-19 games at National & international level. As of now there are about 35 outstanding sportspersons of National & International level from the community. Few luminaries are;

(1) **Sh. Sher Singh Sher:** Born on 23 September 1923 in Khedi Ram Nagar of Kurukshetra dist. was a wrestling & Kabaddi champion. He captained Indian wrestling & Kabaddi team for 13 years w.e.f 1945 to 1958. In 1952 Delhi Asian Games, while captaining Wrestling & Kabaddi team, he won individual gold medal. He was bestowed with the Title of **"Sher"** for his extraordinary achievements by then Punjab CM Sh. Pratap Singh Kairon. Also, he holds the Title of, **"Punjab Kesari"**, in the field of sports. In 1977 he was appointed OSD to then Dy PM Chaudhary Charan Singh and remained so till 1982.

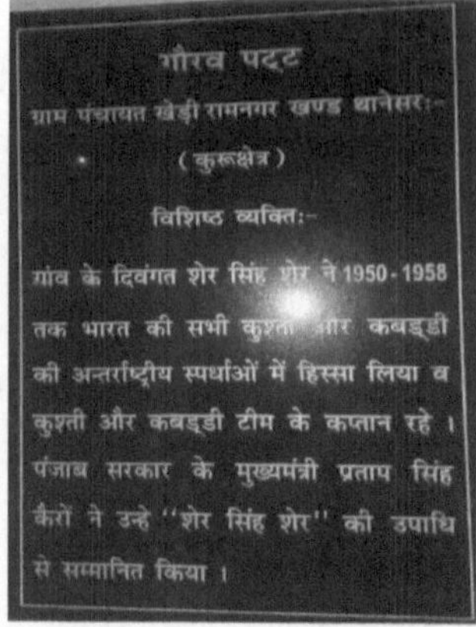

गौरव पट्ट

ग्राम पंचायत खेड़ी रामनगर खण्ड थानेसर:-

( कुरूक्षेत्र )

विशिष्ट व्यक्ति:-

गांव के दिवंगत शेर सिंह शेर ने 1950-1958 तक भारत की सभी कुश्ती और कबड्डी की अन्तर्राष्ट्रीय स्पर्धाओं में हिस्सा लिया व कुश्ती और कबड्डी टीम के कप्तान रहे । पंजाब सरकार के मुख्यमंत्री प्रताप सिंह कैरों ने उन्हे ''शेर सिंह शेर'' की उपाधि से सम्मानित किया ।

| 1. With PM Ch. Charan Singh | 2. Gaurav Patt; Khedi Ramnagar | 3. Captain Kabaddi 1952-57 |
| --- | --- | --- |

In 1990, he established a Girls Volleyball nursery, in his native place Khedi Ram Nagar & enrolled aspiring girls from Khedi Ram Nagar, & Chander Bhanpur etc. The team from this nursery captured the Women Volleyball championship, until then which was being held by Tamil Nadu, and retained it from 1991 to 2011. He has gone unsung in the absence of proper documentation of the Who's & Who of the Ror Samaj by its apex welfare body. He breathed his last on 28 January 2011. A Gaurav Patt has been erected on the entry gate of his villages in his honour under a scheme of Haryana govt for honouring its great & special sons. (Photos courtesy; no 1. Yog Guru Narender Singh Mehla; Photo no 2 & 3, Ms Raj Dabur w/o Col Ajay Dabur; Amargadh (Karnal))

**(2) Sh. Balwant Singh Sagwal:** Popularly known as Ballu, 1st from the Ror community to be awarded country's top honour, *the Arjuna Award* in volleyball in

Balwant Singh *Ballu* in a photo

1972, was a star player of *India's national volley ball team.* An unassuming 6 feet 6 inches tall youth, employed with Border Security Force (BSF) posted at Jalandhar, which that time had a reputation of producing quality volleyball players of repute in the country. From the mid-1960s to 1970s, he catapulted the team to achieve national success. He played for India in Asian Games of 1970, 1974, and 1978. Sagwal ran a volleyball academy at his native place Kaul, where a stadium is also named after him. He breathed his last on 14 November 2010. Kaul village panchayat organises, Balwant Singh Memorial tournament in his memory every year for budding youths. He was well known for his simplicity & humble manners and carried every team member with him very well.

**(3) Sh. Ajmer Singh Chopra:** An ace basketball player, born in 1953 in Rukanpur village of district Karnal, was awarded country's highest sporting honour Arjuna Award in 1982, a 2nd person from the community of few lakhs. From 22 consecutive national championships for Haryana, Rajasthan, & Railways, he grabbed 8 gold medals. Internationally, he represented India in multiple FIBA Asia Championships. This 6'6" tall swingman is one of the most-accomplished Indian hoopers in the history & is the first inductee into the Hoopistani Indian Basketball Hall of Fame. His career highlights include as best player in India's first & only time Olympic basketball participation in 1980 Summer Olympics-Moscow.

Although India lost all the seven games, but he shone individually, averaging a team-high of 21.3 points per game. He ended up as one of the top scorers in the tournament. In 1982 Asian Games, 2 years later, he was again the tournament's top scorer. He was known to be an unstoppable scorer, & country's top option during the "golden age" of basketball in 1970/80s.

**(4) Dr Dalel Singh:** The third Arjun Award recipient from the Ror community was born on 10 June 1956 in the Mahabharat fame Amin Village, of district Kurukshetra Haryana. He is another Indian volleyball star player from the community who captained the Indian National Team in Asian Games. He was awarded, "Bhim Award" by the Govt of Haryana in 1984, and the country's highest sports honour, "Arjun Award", in 1990. After completion of M.A. (Hindi), Dalel Singh took completed D.P. Ed & M.P. Ed in 1979 from PU Chandigadh and 1980 respectively and was selected for senior Indian Volley Ball team.

In 2009, he was appointed as Director Physical Education & Sports, Kurukshetra & retired from this post in 2016. He represented Kurukshetra University in All India Inter University championships 5 times, winning silver Medal 2 Times (1976, 1978) & Bronze Medal in 1977. He represented HSEB in All India Inter State Electricity Board Tournaments for 13 years (1980-1992) and won gold medal 9 times and silver medal 4 times. On national level he holds the Captainship of Haryana Team which won Gold Medal 1st time in National championship in 1982 at Bhopal. On international level he played in

10th Asian Games at Seoul in 1986 & Indian team won Bronze Medal. (Ref: *A case study: Vikash Kumar Research Scholar Dept. of P. Ed, MDU, Rohtak, Email: Vikas4700@gmail.com*)

**(5) Mr. Manoj Kumar:** He is fourth Arjun Award receipent (2014) from the Ror community, & was born on 10 December 1986, in Rajound village, Kaithal Haryana. Haryana Govt has appointed him as Dy Director sports for his achievements in sports.

He became national Champion 1st time by defeating defending champion Som Bahadur Pun in 2008, in the unconventional field of boxing for a Ror youth from Haryana. Before that he had won a bronze medal in 2007 in Asian Amateur Boxing Championship in Ulaanbaatar Mongolia, another Bronze in 2009 Czech Grand Prix in Prague Czech Republic. He won gold medal in the boxing under light welterweight category in 19th Commonwealth Games-2010 held at Delhi. He won another Bronze in 2013 in Asian Amateur Boxing Championship held in Amman, Jordan. He won another gold medal in 2016 South Asian Games at Guwahati. He is boxer of international repute with 5 medals under his belt, 2 Gold and 3 Bronze, pride of the community, and presently have a sports academy at his native place for training young generation.

**(6) Mr. Neeraj Chopra:** The Golden boy, 1st Khel Ratan receipent, and 2nd person to recieve a Padam Shri from the Ror communtiy. He is the first Indian to win a Gold Medal in Athletics, in Tokyo 2020 Olympic (held from 23 July to 8 August 2021 due to covid-19 pandemic) on 7th August 2021, the first ever after 121 years in the history of Olympic games, India started participating and 2nd Indian, after Abhinav Bindra shooter in 2006, to win individual Gold Medal. Born on 24 December, 1997, he is a track and field athlete of the javelin throw. Mr Neeraj Chopda, nicknamed Mr "Thunderbolt", from Khandra (Khanra) village near Panipat, in his twenties created history in Asian Games 2018 by winning Gold medal in Javelin throw, an unconventional field for a youth from Haryana, where village kids aspire to be Kabaddi player, or Wrestler or vollyball or Hocky players etc. Neeraj Chopda burst on the athletics scene with a record throw in the Junior World Championship in Poland in 2016. Since then, he kept on improving, winning honours; starting with the South Asian Games 2016, followed by Asian Championship title 2017, gold medal in the Gold Coast CWG & then another Gold Medal in Asian Games 2018.

He is India's first ever gold medal winner in men's Javelin with a throw at 88.06m, a national record in Olympic games. Neeraj Chopda is the 1st Indian athlete to win CWG & Asian Games gold medals in a year after Milkha Singh won in 1958. His life-size Olympic gold medal replica with national flag was showcased by Haryana Govt Tableau in R-Day parade of 2022.

**(7) Mr. Surender kumar:** Mr. Surender kumar, who plays at defender position, was part of Indian National Hockey team, which created history by winning a Bronze medal in Tokyo olympics-2020, after 40 years of wait. He is born to Sh Malkhan Singh & Smt Neealam Devi on 23 November 1993, in Baraani Village of Karnal district. He is the 1st youth from the Ror community, who has played Hockey in Olympic team. He met the challenge of playing in the olympic even afer suffering a bout of covid-19. He works with Food Corporarion of India.He was part of Rio Olympic-2016 team also. He is part of the team which has been awarded Major Dhyan Chand Khel Ratna-2021.

Mr. Surender Kumar    Naina Kainwal - wrestler    Vinka Samdhyan-boxer

**(8) Ms Naina Kainwal:** Now, even girls of the Ror community are shining in big way in conventional sports like wresting, boxing etc. One such sportswomen is Ms Naina Kainwal, who has excelled in wrestling at national and Asian Games level by winning Gold Medal. Naina Kainwal born on 2nd February 1996 in Sutana Village, dist. Panipat, started her wrestling career in 2011. Her father was himself a wrestler so, it was his dream to represent the country in wrestling, which now she is fulfilling. Her favourite wrestling moment was when she won Bharat Kesari Title in 2017 in

Mehrauli. She has won gold medal; in U-23 Asia Championship Mongolia 2019, Silver medal; Senior National Championship 2018, Gonda; UP, Gold medal; All India University 2018, Aurangabad, Bronze medal; Senior National Championship 2017, Indore.

**(9) Ms Vinka Samdhyan:** Another sportswoman from Ror community Ms Vinka Samdhyan belongs to village Shimla Molana. Her elder sister Monica is a hockey player. But Vinka opted for boxing in 2014 and won Gold Medal in U-20 Youth National Games in 63 kg category in 2018. It was followed by Vinka's first international medal; a Gold–at 7th Nations Cup in Serbia in January 2019.

**(10) Lt (IN) Rahul Turan:** This young officer of the Ror community from Sirsal village of Kaithal district Haryana, born on 5 June 1995, s/o a Warrant officer Karan Singh (Retd), has achieved a great feat by winning the title of, 'Ironman World Championship-2022', in Triathlon (consist of 3.8 kms Swimming, 180 Kms Cycling, & a Marathon of 42.2 Kms which needs to be completed in 17 hrs), held in Kona, Hawaii (USA) by clocking 15:37:54 hrs.

He is 1st such Officer among Rors in the Military service. He is B.Tech in Applied Electronics from Indian Naval Academy & was commissioned on 25 May 2018 in Indian Navy. He was best Marcos Commando in his Naval Commando course. He represented India in World Military Games 2018 at Jakarta in 1500 metres freestyle swimming. Has completed 12 hrs run in Panchkula clocking 101Kms, and also 600 Kms BMS cycling race in 40 hrs from Mumbai to Dhule Maharashtra & back.

A comprehensive list of Sportspersons from the Ror community is as below;

| Table: A Comprehensive list of Ror Sportsperson as in Ror Mahasabha website except S. No; 1&11 | | | | |
|---|---|---|---|---|
| Sno | Names Sh/Ms | Village | Game | Awards/Achievements |
| 1 | Sher Singh Sher | Khedi Ram Nagar | Kabaddi/ wrestling | Gold Medal Asian Wrestling championship1952, Title of Sher, Punjab Kesari, Indian Kabaddi team Captain 1945-52, OSD to PM 1977-82 |
| 2 | Balwant Singh | Kaul | Volley Ball | Asian common Wealth Games 1970, Arjun Awardee-1972 |
| 3 | Ajmer Singh | Rukanpur | Basket Ball | 22 National Championship: won 8 Gold Medal, FIBA Asian Basketball Championship, Asian Games1982, Arjun Awardee 1982; |

| 4 | Dr. Dalel Singh | Amin | Volley Ball | Captain: Indian Team, Asian Games, Arjun Awardee 1990 |
|---|---|---|---|---|
| 5 | Manoj Kumar | Rajaund | Boxing | Gold Medal Common wealth Games 2010- Gold medal; Asian Games& Quarterfinalist in Olympics, Arjun Awardee |
| 6 | Neeraj Chopda | Khandra | Javelin | Padam Shri & Khel Ratan 2021, Gold Medal in Tokyo Olympic 2020, U-19 World Championship 2016, Asian Games 2018, Gold Cost CWG 2018, & Arjun Awardee-2018 |
| 7 | Surender Singh | Barani | Hockey | Tokyo Olympic 2020- Bronze Medal, Bronze Medal-Asian Games |
| 8 | Naina Kainwal | Sutana | Wrestling | U-23 - National Games Gold Medal, Asian – Gold Medal |
| 9 | Vinka Samdhyan | Shimla Molana | Boxing | Youth U-20 National Games – Gold Medal |
| 10 | Lt (IN) Rahul Turan | Sirsal | Triathlon Ironman | 1st serving defence officer of Ror community to win Triathlon-Ironman championship held in Kona (Hawaii-US) on 6 Oct 22 |

## 10.6 Freedom Fighters from the Community

It is said, couple of Rors participated in the 1ˢᵗ war of Independence of 1857, quit India Movement in 1942, etc. but unfortunately, no records of such persons are available. Few names as gathered from some samaritans are as below;

1. Babu Anant Ramji; born in village Kaul in 1909, first Ror to become MLC, participated in Hyderabad, & Kashmir Satyagraha as Arya Samaji under Arya Samaji Parmanand ji.

2. Sh. Dharam Singh, of Mirzapur (Kurukshetra): Who after untimely demise of his parents shifted to his maternal parents' village Chor Karsa, & was in the service of Swamy Shraddha Nand ji as personal security guard, and actively involved in the Arya Samaj movement & national independence movement. He remained in the services of Swamy Shraddha Nand ji all along his activities of Hindu Purification, participation in meetings after Jallianwala Bagh massacre, protest & strikes against Rowlett Act in 1919, & incarceration without trial. He travelled to Burma with Shraddha Nand ji in support of Savrajya Movement & then to Kerala Viakkum for Dalit upliftment programme of Swamy ji. (Courtesy Samardeep Singh Barsana via WA)

3. Few Rors from Bhojpur in 1885 & Goshgadh in 1890 revolted against British, burnt Police station & were hanged. But no details about their identity also are available. *(Courtesy; Sh. Mahak Singh, of Bhojpur Ex ZE, DJB)*

4. Ch. Ramji Lal, Village Amargadh: was in Azad Hind Fauz (Indian National Army) of Netaji Subhash Chandra Bose and fought in the east, north east & Burma against British. *(Courtesy Suresh Dabur via WA group)*

5.  Ch. Madho Ram, Vil. Barsaana: also, was in **Azad Hind Fauz** (Indian National Army: INA) of Netaji Subhash Bose and fought in north east against British. *(Courtesy Samardeep Singh Barsana via WA group)*

6.  Senani Rishal Singh Kharngad: From vil. Chor Karsa, fought in the INA of Netaji in the northeast against British for independence of the country. *(Courtesy Master Gurdiyan Singh, Sambhali Karnal via WA group)*

7.  Also a Ror from Jwara village, who later became a teacher, was in the INA of Netaji Subash Chandra Bose and fought in north east against British. *(Courtesy Sh. Narender Singh Mehla, Yog Guru Mohana via WA group)*

There may be many more unsung heroes but due to dismal status of keeping the records, nothing is known.

## 10.7 Civilian & Other Award Winner Rors

**Padam Shree;** Two outstanding persons in varied fields, from the Ror community have been awarded till date;

**(1) Sh Sultan Singh;** A first from the community, in a non-conventional field from that of his parents, a proud owner of largest fish breeding farm in the North India from the Butana Village of Nilokheri, Haryana, born in 1963, won this civilian awards in 2018 for his exceptional contribution to the fish farming industry. He has set up the first-of-its -kind Recirculating Aquaculture System that helps indoor fish farming & increases the production by 10X. His success story has charted new path of entrepreneurs & doers.

**(2) Sh Neeraj Chopda;** 2nd from the community was awarded Padam Shri-2021 in January 2022, for bringing laurel to the nation by his outstanding performance in the field & track athletic games by winning individual gold medal for the first time in Indian sports history, in Javelin throw at the Tokyo Olympic-2020, held in 2021. Also, Mr Neeraj Chopda, a Subedar in 4 Rajputana Rifles, a JCO, has been awarded PVSM; an award for distinguished services of the most exceptional order by Military, (Param Vishisht Seva Medal) 2021, a preserve of three-star generals, in a first such instance.

**President's Police Medal;**

**(3) Mr Ramnish Geer;** An Engineer by education, but a bureaucrat by profession, a BE from RECK of batch 1982-87, now NITK, from Karnal, joined CBI as DSP through civil services exam. He was awarded, this prestigious President Police Medal-2021 in Jan 2022 on Republic Day, for his distinguish services. He was awarded a Gold Medal as best Investigating Officer in CBI and also was awarded Independence Day Medal in 2014 for his Meritorious Police Services

* * * * *

# Chapter-11. Rors and Social Life

## 11.1 General

To know the profile of a community, knowledge of its social life is the way-out. So, study of social life in r.o.; Daily chores; habits, dress & personal adornments, Birth, Betrothal, Wedding & related ceremonies, remarriage of Widows, religious life; modes of worship, pitr-ancestors, festivals, and inter-caste relations among the people, is inevitable. Social life of Rors as vividly described in the Karnal district gazetteer, as existing that time, where majority of them were inhabiting, is abstracted in this chapter. (Ref Page; 44 to 80, Chapter I-C: Population Part A)

## 11.2 Social and Religious Life of Rors

Social & religious life of Rors was similar to other principal castes of the Karnal district. Customs existing that time are still being followed in villages, but to a lesser extent 1$^{st}$ly due to Arya Samaj effect & 2$^{nd}$ly modern education have changed mindset of the people or in the urbanised villages or among the educated Rors, who post-retirement have settled in cities. In this section the social & religious life of Rors, as existing now vis-a-vis old shall be described.

(a) **Village Setups:** In Haryana, Karnal dist. is unique as it has seen epic wars & battles in its territory. All old villages were republics in themselves (like Janpada of old times) & were built on elevated sites above the ground level, on the heaps of accumulated rubbish of older villages & towns ravaged in wars and battles. (As described by Charles Metcalfe; In times of trouble, they arm & fortify themselves; a hostile army passes through the country; the village communities collect their cattle within their walls, let the enemy pass unprovoked. If the country remains scene of continued pillage for years leaving villages uninhabitable, they return whenever the peaceful possession revived. A generation may pass away but the next generation will return. The sons will take the place of their fathers at the same site, same position for the houses, and same land in the village will be re-occupied." My village Gudha; was a fortified village having a security wall all around with a guarded gate.)

(b) **New Villages:** A Village was normally built on the spoils; or as old houses fell, new ones were built over them, thus the village used to rise high above the surrounding plains; in some of the old Nardak, villages are as high as 200 ft. A new village, even now also, when formed is called a *Dera, Majra or Gadhi* as few families/brothers from some other location purchase agricultural land in that area, shift & settle there. Plenty of Ror villages have sprung up on account of this reason only as they had less land holdings in their ancestral village.

**(c) Village Connectivity & Facilities:** Most of the Ror villages now are well connected by road or Railways. All streets are pucca paved with bricks having covered drains. All houses are pucca customised brick masonry, including multi-storey imposing mansions, with modern furniture, Television & Radio, plumbing, fans, coolers, even air conditioners, kitchen with LPG, & running tap water including toilet facilities.

**(d) Domestic Utensils and Furniture:** Earlier mostly Pottery types of utensils were used & vessels made of brass and bell-metal (kaansi) were used by rich people only. The furniture of an ordinary village house was very functional, durable, and cheap. The string of bedstead was made at home; while, the carpenter made the bedstead & other furniture, & the village potter supplied the earthen vessels as part of their services; was paid at the time of crop arrival cycle as per the rate fixed by the village committee. But now it is all steel utensils, crockery and even pressure-cooking vessels used by the village folks. Modern furniture and gadgets like electric grinder, washing machine, grass cutting machine for feeding livestock, milk churning machine to prepare lassi, butter etc are used on large scale. Now in addition to bedstead (khaat), customised beds with mattresses are more prevalent.

**(e) Daily Life;** The daily life with the division of time, people's chore & their work schedule also, a vivid description of village's field life along with female's help & her role in the field, cattle rearing & household chores, including staple & special food has been detailed in the district gazetteer. Daily life now due to availability of modern farm implements & reduced land holding has changed drastically. Now Rors are not keeping much livestock except required for the self-need or the ones doing dairy business. Due to use of modern farm implements & less live-stock, now less women folks are extending help even in rearing of cattle's and in the field. (ibid46)

**(f) Clothes and Ornaments;** The dress of rural folks, male & female both, was simple. Everyday dress was made of coarse cloths. Old village folks still wear the same simple dress. But, new generation, now even in villages, have taken to modern western pant shirt & few people only wear the traditional dhoti, Kurta & Pagdi. All service class people wear pant shirt in summer & suit in winter. Earlier people used to wear ear rings called 'baali' and finger ring. But now they wear finger ring but not ear-rings except few as fashion statement or the seniors of earlier generation. In olden days, females used to wear Kurti, Ghaghara with

Odhna. The young ones used to wear an angia (bodice) also. Now a day almost all females wear salwar kameez, educated one's sari & pant shirt, including jeans also. Lot of jewellery, is worn now also, but of modern design, including pendal (Mangalsutra). (ibid47-49)

**(g) Birth:** The whole process of birth detailing all ceremonies like: beating of *brass thali* if boy is born; hanging of *Bhandarwar of mango leaves* on the doorways etc and naming of child as per Zodiac, tying *Taagadi* around the waist of the child, feasting of all near & dears on *dashutan* is described minutely and it is still observed in the villages. Earlier child birth used to take place in home only & Dai (mid-wife) used to help the female in delivering the child. But now there is a drastic change & birth takes place in the maternity homes. (ibid50)

There was another tradition of *swaddling clothes*, which were got from the neighbour's house, but now it's not in vogue even in villages. They were called *Potdes thus, "Potadon ka Amir"* is equivalent to, "a gentleman from his cradle." For 3 days the child was not suckled; 5 days no one, except the mid wife, used to go into the house; on 6th day night the whole household used to sit & watch the child; as on this day the child's destiny is written down, especially as to his immunity from small-pox etc. If the child goes hungry on this day, he will be stingy all his life; and a miser is accordingly called," *Chhate ka Bhukha* ", a prosperous man is called" *Chhate ka Rajya.*"

**(h) Marriages & related ceremonies:** Jats marry at 5 to 7; Rors & Gujars12 to 14; Rajputs 15 to 16 or even older. Foster relation-ship is equivalent to blood relationship as a bar to marriage. Any number of wives may be married, but a second wife is seldom taken unless the first is childless. A sister of first wife may be married or any relation in the same degree; but not one above or below. Brahmin fixes an auspicious day & decides ceremonial oiling (baan). It must be 5, 7, 9, or 11; but the girl will undergo two fewer than the boy. (ibid51 to 60)

**(i) Marriage Rituals:** Earlier Rors used to marry at 12 to 14 & after marriage when the girl used to turn 18, there was muklawa. Now marriage ceremonies, time & modalities have drastically changed and entire process is a work of at the most one week unlike earlier it used to be of the months together. Most of the marriage ceremonies now take place in the winter unlike earlier when it used to take place in the summer after the harvest of Rabi crop & summer holidays of schools as it were used for stay of Baraat. There is hardly any significant role of *Nai* now except ceremonials, whereas earlier he had very important role of finding the suitable match. Now a day's all venues, preparation of sweets for marriage, feast for Baraat and Bhaaji including the normal food for household guests are outsourced unlike earlier days wherein it was prepared in-house by engaging the Halwais for weeks together. Earlier *Ror* bridegroom used to wear Dhoti-Kurta or later Pant shirt and sport a Mor(crown); a lofty floral crown fixed on the head with Pagdi but now groom go far designer's wears, Churidars/westerns/Bandgala or ensembles & a designer headgear with a small crown fixed on it. (ibid50 to 60, describes the Marriage formalities starting from betrothal to after marriage relations prevalent in all principal communities including Rors of Karnal district.)

**Satta;** Rors, dwelling in villages, still practise marriages through exchange of girls directly or indirectly called *satta*. This system, started for purity of blood, though some demeans it, but it has many advantages like; the safety of the girl on both sides. Another big advantage of this *satta system* was complete absence of dowry except the voluntarily bare necessities of household use items to the girls, applicable for both sides. Educated, employed and forward looking Rors however now do not practice satta system for the marriages since the latter half of the 20th century. Majority of the marriages are arranged but now-a-days among the service class Rors residing in metro cities where girls are highly educated, even in professional streams, there are lot of inter-caste marriages also.

**(j) Remarriage of Widow or Karewa:** The ceremonies for a daheju are same as for a man's different marriages. But a woman cannot perform pheras twice in her life. Except Rajputs, Brahmin & Tagas, who do not allow Karewa, a widow of other castes can remarry under the above name. In Karewa, on the death of a man, his younger brother has the first claim to the widow, then his elder brother, & after them other relations in the same degree. Karewa cannot be performed while the girl is a minor, as her consent is must. But it has been extended so that a man may marry a Widow whom he could not have married as a virgin, the only restriction being that she is not of his own clan. *Thus, a Gujar may marry a Jat or Ror widow of any clan but not his own.* (ibid60-61)

**(k) Family Structure:** Joint family system among Rors started disintegrating in the last quarter of 20th century and by early 21st century most of them had become nuclear families, even in villages. This further reduced land holding & more dependency on other avenues to earn livelihoods. This way they diversified in jobs outside the agriculture sector & as such lot of them migrated to cities and towns for jobs & other related vocations in other sectors. Now there are hardly any joint-families, and it has taken irreparable toll on the social fabric of the family ties, relative relations & ethics of the community. Plenty of Rors are dwelling in isolation in urban cities now?

**(l) Status of women:** Ror women enjoy full liberty almost in all spheres. Now they own share in parental property as well as perform the role of head of the house in the absence of male successor. Girls especially from educated families, are in all the fields, be it Engineering, Medical, Business Administration, legal and off late in Military, and other service sectors. Girls from village background are shinning in sports, and also choosing diverse careers like nursing, police, bus conductor etc in addition to the conventional teaching initially.

**(m) Life cycle Rituals:** Rors being an agrarian community, *there was & also is not much emphasis on life-cycle rituals.* But on occasions like birth of a male-baby, a feast called *Dashutan* is organised and celebrated by inviting all near & dears. Marriage is big ritual after the birth & all close-relatives, friends, & members of the kunba are invited to the ceremony. Death is a cause of grief; all relatives, friends, Kunba members visit to console the family. In fact, in villages everyone consoles and take part in the cremation. Earlier rituals for salvation of the deceased used to last a year and thereafter annually for couple of years. But now due to busy life schedule of every one whether in village or in service, all the rituals are completed within 7 to13 days of the death. In case of an old patriarch, however, who on the death is blessed with grandchildren, now also a feast known as *Jimna (Brahm Bhoj)* is arranged by the family for all near & dears, relatives, including a member from each family in the village.

**(n) Food Habits:** Still majority of the Rors, are vegetarians only. Though there is some shift to non-vegetarian diet but not in the home. It is mostly in the mess by defence people, in clubs, hotels or restaurants by civilians. There is almost no non-vegetarian cooking in homes even in the villages except perhaps among Ror-Sikhs. Perhaps, it may be due to the influence of *Arya Samaj* & also the availability of abundant vegetarian food & milk etc as they are mostly concentrated in the most productive grain bowl of the country. Social drinking including in marriages is more prevalent. Compulsive and excessive drinking is discouraged and looked down as a bad virtue.

**(o) Arts, Crafts, Festivals & Folklores:** Rors have not much worth mentioning in arts & crafts field. However, in folk traditions, the ladies in the villages do make lot of display art objects & wall hangings, Bhandarwar for doorways for decorating their homes. They make storing baskets from straws, storing bins from old papers & rags. Women folk in winter used to work on Charkhi to separate seeds from the cotton balls, spin yarn from cotton wool with spin wheel (Charkha) to weave khesh Duries etc, from the thread made so, and also make door mats from the old & torn cloths.

Choir singing during marriage on Daal dhona, Baan Baithana, Bhaat Lena, expletives on the reception of Baraat, emotional Geets on Pheras, and at Bidai are very much prevalent still in villages and a must for the ceremony. Young & newly-wed women in groups after completing their household chores indulges in dance, songs, & merry making especially in Phagun, & community swings on Teej festival in the month of Shravan, the time of Khotlis & Ghevar etc.

They celebrate all festivals starting with Buddhi/Shitala Mata, Durga Mela in Chaitra month, Ganga Dashhara in June, Teej, Raksha Bandhan (earlier limited but now with full gusto), Janmashtami, observe Pitru Shraddh, Navratri with hoisting of Sanjhi on cow dung plastered wall, Ashtami ki Kadhai, immersion of Sanjhi on 9th day, Dashhara, naumi ki kadhai every month, Pitru Puja (Kul Devata) before Diwali, Govardhan Puja, Bhai Dooj, Ahoi, Karva Chauth, Hingo, Sankranti, & Holi etc. Rors are very much fond of swang; story telling of past kings, folk-tales by stage performing artists, a great pass-time after harvests & perpetuation of history by words of mouth as well means for mustering money for community cause of constructing Dharmshalas, & village schools etc.

**(p) Economic Status:** Being an agrarian community, main source of income of Rors was from agriculture produces supplemented by animal husbandry. With the growth of family land holdings declined further, so to sustain themselves with the expanded population, they took to education & migrated to urban areas and took up military/govt jobs and also ventured in occupation like business, services in Pvt sector including in tertiary areas.

**(q) Social division;** It is demonstrated by various endogamous caste groups. The exogamous category locally termed as *got* is considered the most popular social division & 80% of the communities consider it to be the most common attribute. The hierarchical divisions considered important by about 44% of communities, is the basis for regulating marriages. Avoiding marriage into father, mother & grand-mothers got', is the Norm. Sagotra marriage & marriage within the village is big No & as it is violations of Norms including in the neighbouring village due to, 'Simjor ki Biradari.'

**(r) Social intercourse among various castes:** Broadly speaking no superior caste will eat or drink from the hands or vessels of an inferior one or smoke its pipe. All food is divided into *pakki roti;* fried with *ghee,* and *kachchi roti;* not so treated. Except Brahmins & Tagas, each caste will drink water from a metal vessel, if scoured *(cleaned)* with ash/soil, and will smoke from a pipe (Hukka) with brass bowl, taking out the stem & using the hand with the fingers closed instead, from the same people with whom they will eat *pakki* roti; but they will not drink or smoke from earthen vessels or use the same pipestem, except with those whose *kachchi* roti they eat. *Jats, Gujars, Rors, and Ahirs* eat & drink in common without any scruples. Brahmins & Rajputs will not eat from anyone below a *Jat, Gujar, or Ror*; while these 3 tribes themselves do not eat or drink with any of the menial castes; and the castes: Leather-maker, washerman, barber, blacksmith, sweeper, Dum, & Dhanak including Potter. Hukka or smoking pipe in a village, often left out in the Baithak & fields, are generally distinguished by a piece of something tied round the stem: (red for a Hindu, leather for a Chamar, string for a sweeper, blue rag for a Musalman), and so on, so that someone wishing for a smoke may not defile himself by mistake. *Gud &* most *sweetmeats* can be eaten from almost any body's hand even from that of a leatherworker or sweeper, but in that case, it must be whole, not broken. (Karnal Dist. Gazetteer-1883-84 page; 88-89)

**(s) Exogamy among clans;** Every clan is exogamous; but every man must marry into his own tribe. No man usually marries into a family of any other clan even of adjoining village; the prohibition is based upon "simjor ki Biradari," the relationship of common boundary. The old rule of marriage is becoming less rigid, due to two social reasons to strengthen its vitality:(1) It was important to marry one's daughter where one can get grazing for his cattle in the seasons of dearth. (2) Another point though not very important is, to live away from father-in-law's place. (ibid87-88)

## 11.3 Caste Councils/Associations/welfare bodies

There are no caste councils in Ror community like Khap Panchayat of Jaats. At the village level, the committee consisting of influential persons of the village from different castes decide the issues of the village. The Ror community (if it is dominant in a village) plays an important role in deciding the issues related to other castes also if its own peoples, failed to do so. Ror community, however, have following welfare bodies and associations;

**(a) Ror Mahasabha:** Constituted in 1958 with its head office at Karnal, earlier registered vide no: ROS-51 dated 21.09.1959, has now been re-registered on May 8, 2014; vide no:HR-KNL-2014-01248 under Haryana Registration & Regulation of Societies Act, 2012. The aims & Objectives are; (a) To raise the social, Economic and Educational standard of the Ror community; (b) To establish educational and other Institutions for the furtherance and implementation of its aims and to help such institutions already established; (c) To construct Sabha Bhawan(s), Dharmshala, Rest Houses or any other building for its use; (d)To award stipends/scholarships to students and persons for carrying on their studies and for the development of their faculties and talents-bodily, mental and spiritual; (e) To make provisions for lecturers and teachers for the upliftment of the community; and (f) To establish its Up-Sabhas.

Bye-laws endeavours to bring social reforms among community members, lay emphasis on the education of girls, to reduce expenditure on marriages & other social ceremonies. Though the meeting of this organisation is called once a year, but its executive members are active throughout the year for implementing its decisions. Though the basic purpose of this Sabha is to bring about social and cultural reforms among the Rors, but it also acts as a political instrument mainly at the time of elections (?). In the past 62 years, the Mahasabha have done lot of works but still there are many more miles to go & very crucial things to do, to catapult this caste to center stage? The founding members of the Ror Mahasabha are listed below in table 11.1;

| Table 11.1: List of founding members of the Ror Mahasabha * Numbardar; ** Head Master | | | | | | |
|---|---|---|---|---|---|---|
| S. No | Name | Village | Post | S. No | Name | Village | Post |
| 1. | Ch. Shiv Ram Verma | Jhanjhadi | President | 16 | Ch. Tungal Singh * | Ahmadpur | Ex member |
| 2 | Ch. Hukam Singh | Kunjpura | Vice President | 17 | Ch. Bhulla Ram | Aahun | Ex member |
| 3 | Ch. Chanda Singh | Butana | Vice President | 18 | Ch. Multan Singh | Kutail | Ex member |
| 4 | Vaidya Rati Ram | Karnal | Secretary | 19 | Ch. Chambel Singh MLA | Amin | Ex member |
| 5 | Ch. Sadhu Ram | Shamgadh | Jt. Secretary | 20 | Master Ishwar Singh** | Staundi | Ex member |
| 6 | Ch. Hade Ram | Karnal–KM | Cashier | 21 | Ch. Mahender Singh** | Bastali | Ex member |
| 7 | Sh. Ram Singh | Karnal– DP | Press Secy | 22 | Ch. Tara Chand | Kaul | Ex member |
| 8 | Sh. Dhan Singh | Bhaini Khurd | Press Secy | 23 | Ch. Balwant Singh | Bastali | Ex member |
| 9 | Ch. Nand Ram | Saanch | Press Secy | 24 | Ch. Chattar Singh | Hebatpur | Ex member |
| 10 | Ch. Amar Singh | Mohana | Press Secy | 25 | Ch. Bakhtawar Singh | Majra Rodan | Ex member |
| 11 | Ch. Mam Raj Singh | Lakhnaur UP | Press Secy | 26 | Ch. Rati Ram | Gudha | Ex member |
| 12 | Ch. Anant Ram | Mirzapur | Ex member | 27 | Ch. Mam Chand* | Dhathrat | Ex member |
| 13 | Ch. Naurang Singh | Ahar | Ex member | 28 | Ch. Maan Singh | Lakhnaur | Ex member |
| 14 | Ch. Bhagat Maan Singh | Sutana | Ex member | 29 | Ch. Harful Singh | Dadupur | Ex member |
| 15 | Ch. Bhag Singh MLA | Rasina | Ex member | 30 | Ch. Mugla Ram | Morkhi | Ex member |

**Ror Bhawan/Dharamshala**: A community Bhawan or Dharmshala, as it occupies physical space in real time, is speaking and visual history of any caste being an ever-present symbol of the community. Histories & civilisations are sustained through such permanent physical structures since time immemorial. Hence the construction of such buildings at prominent locations in the Religious, tourist, and other important cultural or business centres or the capital cities of the state or the country, is one of the best ways to make known the existence of the community in addition to being an affordable accommodation & social gatherings facility for its community members.

So, with this philosophy in view, Ror community have got constructed 5 Dharmshalas called Ror Bhawan at Haridwar (1934), Karnal (1960), Kurukshetra (1984), Panipat (1996), and Panchkula (2011) which are fully functional. Ror Bhawan at Asandh is under construction w.e.f. 5 March; 2017, and land for constructing another at Pundri has also been purchased. For more facilities at Karnal, 3000 sq. mtr land in sector-32, UE Karnal also has been purchased. Now, there is in-principal approval from the current (2021-23), Governing Body of the Ror Mahasabha headed by Pradhan Sh. Nasib Singh for constructing a Ror Bhawan in the capital of the country at Delhi also.

**(b) Ror Employee Association:** Under the aegis of Ror Mahasabha, for uplifting the educational standard, other in-service needs, and welfare of the Ror employees, Ror Employee Association with the jurisdiction to cover the Ror employees of Haryana, Uttar Pradesh, Uttarakhand, Chandigarh, and Delhi, was formally constituted on 29.5. 1986.This association is located at Karnal with its registered office in Ror Bhawan, G.T. Road, Karnal, (132001) Haryana. The main aims and objectives of the association are; (a)To establish an information and guidance bureau to provide guidance for admission in different educational/technical/ professional institutions and for better employment opportunities; (b)To arrange coaching for competitive examinations for (i) Seeking admissions (ii) carrier advancement; (c) To provide scholarships to the poor and meritorious students for higher studies; (d)To start and maintain libraries; (e)To provide better educational facilities by opening model schools/ Institutions; (f) To bring out a publication on social reforms; and (g) To establish its sub-units (District/Block level).

The Governing Body of the Ror Employees Association consisting of 21 office bearers and executive members; President, Vice-President, General Secretary, Joint Secretary, Treasurer, Press Secretary (2no), and Executives Members (14 no). (Note: By-laws have provision for two special invitee/honorary members to be co-opted by the Governing Body from amongst the associate or retired members).

Dr Ram Swarup Chauhan, a prominent face of Ror community, a distinguished professor of Mathematics in RECK is the founding president of the association and remained so w.e.f 29.5.1986 to 6.9.1998. The other founding office bearer is; Dr Mahender Kumar Chaudhary as General Secretary and later as President w.e.f 6.9.1998 to 20.6.2010. During the tenure of Dr Rishi Pal Mathana, a lecturer in Eco, the association did a herculean & humongous job of publishing a directory having the details of about 4100 Ror Employees of all sorts and types, which is learnt to being revised to about 8000 employees. It is a yeoman service the body have done for the community. However, there are some inadvertent omissions of high-ranking officers and executives especially of the central govt and defence forces from the directory. With these omissions number of employees perhaps could be more than 10000. The employees have been categorised as below in table 11.2.

| Table 11.2: A Gist of categories and numbers of the Ror employees as in Directory 2011 | | | | | | | | | | | | |
|---|---|---|---|---|---|---|---|---|---|---|---|---|
| S. No | Category | Directory S. No | | Page no | | Total Employee | S No | Category | Directory S. No | | Page no | | Total Employee |
| | | From | To | From | To | | | | From | To | From | To | |
| 1 | Civil & Judicial | 1 | 52(a) | 1 | 4 | 53 | 9 | Agriculture** | 2836 | 2964 | 162 | 169 | 130 |
| 2 | Education & Research | 53 | 1437 | 5 | 84 | 1385 | 10 | Roadways | 2965 | 3083 | 170 | 175 | 119 |
| 3 | Health services | 1438 | 1560 | 85 | 92 | 123 | 11 | Railways etc | 3084 | 3099 | 176 | 176 | 16 |
| 4 | Def.: Army Navy IAF | 1561 | 1802 | 93 | 105 | 242 | 12 | Banking | 3100 | 3153 | 177 | 179 | 54 |
| 5 | Police * | 1803 | 2498 | 106 | 141 | 702 | 13 | Corporate*** | 3154 | 3580 | 180 | 206 | 428 |
| 6 | Electricity Dept | 2499 | 2717 | 142 | 153 | 219 | 14 | Local Bodies | 3581 | 4079 | 207 | 233 | 499 |
| 7 | Irrigation & PHE etc | 2718 | 2797 | 154 | 158 | 80 | 15 | Editors etc | 4080 | 4104 | 234 | 235 | 25 |
| 8 | Excise & Revenue | 2798 | 2835 | 159 | 161 | 38 | | Grand Total | | | | | 4113 |
| *2498(e), **2464(g) ***3580(b) | | | | | | | | | | | | |

Had the tabulation of the directory been done group-wise, it would have been a great asset for seeking proportionate no of service as per population of the caste from the govt.? Also, it would have been helpful in planning the strategy for improvement in deciding the type of education and training for the youth, the community should undertake. Ror Employee association can do a great service to the youths of the community by devising innovative vocational trade and technical training schemes, which however are, yet to be materialised. The EC, who did the humongous job of compiling & publishing the directory-2011 is as in table 11.3 below.

| Table 11.3: List of Executive committee Members of Ror Employee association -2011 | | | | | | |
|---|---|---|---|---|---|---|
| Sr N | Name | Position | Add: VPO, Dist. | Sr N | Name | Position | Add: VPO, Dist. |
| 1 | Dr Rishi Pal Mathana | President | Mathana, KKR | 11 | Dr Devender Singh | Member | Kalsi Saharanpur |
| 2 | Er Jeet Singh | V President | Chhichhdana, PNP | 12 | Prof M S Mehla, NLK | do | Sangrauli Kaithal |
| 3 | Er Mukesh Chauhan | Gen Secy | Raipur, KNL | 13 | Sh. M S Gollen | do | Pundri Kaithal |
| 4 | Sh. Fateh Singh | Secy | Chhichhdana, PNP | 14 | Ram Singh Kandhol | do | Alupur PNP |
| 5 | Sh. Ishwar Arya | Fin Secy | Kaul, Kaithal | 15 | Ram Kumar Mehla | do | Jadaula Kaithal |
| 6 | Sh. Om Prakash | Press Secy | Budhanpur KNL | 16 | Randhir Singh Mehla | do | Sangrauli Kaithal |
| 7 | Sh. Randhir Singh | do | Khandra PNP | 17 | Rajesh Kumar | do | Morkhi Jind |
| 8 | Chattar Pal Mehla | do | Jadaula Kaithal | 18 | Ajmer Singh Mehla | do | Saanch Kaithal |
| 9 | Dr Giyani Devi | Member | Sec -9 UE KNL | 19 | Naresh Kumar | do | Kalsi Saharanpur |
| 10 | Dr Rakesh Sagwal | do | Goshgadh UP | 20 | Sh. Subash Ghari | do | Ghari KKR |
| **Advisory Committee –cum-special Invitee members of Ror Employee association** | | | | | | |
| 1 | Dr R S Chauhan | Rtd. NITK | Raipur Rodan KNL | | H NO 4 sec 13, KKR | Past President (23.3.86 to 6.9.98) |
| 2 | Dr M K Chaudhary | HAU-Hisar | Goshgadh, Muzaffarnagar | | Sagwal House KNL | Past President (6.9.98 to 20.6.10) |
| 3 | Sh. Jogi Ram | SE-HEDA | Pai Gate Pundri | | 615Amravti Panchkula | Founding Member |

**(c) Ror Chetna Manch:** In nineteen eighties thousands of Rors officers and employees working in Central Govt, Delhi Police and other departments of Delhi UT residing in Delhi and NCR, were experiencing a void on account of absence of interaction among themselves and about the development in the community. So, a group from them decided to form a Manch of Rors residing in Delhi–NCR and thus came into existence the, "Ror Chetna Manch" (RCM) in 1989. The aims and objectives of the Manch as per bye-laws are: (1) To imbibe/ awaken the moral and spiritual awareness among Ror community; (2) To endeavour to solve the educational and social problems plaguing the community; (3) To prepare interesting and creative material for reorganisation of the community; (4) To cooperate with other societies with similar aims & objectives for the development of the Ror community; (5) To award scholarships and facilitations of Ror youths excelling in their field; and (6) To establish unity, integrity, faithfulness, feeling of well-being and brotherhood among the community, open sub units in villages, districts, states, and hold seminars, conferences, workshops, establish libraries, to publish magazines/books, information bulletins/pamphlets, and hold various competitions.

The Manch is registered with registrar of Society Delhi vide society registration Act XXI of 1860 no: S-20285 of 1989 dated 25th August1989. The Manch had permission for publishing a news Magazine named, "Ror Drashta" from Registrar of News Papers of India vide approval no: 50918/87 dated 16/4/1991. *Ror Drashta* was published monthly/quarterly from Delhi highlighting the socio-economic and political aspects of Rors. Also, it had a series of articles on the history of Rors vis-a- vis Maratha. Founding members of the RCM are as below;

| S. No | Name | Address | Occupation | Society Post |
|---|---|---|---|---|
| 1 | Sh. Surender Singh Kadiyan | Y-454/455, camp no.1, Nangloi, Delhi | Govt Service | President |
| 2 | Sh. Ishwar Singh Mehla | 811, Tagore Road Hostel, Minto Road, New Delhi-2 | Govt. service | Vice President |
| 3 | Sh. S.P. Verma | 110, MS Apts, Blk-3, Timarpur, Delhi | do | do |
| 4 | Sh. Multan Singh | WZ-395, GaliNo.6, Sadh Nagar, Palm Colony, Delhi - 45 | Personal | General Secy |
| 5 | Sh. Jay Chand | 100, Chara Mandi, Jakhira, Delhi | Personal | Jt. Secy |
| 6 | Sh. Som Nath Chaudhary | 246/1, LIG flats, sector 6, Rohini, Delhi -34 | Personal | Jt. Secy |
| 7 | Sh. Surender Kumar | 39, Grand Hotel, civil lines, Delhi -7 | Govt. service | Treasurer |
| 8 | Sh. R.D. Mehla | RZ-207 GalNo17, Sadh Nagar, Palm Colony, Delhi-45 | Govt. service | Librarian |

The Manch continued its publication and other activities till December 1992 and intermittently up to 2003. But after the Jan-Feb-March 2003, issue, the publication of Ror Drashta also stopped as everyone lost interest.

**(d) Misc Welfare bodies/Manch:** There are couple of misc. welfare groups like Ror Jagriti Manch, Ror Seva Dal, Ror Raja Seva Dal, Guru Brahmanand Seva Dal etc who arranges community Bhandara & provides social services during natural calamities or in teerth Kshetras during baths on the occasions like Eclipses, Kumbh etc.

## 11.4 Educational Institutes of Ror Caste

Two dynamic leaders of the community, Babu Anant Ram ji, & Ch. Ishwar Singh ji, established Janta College Kaul in 1954, & Kanya College Fatehpur Pundri, & Dhandh. Inspired by the ideology of Arya Samaj & Swami Dayanand Saraswati Ch. (late) Shiv Ram Verma ji, Ex Minister of Haryana, & Ch.(late) Ishwar Singh ji, Ex speaker Haryana Assembly, along with prominent people of the area took an initiative with an aim of propagating girl's education in this rural area for Ror caste & other communities also, and established Kanya Gurukul Samiti on 12.10.1980. This Samiti is running two educational institutions; Arya Kanya Gurukul Senior Secondary School & Guru Brahmanand Kanya Mahavidhyalaya established in 2015, offers course in B.Sc., B. Com, & B.A. Both these institutions are situated in the lush green eco-friendly environment in the legendary village Anjanthali (of Mahabharat fame), near Nilokheri.

## 11.5 Spiritual Institutions

Guru Brahmanand, is the only spiritual guru from the Ror community, born to Smt. Rani Devi & Shri Badama Ram, a humble farmer of village Chuhad Majra, Dist. Kaithal Haryana, on 24th Dec, 1908, as Chhotu Ram. He had spiritual inclination since childhood, so while studying in Kurukshetra Gurukul, he left for Haridwar. At Haridwar seeing spiritual bent of his mind he was renamed, 'Brahmanand.' He established couple of Gurukul, Ashram, Gaushala, and Vedic Yagya Shalas. He was a social reformer and fought against orthodoxy, illiteracy, and lower status of women in the society. Swami Brahmanand wrote five books; Brahmanand Pachasa, Braham Vichar, Neeti Vichar, and Sharirko Upanishad. He completed his mortal journey on 16th May, 1973 on Budh Purnima Day. Today lot of Brahmanand Ashrams are operational throughout the Ror belt of Haryana for propagating his teachings and philosophy.

* * * * *

# Chapter-12. Rors and Occupations

## 12.1 Basis of occupation

In India the occupation of the great masses of what we call upper or yeoman classes, is same. If we set aside pujaris & traders, artisans & menials, remaining are Agriculturists, who constitute the larger portion of the population. Also, these people subsist by husbandry & cattle-farming. They are also the owners of the land, the holders of territories; are overlords as well as villains. Hence springs the cardinal distinction between the occupation of the ruling & being ruled. Also, most of the Military & other forces of the country consist of them only.

So, occupation decides the status & standing of a caste in the social hierarchy. The agriculture is occupation of martial races; the slogan by our Late PM Shastri Ji, *"Jai Jawan Jai Kishan"*, reverberates its importance. In modern times in addition to agriculture, service sector assumes an important place & is a status index of a caste in society.

## 12.2 Educational and Employment status of Rors

Establishment of Kurukshetra University, Regional Engineering College, Shri Krishna Ayurvedic college at Kurukshetra, Agriculture College at Kaul; Govt Polytechnic at Nilokheri; NDRI at Karnal, among The Ror citadel perhaps proved boon & a catalyst in pursuit of education by the youths of this community. A progressive, well-informed Society and Nation are built on the foundation of good education. Pre-independence, one could count educated Rors on finger tips, employed as clerks, police constable or as army soldiers. But post-independence with the opening of schools in villages after matric lot of youth took up JBT for teaching job & BA degrees for services in other govt depts. Around 1962 there were few as post graduates in the community. But by 1965 they expanded into science stream, agriculture engineering, engineering, and in medical stream. Around 1975 they went for MBA, the latest stream in education that time. With the 1st generation of Rors in teaching, police, army, & clerical services in govt dept, residing in cities, their girl wards also seized the opportunity, though initially they took up the art stream only, but by the end of 20th century, there was no stopping them also from enrolling into Science, Medical, Engineering, & MBA streams.

A compilation of 2011 by Ror Employee Association, for all types of services gives a figure of about 4000 Ror employees. But as of now, as a rough estimate total employees from the community in all sectors including private & multinationals, may be around 10000. As a rough estimation there may be about 200s of Group-A officers in the central govt services across all govt departments and in corporate sector. Presently there are lot of Rors; both boys and girls, besides; Doctors, Engineers, Agriculture scientists, & IT professionals, who are gainfully working in foreign countries like US, Canada, Australia, Europe, UAE etc. This became a trend in early 21$^{st}$ century, and now more than 1000s youths from lot of villages in Karnal and Kurukshetra district have secured jobs overseas in misc. sectors.

**(a) Employment Status in state Govt Services:** Haryana Govt., to assess the share of each community vis-a vis its population compiled & published caste & group-wise data of its employees as on December 2017, for 19 communities, to prepare a plan to bridge the share gap in govt service among them as part of social equality. Most of the remaining castes out of 82 of Haryana, are nomadic, and as such are not accounted for in the data. As seen from the table below, there are 28 Group-A, 309 Group-B, 2161 Group-C, & 199 Group-D employees, totalling to 2697 from the Ror community, a share of 1.11 % whereas their population share in Haryana is about 2%.

Castewise and groupwise employees in Haryana as on 15-12-2017

| Group A | | | Group B | | | Group C | | | Group D | | | Total | | |
|---|---|---|---|---|---|---|---|---|---|---|---|---|---|---|
| Caste | Emp | Percnt | Caste | Emp | Percnt | Caste | Emp | Percnt | Caste | Emp | Percnt | Caste | Emp | Percnt |
| Jat | 1148 | 24.48 | Jat | 9201 | 30.22 | Jat | 52915 | 31.08 | Balmiki | 7721 | 21.11 | Jat | 68427 | 28.28 |
| Baniya | 610 | 13.01 | Brahman | 4099 | 13.46 | Chamar | 18471 | 10.85 | Jat | 5163 | 14.12 | Chamar | 26333 | 10.88 |
| Panjabi | 557 | 11.88 | Panjabi | 3094 | 10.16 | Brahman | 16879 | 9.92 | Chamar | 4378 | 11.97 | Brahman | 25236 | 10.43 |
| Brahman | 491 | 10.47 | Chamar | 3022 | 9.93 | Ahir | 11391 | 6.69 | Brahman | 3767 | 10.3 | Ahir | 14581 | 6.03 |
| Chamar | 462 | 9.85 | Ahir | 1841 | 6.05 | Panjabi | 8785 | 5.16 | Ahir | 1163 | 3.18 | Panjabi | 13158 | 5.44 |
| Ahir | 186 | 3.97 | Baniya | 1642 | 5.39 | Khati | 4471 | 2.63 | Saini | 976 | 2.67 | Balmiki | 11205 | 4.63 |
| Yadav | 98 | 2.09 | Khati | 590 | 1.94 | Kumhar | 4284 | 2.52 | Dhanak | 926 | 2.53 | Saini | 5600 | 2.31 |
| Saini | 80 | 1.71 | Saini | 577 | 1.9 | Saini | 3967 | 2.33 | Gujjar | 860 | 2.35 | Baniya | 5474 | 2.26 |
| Jat Sikh | 71 | 1.51 | Kumhar | 476 | 1.56 | Dhanak | 3486 | 2.05 | Panjabi | 722 | 1.97 | Khati | 5443 | 2.25 |
| Kumhar | 56 | 1.19 | Jat Sikh | 434 | 1.43 | Balmiki | 3121 | 1.83 | Kumhar | 619 | 1.69 | Kumhar | 5435 | 2.25 |
| Kamboj | 53 | 1.13 | Dhanak | 372 | 1.22 | Gujjar | 3001 | 1.76 | Meo | 479 | 1.31 | Dhanak | 4836 | 2 |
| Dhanak | 52 | 1.11 | Yadav | 351 | 1.15 | Baniya | 2953 | 1.73 | Yadav | 385 | 1.05 | Gujjar | 4160 | 1.71 |
| Khati | 52 | 1.11 | Balmiki | 316 | 1.04 | Jat Sikh | 2423 | 1.42 | Khati | 330 | 0.9 | Jat Sikh | 3101 | 1.28 |
| Balmiki | 47 | 1 | Ror | 309 | 1.02 | Ror | 2161 | 1.27 | Baniya | 269 | 0.74 | Ror | 2697 | 1.11 |
| Sunar | 44 | 0.94 | Sunar | 298 | 0.98 | Kamboj | 1908 | 1.12 | Sunar | 250 | 0.68 | Kamboj | 2406 | 0.99 |
| Ror | 28 | 0.6 | Gujjar | 271 | 0.89 | Sunar | 1769 | 1.04 | Lohar | 237 | 0.65 | Sunar | 2361 | 0.98 |
| Gujjar | 28 | 0.6 | Kamboj | 267 | 0.88 | Meo | 1715 | 1.01 | Ror | 199 | 0.54 | Meo | 2336 | 0.97 |
| Meo | 20 | 0.43 | Lohar | 135 | 0.44 | Lohar | 1605 | 0.94 | Kamboj | 178 | 0.49 | Yadav | 2054 | 0.85 |
| Lohar | 14 | 0.3 | Meo | 122 | 0.4 | Yadav | 1220 | 0.72 | Jat Sikh | 173 | 0.47 | Lohar | 1991 | 0.82 |

**(b) Status in Central Govt & all India Services:** There is no such caste-& Group-wise tabulation by Govt of India. But as of now there may be about 200 officers of the level of administrative grade in Civil, Engineering, Military, & all India services in central govt, public sector undertakings & other misc. services. Also, there are thousands in IT cum BPO across junior & middle level, and in private sector even at corporate level.

## 12.3 Overview of Employment Status of Rors

An overview of Employment Status of the Ror community, as gathered mainly from Ror Employee Directory -2011 & other sundry sources is briefly as below.

**(a) Academic & related Services:** Education provides best employment opportunities leading to prosperity, upliftment of social status of the family directly, & of the community indirectly. Perhaps, less land holding is one of the reasons, the community youth started looking for other avenues of livelihood, which education only could provide.

Not aware of first graduate from the community, but first post graduate Ror, perhaps is *Dr Ram Swarup Chauhan* of Raipur Rodan, who did his MA in Math in 1962 from the Punjab University Chandigarh. He is also the 1st lecturer in a professional institute (RECK) from the community & did his PhD in 1971. His other contemporary Rors who did PhD are Dr Babu Ram, a professor of Maths in MDU Rohtak from Bastada, and Dr Randhir Singh, a professor in Bio-chemistry in HAU Hisar, from village Saanch. Haryana Agriculture University Hisar had once more than fifty scientists and teachers serving it at one time but presently this number has fallen to a mere dozen or so. All these scientists have contributed immensely at National and International level publishing quality research papers & received many coveted awards. Even now, few of them are visiting experts in many South African countries in agriculture & its allied fields. Dr Randhir Singh, a bio-scientist of national repute, was dean, college of Basic Sciences & Humanities, HAU Hisar. Dr Mewa Singh Turan, had been registrar, Chairman, Dean & Director of Guru Jambeshwar University of Science and Technology Hisar. Dr Manjula Chaudhary of Amin, 1st woman from the community, served as Dean Academics affairs Kurukshetra University. Presently more than 150 Rors are working in the academic field as lecturers, professors, chairman, Deans and Registrars'. An extract of Ror professors, HODs, Dean etc in academic from REA Directory-2011 is as below;

| A part extract of the employees of the Ror community, in Education & Research, from REA Directory-2011 | | |
|---|---|---|
| Post | Nos | Few initial prominent/latest |
| Vice Chancellor | 1 | MPHU Anjanthali Samar Singh; a retired Agronomist from HAU Hisar |
| Dean/Director Universities/college Principal | 5 | Presently; Dr B.S Bodla Director, IMS, KUK, |
| Chairman/Head of Department | 20 | Few First; Dr R S Chauhan, Dr Babu Ram, Dr Randhir Singh. |
| | | Few Presently; Dr Pal Singh Mehla, Dr Sunita Mehla, |
| Scientists | 30 | Anish Chaudhary GRA Texas, Dalbir Singh DRDO, Devender Singh |
| CSWRI, Devender Kumar NGRI, Ishwar Singh Mehla Du Pont, Jagdish Chand Tamak ITR&D, Jagdish Tamak ITC, Jitender Mehla | | |
| Minnesota, Jogender Mehla AIIMS, Karan Singh GVK Bio, & R K Mehla NDRI (These are other than Agricultural Scientists) | | |
| Professor/Principal of colleges | 30 | Few from past; Sh (Late) Ajmer Singh Dabur, Dr Mehar Singh Khanchi |
| | | Few Presently; Dr Sultan Singh, controller of Exams, CDLU, Sirsa |
| Asso. Professor/Readers Lecturers etc | 341 | Principal Schools = 65; Headmaster/Registrar/Dy Registrars = 20 |
| PGT/TGT, JBT/Teacher/ Masters etc | 580 | DPE/PTI          = 100 |

Dr *Samar Singh*, a retired scientist from HAU Hisar, a 1st from the Ror community, was appointed on December 10, 2019 Vice-Chancellor of Maharana Pratap Horticulture University situated at Anjanthali, Nilokheri, Karnal.

**(b) Administrative & Civil Services:** Till 1980, there was no one from this community in proper all India civil services, except some solitary soul in state civil services at class II level like HCS, PCS etc. Mr Maha Singh from Kalkha, Panipat, a Physics Graduate with MBA from KUK, is the 1st IAS from the Ror community. There are couple of others but countable & less than two dozen including allied & state civil services, from a community of about 9~10 lakhs. Now few girls from the Ror community also, have broken the glass-ceiling by getting selected in civil services. A list of civil services officials from the community is as below;

| S. No | Name S/Sh/Ms | Service type | Native place | Posting/Status | Remarks |
|---|---|---|---|---|---|
| 1 | Maha Singh | IAS | Kalkha, Panipat | Retired; Ad Chief Secy | |
| 2 | Balkar Singh Khanchi | IAS | Munerhedi, Karnal | DM, Etah UP | |
| 3 | Gulab Singh | IAS (State Quota) | Divalhedi, UP | Retired (Guj. Cadre) | |
| 4 | Krishan Kumar | Danics | Karnal, HR | Retired | |
| 5 | Devender Kalyan | IRS | Kutail, Karnal | Ad Com. IT Delhi | |
| 6 | Balwan Singh Jaglan | Danics | Kurana, Panipat | UT, Delhi | |
| 7 | Randhir Singh | HCS | | Retired | |
| 8 | Virender Verma | HCS | Jhanjhadi, Karnal | Retired, Haryana | |
| 9 | Ritu Lather | HCS | Dinger Majra | BD&PO KKR | |
| 10 | Narender Singh | HCS | Kunjpura, Karnal | HSAMB Haryana | |
| 11 | Sat Pal | HCS | Dathrat, Jind | SDM Narnaul | |
| 12 | Asha Chaudhary | Danics 2009 | D/O Krishan Kumar* | Dir Civil Aviation, A&N | at *S.No.4 |
| 13 | Rajinder Singh | RAS | Kurana, Panipat | Com TO, Alwar Raj | |
| 14 | Vikas Kumar | HCS(Allied) | Kutail, Karnal | BD&PO Gurugram | |
| 15 | Vinesh Singh | PCS | Divalhedi, UP | DM office Kheda | |
| 16 | Apurva Singh | PCS-2012UK | Roorkee Haridwar UK | ADM-UK | |
| 17 | Swati Chaudhary | PCS-2016 UP | Bahlolpur UP | DSP –UP | |
| 18 | Harit Chaudhary | HCS2018 | Shekhpura Karnal | ETO – HAR | BE NITK |
| 19 | Monika Balda | HCS | D/O Karan Singh Balda | SDM | Dathrat Jind |

**(c) Agriculture & allied Services:** This sector in addition to major service provider to unorganized manpower has immense scope for regular & organised employment of high calibre for marketing officials, agriculture scientists, veterinary experts, horticulture, mining, and agro based food processing & packing industries. *Maximum numbers of PhD, Scientists, lecturers, Agro Industry based officers in govt, corporate or MNC sectors, including the only Vice Chancellor from the Ror community, is from this sector.* In common parlance saying goes, *"Agriculture is the culture of Haryana."* Agriculture College at Kaul proved boon for the youths from this agrarian community in agriculture education. There are about two thousand Rors executives & employees in this sector. It may not be out of place to mention that this sector alone single handily can be given credit for raising the educational, social, & financial status of the Ror community in Haryana. A list of few prominent agriculture scientists from the Community, is given below.

| A list of Prominent agriculture scientists from the Ror Community; | | | | | |
|---|---|---|---|---|---|
| (list courtesy Dr Rishi Pal, ex-Principal Scientist) | | | | | |
| S. No | Name S/Shri; Ph D/Dr | Speciality | Position at retirement | Village | Settled |
| 1 | Samar Singh | Agronomist | V C, MHU, Anjanthali | Prem Kheda | Karnal |
| 2 | Randhir Singh | Bio-chemist | Dean college of Basic Science, HAU, | Saanch | KKR |
| 3 | Dharm Singh Chopra | Bio-chemist | HOD, Hisar | Khandra | Delhi |
| 4 | Mahender Kr Chaudhary | Agri-economist | Regional Director HAU, RRR Stn Knl | Gausgadh (UP) | Delhi |
| 5 | Chandgi Ram | Seed-Technologist | Principal Scientist | Popdon | Karnal |
| 6 | Rishi Pal | Plant-Breeder | Principal Scientist | Kot Mohalla | Karnal |
| 7 | Jai Pal Singh | Soil-Scientist | Project Director; HOD, Hisar | Mundadi | Karnal |
| 8 | A S Mehla | Plant-Breeder | Principal Scientist | Saanch | Karnal |
| 9 | Kali Ram | Nematologist | HOD, Hisar | Aahun | KKR |
| 10 | Devi Singh | Horticulturist | Principal, College of Agriculture, Kaul | Kutail | KKR |
| 11 | Ram Singh | Plant Pathologist | Scientist I/C, HAU RR Stn Kaul | Pabnawa | KKR |
| 12 | Ram Singh | Entomologist | Head, HR Department HAU, Hisar | Amupar Majra | -- |
| 13 | Labh Singh | Ext -Specialist | Head, HAU Ext Training Institute, NLK | Jadaula | -- |

**(d) Defence or Military services:** Rors being agrarian & martial caste, traditionally are more suited to military services, but ground reality is starkly different. An effort was made by the Ror 'Who's Who' for a *Ror Regiment* by taking up the matter with the Defence minister of India in late sixties, but it could not fructify. Enrolment in military among Rors took an upward move only after 1962 war. In1962, few Rors already in military services became commissioned officer through a onetime scheme of emergency commission. There is no record of Rors in the military services during British period upto WW-I or earlier in any book or with any Ror institution or with any individual. There were four sepoys; Raja Ram in ASC (uncle of col Uday Singh) in 1941-46 along with Bir Singh, Phool Singh & Ch Neki Ram in infantry from Dadupur Rodan, village having maximum numbers in Military service. Sh Baru Ram, of my Village Gudha, a sepoy also served in Burma during WW-II in British army & later his younger brother also was in army. Perhaps There was also a JCO Subedar Major Daya Singh of Village; Duserpur Dist. Kaithal in 1933 (info WA post). There was a Risaldar also, by Name Bhagirath Ram of 18 CAV from Feb1943 – Jan 1971 from Dadupur (Rodan).

1st commissioned officer (IMA cadet-1956) is Lt Col Dei Chand from Amargadh (Kala Majra). Lt Col Sunehra Singh of Mohana is 1st officer, to receive the Gallantry Award; Vir Chakra; from the community. Other officers are/were; Lt Col Sewa Singh of Amargadh (Kala Majra) (Author's father-in-law), Col Ram Chander (VSM) of Rasina, and Major Chandgi Ram (a commando trainer) of Kurana.

Highest rank achieved by Ror officers till date is Brigadier and 1st among these is; Brigadier (Dr) Zile Singh, of AMC from Kurana (settled in Pune), 2nd is Brigadier Jai Pal Singh Mehla of Military Farms, from Mohana, 3rd is Brigadier Randhir Singh (VSM) of Mechanised Infantry, from village Kaarkhana (settled in Karnal), & 4th still serving is Devinder Singh, of RVC (Remount Veterinary Corps) from village Khanpur (UP).

| 1st Brigadier from Ror community Brig (Dr) Zile Singh, MBBS & MD | 1st Commissioned officer (1956) from Ror community; Late Lt Col Dei Chand | 1st Ror Gallantry Awardee; Vir Chakra Lt Col Sunehara Singh |

Brigadier (Dr) Zile Singh is a M.D in PSM & an academician, was HOD in AFMC Pune, Director (administrator) of 1000 bedded super speciality Military Hospital Jalandhar and has contributed many articles in national & international medical Journals on preventive and community medicines practices. Also, post retirement stint he was HOD and PhD thesis evaluator at a private medical institute and hospital, PIMS, Pondicherry.

2nd Generation Col Ajay Dabur, s/o

Col Sewa Singh -ASC

गाँव का गौरव पट्ट: सरकारी योजना पंचायत द्वारा गाँव के खेल रत्न, स्वर्ण पदक विजेता आदि खिलाड़ियों, सेना में व सिविल सेवा में कार्यरत उच्चाधिकारियों या किसी और क्षेत्र में गाँव का नाम गौरवान्वित किया है, तो उनका नाम व गाँव का संक्षिप्त इतिहास लिखकर गाँव के प्रमुख प्रवेश मार्ग पर गौरव पट्ट लगाना वांछनीय है। Names on above Patt are; Late Lt Col. Sewa Singh, Late Lt col Dei Chand & Col Ajay Dabur

Most of the Rors are 1st generation officers except couple of 2nd generation, and a lone 3rd generation officer in the Military services Col Uday Singh s/o Hon Capt (late) Bharat Singh, & Col Ajay Dabur s/o Lt Col Sewa Singh (as shown above) are 2nd generation officers.

Major Gaurav Choudhary s/o Brig Randhir Singh (Retd); in addition to being 2nd generation officer, is also the 1st ADC of the two Presidents of India (Late) Pranab Mukherjee & Sh Ram Nath Kovind), among Ror Army offices. Now there are 3 women officers also Viz; Sq. Leader Era Chopda, of Khandra village, Major Shreya Chaudhary in ASC from Beed Majra, & Flt Lt Sukanya Singh. Incidentally Major Gaurav Chaudhary & Sq. Ldr Era Chopda are the 1st couple in the Military services from the community.

1st Ror ADC to President of India & 2nd Gen Major Gaurav Choudhary

1st Ror Woman Défense officer Sqn Ldr Era Chopda & w/o Maj Gaurav

Brig Randhir Singh,3rd Brig. from Ror community & F/O Maj Gaurav

Interestingly, there was, also a lone lady officer in Military Nursing Services, Lt Col Saroj Bala, now retired from Ror community of village Dadupur Rodan. There are 2 helicopters pilots also in the Army aviation corps; One is Major Ankit Kumar, of Rahda village and 2nd is Captain Man Mohan Singh Dahiya, village Gudha (Gharaunda).

Major Sahdev Dodain of Dadupur Rodan at sr no 34 in the tabulation below is a 3rd Gen officer, who is s/o Col Rajinder Singh (Retd) of Arty (Sept 1976-July 2017) s/o Risaldar Bhagirath Ram.

| 3rd Generation Lt col Sehdev Dodain | s/o Col Rajinder Singh (Retrd) | Hon Capt Bhagirath Singh |
|---|---|---|

As on date there are about 400 personnel in military services which includes about 85 officers, from the Ror community from an approx. strength of estimated 10 lakhs. A comprehensive tabulation is as below;

| Comprehensive list of Ror officers (including the deceased) in Defence/Military services, as on June 2020/21 | | | | | |
|---|---|---|---|---|---|
| Sr | Rank | Name | Village | Settled at | Remarks |
| | **ARMY** | | | | |
| 1 | Brig | (Dr) Zile Singh (Retd) | Kurana | Pune | AMC |
| 2 | Brig | JPS Mehla (Retd) | Mohana | Panchkula | Army Farm Services |
| 3 | Brig | Randhir Singh (Retd) VSM | Kaarkhana | Karnal | VSM: Vishisht Seva Medal |
| 4 | Major General | Devender Kumar | Khanpur (UP) | Karnal | |
| 5 | Col | Ram Chander VSM (Retd) | Rasina | Jaipur | VSM: Vishisht Seva Medal |
| 6 | Col | (Late) Devender Singh | GyanaMajra UP | | |
| 7 | Col | (Late) Balbir Singh | Subhri | | |
| 8 | Col | Satpal Singh Sagwal (Retrd) | Kaul | | |
| 9 | Col | Sultan Singh Ralhan (Retrd) | Karsa Dod | | |

| 10 | Col | Manoj Kumar | Shamgadh | Delhi | |
| 11 | Col | Ajay Dabur (Retd) Artillery | Amargadh CHD | 2nd Gen | s/o (late) Lt col Sewa Singh |
| 12 | Col | Amit Prakash Kadiyan, SC | GyanaMajra UP | Faridabad | SC: Shaurya Chakra |
| 13 | Brig | Sukhbir Singh | Munerhedi | | |
| 14 | Col | Uday Singh Battan (Retd) | Dadupur Rodan | 2nd gen Delhi | s/o Hon Capt. (late) Bharat Singh |
| 15 | Col | Madan Pal (Retd) | Bhaini Khurd | | |
| 16 | Col | VP Mehla | Mohana | | |
| 17 | Col | Rajinder Singh Dodain (Rtrd) | Dadupur Rodan | 2nd Gen | s/o Hon Capt Bhagirath Singh |
| 18 | Col | Satyavir Singh (Retd) | Mohana | | |
| 19 | Col | Ranbir Singh (Retd) | Staundi | Delhi | |
| 20 | Col | Narender | Budhanpur | | |
| 21 | Lt Col | Sunehara Singh, Vr C (Retd) | Mohana | Karnal | 1st Vr C: Vir Chakra awardee; Ror |
| 22 | Lt Col | (late) Dei Chand: IMA 1956 | Amargadh | Pune | 1st Commissioned Officer; Ror |
| 23 | Lt Col | (late) Sewa Singh ASC | Amargadh | | |
| 24 | Lt Col | Zile Singh (Retd) | Peont | | |
| 25 | Lt Col | Joginder Singh | Badsalu | | |
| 26 | Lt Col | Multan Singh | Alupur | | |
| 27 | Lt Col | Ishwar Singh Dahiya, SC | Gudha | Karnal | SC: Shaurya Chakra |
| 28 | Lt Col | Amit Kadiyan | Katlahdi | | |
| 29 | Lt Col | Sudhir Samdhyan | Bhaini Khurd | | |
| 30 | Lt Col | Pradeep Khenchi | Shera | | |
| 31 | Lt Col | Sandeep Kumar | Jauli Kheda | | |
| 32 | Major | Chandgi Ram (Retd) | Kurana | Delhi/G Noida | |
| 33 | Major | Malkhan Singh (Retd) | Shamgadh | | |
| 34 | Major | Sahdev Dodain | Dadupur Rodan | 3rd Gen | s/o Col Rajinder Singh (Retrd) |
| 35 | Major | Rakesh Kandhol | Alupur | | |
| 36 | Major | Vivek Bodla | Pabnava | | |
| 37 | Major | Jitender Sagwal | Kaul | | |
| 38 | Major | Gaurav Choudhary Sena Medal | Karnal | 1st Ror ADC | 2nd Gen; s/o Brig Randhir Singh |
| 39 | Major | Amit Kumar | Belda UP | | |

| 40 | Major | (Dr) Amit Chaudhary (Retd) | Dadupur Rodan | Delhi AMC | SSC; s/o Adv Multan Singh |
|---|---|---|---|---|---|
| 41 | Major | Ankit Kumar | Rahda | Aviation Pilot | s/o Hon Capt. Mohinder Singh |
| 42 | Major | Manmohan Dahiya | Gudha | Aviation Pilot | s/o ex-servicemen Rajbir Singh |
| 43 | Major | Sukhwinder Singh | Ahar | | |
| 44 | Major | (Dr) Abhishek Kadiyan | GyanaMajra | Karnal | AMC |
| 45 | Major | Pankaj Singh | Ramgadh | Karnal | |
| 46 | Major | Praveen Kumar | Jwara | | |
| 47 | Major | Shreya | Beed Majra | Karnal | |
| 48 | Major | Sumit Dahiya | Gudha | | |
| 49 | Capt. | Krishan Kumar (Retd) | Karnal | Delhi | SSC; short service com |
| 50 | Capt. | Mehar Singh (Retd) | Kaul | Karnal | SSC; short service com |
| 51 | Capt. | Paramjit Dahiya | Gudha | | |
| 52 | Capt. | Abhishek Mehla | PandoKhedi UP | | |
| 53 | Capt. | Ajay Sagwal | Kaul | | |
| 54 | Lt | Jatin Gadtan | Bastada | | |
| 55 | Lt | Dhruv Mehla | Mohana | | s/o Col VP Singh Mehla |
| 56 | Lt | Shubhankar Kanyan | Kunjpura | IMA 2020 | |
| 57 | Lt | Harsh Chaudhary | Gorgadh | | |
| 58 | Lt | Rohit Kumar | Snehadi | IMA2021 | |
| 59 | Lt Col | Saroj Bala (Retd)-MNS | Dadupur Rodan | Panchkula | D/O (late) Sub. Chanda Singh |
| | **Navy** | | | | |
| 60 | Cmndr | Amit Turan | Jauli Kheda | Karnal | |
| 61 | Cmndr | Vinod Kumar | Neval | | |
| 62 | Lt Cmdr | Mayank Chaudhary | Butana | Karnal | |
| 63 | Lt Cmdr | Siddharth Chaudhary | Shamgadh | | |
| 64 | Lt | Sandeep Khenchi | Bazida Jattan | | |
| 65 | Lt | Dinesh Kumar | Bibipur Jattan | | |
| 66 | Lt | Vinay Domiyan | Kurukshetra | | |
| 67 | Lt | Rohit Turan | Sirsal | s/o | ex-warrant officer Karan Singh |
| 68 | Sub Lt | Praveen Kumar | Katlahedi | | |

| | AIR | Force | | | |
|---|---|---|---|---|---|
| 69 | Gp Capt | Rajinder Singh | Mohana | Gurugram | |
| 70 | Gp Capt | Pramod Kumar | GyanaMajra UP | Karnal | |
| 71 | W. Cdr | (late) Chandra Singh YSM(P) | Dadupur Rodan | | s/o (late) Hon. Capt Bharat Singh |
| 72 | W. Cdr | Rajbir Chaudhary (Retd) | Badsalu | | |
| 73 | W. Cdr | Surender Khanchi | Shera | Kurukshetra | s/o Prof. Mehar Singh Khanchi |
| 74 | W. Cdr | Vikas Sagwal | Goshgadh UP | | |
| 75 | W. Cdr | Aditya Kadiyan | GyanaMajra UP | | |
| 76 | Sqn Ldr | (Late) Dharm Singh Taya | Dadupur Rodan | | |
| 77 | Sqn Ldr | Ishwar Singh Taya (Retd) | Dadupur Rodan | Delhi 2nd Gen | s/o (Late) Dharm Singh sr76 |
| 78 | Sqn Ldr | Sanjay Singh | Dadupur Rodan | Kurukshetra | |
| 79 | Sqn Ldr | Narinder Mehla | Mohana | | |
| 80 | Sqn Ldr | Sanjay Singh | Mohana | | |
| 81 | Sqn Ldr | Amardeep Sagwal | Kaul | | |
| 82 | Sqn Ldr | Sumit Turan | Sirsal | Son-in-law of | Gp Capt Pramod Kumar |
| 83 | Sqn Ldr | Era Chopda | Khandra | w/o | Major Gaurav Chaudhary |
| 84 | Sqn Ldr | Avesh Kumar | Khedi Sakra | | |
| 85 | Flt Lt | Sukanya Singh | Dadupur Khurd | Karnal | |

**NB**: List Courtesy; Brig Randhir Singh & Lt Col Multan Singh. For any discrepancy please contact: 9419232239

**(e) Engineering & IT Services:** After academics/Agriculture, Engineering professionals are more in numbers than in any other discipline from the Ror community. As a rough guess there are more than 1000s of Engineering degree, diploma holders, and IT professionals in the community as on date, employed in govt, public, multinationals & private sectors including overseas. Perhaps, 1st to enrol in diploma (Civil Engineering) in 1957 in Ramgadhiya Polytechnic Phagwada (Punjab), is Shri Anant Ram from Pabnava. Few pioneers in Diploma are tabulated below;

| | A list of few pioneers & prominent Diploma Engineers from the Ror community | | | | |
|---|---|---|---|---|---|
| S. No | Name/s Shri | Village | Diploma in | Year | Remarks- Retired as |
| 1 | Anant Ram | Pabnava | Civil Engg | 1957-60 | XEN, KUK |
| 2 | Ajmer Singh Sagwal | Kaul | Elec. Engg | 1960-63 | Sg. E, Frmr Board Member HSSC |
| 3 | Ishwar Singh Sagwal | Kaul | Civil d'man* | 1961-64 | Diploma in EE, AMIE & M. Tech, XEN HSEB |
| 4 | Sunehra Singh | ChorKarsa | Civil Engg | 1961-64 | SDO Haryana Govt |
| 5 | Kishan Singh | Shamgadh | Civil D'man | 1961-64 | Circle D'man HSEB |
| 6 | Dila Ram | Taraodi | Elec. Engg | 1962-65 | Director (Engg) AIR&DD, AMIE; ASE AIR in 1974 |
| 7 | Mange Ram Dhanker | Kaimla | Mech. Engg | 1962-65 | XEN UPSEB, AMIE |
| 8 | Prem Singh Kharngad | Kutail | Mech. Engg | 1962-65 | SDO, UPSEB |
| 9 | Hari Singh | Kutail | Civil Engg | 1962-65 | SDO Haryana Govt |
| 10 | Jay Singh Sagwal | Kaul | Civil D'man* | 1962-65 | Circle D'man HSEB *= (d'man: draughtsman) |
| 11 | Bichha Ram | Badsalu | Civil Engg | 1964-67 | XEN, Irrigation dept Haryana, AMIE |
| 12 | Ishwar Chand | Taraodi | Elec. Engg | 1964-67 | Asst XEN, HSEB, AMIE |
| 13 | Suraj Bhan | Rasina | civil | 1966-69 | SDE, PHE |
| 14 | Miya Singh | Rasina | Mech | 1972-75 | JE, Irrigation |
| 15 | Karam Singh | Rasina | E&C | 1975-78 | XEN(IT), Market Board Haryana |
| 16 | Gian Chand | Mathana | Mech | 1975-78 | Sg E, UHBVN |
| 17 | Ishwar Singh | Hathlana | civil | 1976-79 | SDE, PHE |
| 18 | Ram Singh | Kalkha | Elect | 1976-79 | JE, ITI |
| 19 | Hukam Singh | Bastada | Civil | 1978-81 | Diploma & AMIE, Dy CE, Delhi Metro |
| 20 | Maya Singh Gollen | Pundri | Elect | 1978-81 | - |

NB; There may be more from UP State, who might have been missed out due to non-availability of info about them

The establishment of Regional Engineering College at Kurukshetra in 1963, paved the way for studying engineering degree in own area & a list of few pioneer & prominent is tabulated below.

| | A list of few pioneer & prominent Degree holder Engineers from the Ror community | | | | | |
|---|---|---|---|---|---|---|
| S. No | Name/S Shri | Village | Branch | Yr./Batch | Institute | Remarks- Retd as |
| 1 | Arjun Singh | Shahpur | Mec Engg | Not Known | Not Known | 1st from community |

| 2 | Nar Singh | Jyani | Civil Engg | 1958-63 | Not Known | M. Tech |
| 3 | Gyan Singh | Shamgadh | Civil Engg | 1967-72 | RECK | Chief Engineer |
| 4 | Ram Pal | Budhanpur | Elec Engg | 1968-72 | PECC | Director, UHBVN |
| 5 | Mahabir Singh Chauhan | Raipur Rodan | Elec Engg | 1968-73 | RECK | Sg E, HSEB |
| 6 | Multan Singh | Baldi | Elec Engg | 1968-73 | RECK | Sg E, HSEB |
| 7 | Ishwar Singh Mehla | Gudha-Kohand | E&C Engg | 1971-76 | RECK | Dy DG(Engg)-AIR&DD |
| 8 | Rajinder Singh | Ahar | Civil Engg | 1971-76 | RECK | Chief Engineer |
| 9 | Rajpal Singh Mehla | Mohana | Civil Engg | 1974-79 | RECK | EE, DDA |
| 10 | Pradeep Kumar | Belda | Civil Engg | !979-84 | RECS | Civil Engineer |
| 11 | Mohinder Singh Mehla | Sangrauli | Elec Engg | 1980-85 | RECK | Principal H Poly, NLK |
| 12 | Ramneesh Geed | Karnal | Civil Engg | 1982-87 | RECK | Director CBI; Working |
| 13 | Mahak Singh | Bhojpur | Civil Engg | 1982-86 | RECS | ZE, DJB (Retrd) |
| 14 | Sunita Chauhan | Raipur Rodan | Elec Engg | 1983-88 | RECK | Prof; Working NITK |
| 15 | Navneet Geed | Karnal | Civil Engg | 1984-89 | RECK | Business in Delhi |
| 16 | Viswajeet | Kunjpura | Civil Engg | 1984-89 | RECK | Business Panchkula |
| 17 | Mukesh Chauhan | Raipur Rodan | Elec Engg | 1986-90 | NITK | Working; Sg E UHVPN |
| 18 | Rakesh Chauhan | Raipur Rodan | Civil Engg | 1989-93 | NITK | Working; CE Irrigation |
| 19 | Deepika Singh | Pune (Kurana) | E&C Engg | 2002-06 | MIT Pune | UAE-Dubai |

| 20 | Isha Mehla | Delhi-Gudha | E&E Engg | 2003-07 | NIEC-D | IT; Hauge Holland |
|----|------------|-------------|----------|---------|--------|-------------------|
| 21 | Vinay Chaudhary | Delhi-Bastada | Mec Engg | 2004-08 | IITD | Working in Amazon |
| 22 | Ishan Mehla | Delhi-Gudha | E&C Engg | 2006-10 | NSIT-D | Working; IOCL |
| 23 | Romil Sagwal | Kaul | Elec Engg | 2008-12 | NITK | Working; CRRI Delhi |
| 24 | Sakshi Singh | Bhojpur -Delhi | InfoTech | 2009-13 | MNITA | Working -IT |

**NB;** There are many more from NITs, DCE, IITs, etc, but the details are not available, so, could not be included in this list.

**(f) Electricity and Irrigation Services:** There are about 219 & 80 employees respectively in these two departments limited to Haryana. In Electricity there are about 26 officers' including 1 Director of Board, Mr Ram Pal, and SE & member board Mr Ajmer Singh. In Irrigation there are about 8 officers including 3 Chief Engineers namely Sh Gian Singh and Sh Rajinder Singh, both retired now and Sh Rakesh Chauhan still serving.

**(g) Excise, Taxation & Revenue Services:** There are about 38 in all; 1/3$^{rd}$ of them are Patwaris, Kanungo, Naib Tahsildar etc; remaining in assisting services in Land & revenue dept. Only 5 are at Excise & Taxation officer level.

**(h) Finance and Banking Services:** As per REA Directory-2011 there are about 54 Rors employed in this sector & matter of pride is that about 37 among them are officers, of the level of AM to AGM, DGM etc.;

| Sr. | Name S/Sh | Rank | Village | Remarks |
|-----|-----------|------|---------|---------|
| 1. | Bhim Singh Jaglan | AGM; SBI | Kurana | |
| 2. | Devender Singh Khainchi | Branch Manager; ICICI; GGN | Shera- Panipat | |
| 3. | Ishwar Kadian | Sr Manager; OBC; CHD | Katlahedi -KNL | |
| 4. | Kishan Singh (Retrd) | Asst General Manager-OBC; ND | Kaarkhana | |
| 5. | Mahavir Singh | DGM; HSIDC; PNCKL | Staundi -KNL | s/o Ishwar Singh |
| 6. | Radhey Shyam Chaudhary | Sr Manager; Haryana Gramin Bank | Popdan-KNL | Plot -23, Sec-10 |
| 7. | Ram Kumar Jaglan | Chief Manager; UBI | Kurana-Panipat | s/o Dei Ram |
| 8. | Ram Singh | Branch Manager; UP Gramin Bank | Dadhrera-Mzfrngr | s/o R C Singh |
| 9. | Rishi Pal Tamak | Sr Manager; UBI Mumbai | Pabnawa-Kaithal | s/o Surat Singh |

**(i) Health & Medical Services:** In 1970s doctors were rare from the Ror caste except pioneer like; Dr Jasmer Singh from Karnal, Dr Balbir Singh from Aahun, and Dr (Brig) Zile Singh from Kurana, the 1$^{st}$ MBBS from the community. In the latter part of the 20$^{th}$ century many Ror youths, including few girls enrolled in medical stream. There are about 31 MBBS doctors from the community of about 9 lakhs; a miniscule number. A list of pioneers, & others is below.

| No | Name S/Shri; Dr | Position at retirement | Village | Settled at/s/o S Sh |
|---|---|---|---|---|
| 1 | Jashmer Singh, MBBS | Not aware | Karnal | Karnal |
| 2 | Balbir Chaudhary, MBBS | Self-clinic at Karnal | Aahun | Karnal |
| 3 | Brig Zile Singh MBBS/MD | Brigadier, MH Jalandhar, HOO, PIMS | Kurana | Pune (MBBS-1972, MD; 1980) |
| 4 | Satya Pal Singh | BAMS -Verma Clinic Md Pur, N. Delhi | Staundi/VK ND | s/o Ram Kishan |
| 5 | Aditya Chaudhary | PGMS-MC Rohtak | Aahun-Karnal | s/o Balbir Chaudhary |
| 6 | Major Abhishek Kadiyan | Major AMC | GyanaMajra | Karnal |
| 7 | Amit Chaudhary, Major | AMC (Retd; SSC), GGn Hospital | Dadupur/ Ggaon | s/o Adv Multan Singh |
| 8 | Ajay Sher | MO, PHC Rasina | Khedi Ram Nagar | s/o Sher Singh Sher |
| 9 | Suman Sher D/o Dila Ram | MO, Civil Hospital Kaithal, Gynae | Khedi Ram Nagar | KKR-w/o Ajay Sher |
| 10 | Ram Kumar Mehla | Sr MO, Civil Hospital KNL | Mirzapur -KKR | s/o Anant Ram |
| 11 | Sultan Singh Dahiya | MO CHC Pundri | Gudha - Kohand | s/o Shrdha Ram |
| 12 | Rajesh Kumar MD | Holy Family Hospital GGM | Taraodi | GGM s/o Dila Ram |
| 13 | Monica, MBBS | Asst Director, NICO, ND | Kurana | Delhi, w/o BS Jaglan |
| 14 | Dhoom Singh | GD Physician, Main Mkt Devband | Divalhedi-UP | s/o Ram Lal |
| 15 | Chetna Chaudhary, BDS & MBA-HM | Delhi-Everwell HS | Delhi (Bastada) | D/O Hukam Singh Chaudhary |
| 16 | Deepak Turk | MO, PHC, Popdon -Asandh- KNL | Salarpur - KKR | s/o Moti Ram |
| 17 | Sonia, Dental Surgeon | Deepak Clinic -KKR | Salarpur/ UEKKR | w/o DR Deepak Turk |
| 18 | Anuj Kumar, MBBS | GD Physician, Nursing Home Devband | Divalhedi-UP | s/o Dhoom Singh |

| 19 | Poonam Singh | GD Physician, Nursing Home Devband | Divalhedi-UP | w/o Dr Anuj Kumar |
|---|---|---|---|---|
| 20 | Atul Kumar, MBBS | USA-New Jersy | Lakhnaur-UP | s/o Amar Singh |
| 21 | Balwant Mehla | Dist. Ayur Officer, KKR | Jadaula | s/o Inder Singh Mehla |
| 22 | Gulshan Battan | MO, HCMS-II, PHC Saga KNL | Badsalu | KKR s/o Prithi Singh |
| 23 | Hukam Singh Mehla | BAMS- Nursing Home-Rajaund | Jadaula-Kaithal | s/o Nanna Ram |
| 24 | Rajiv Chaudhary | Dental Surgeon, ECHS-KKR | Saanch/KKR | s/o Dr Randhir Singh |
| 25 | Shaifali, Dental Surgeon | Rajiv Dentals KKR Clinic -KKR | Saanch/KKR | w/o Rajiv Chaudhary |
| 26 | Ramesh Kumar Sr Dr | Govt Ayurvedic Hospital Kangra HP | Divalhedi-UP | s/o Nihal Singh |
| 27 | Sandeep MBBS | Govt Hospital Kaul Kaithal | Mirzapur -KKR | s/o Balbir |
| 28 | Satvinder Singh Chaudhary | MO, CHC Kaul Kaithal | Badsalu -KNL | s/o Bichha Ram |
| 29 | Sonia Jood -Gynae | General Hospital Hisar | Mundri-Sec15A | HSR D/o Dr J P Singh |
| 30 | Sunita Kalyan | HCMS- ESI Dis civil lines GGM | Kutail -KNL | w/o Devender Kalyan |
| 31 | Surender Kumar | Apolo Hospital New Delhi | Gohida-KNL | s/o Phoola Singh |

**(j) Judiciary & law Services:** There are about 40 Judicial officials from driver to CJM, though there may be about 1000s of lawyers & law professionals across three states including in the courts of Delhi NCR, & UT Chandigarh. There are couple of district Attorney, & Readers, in Punjab & Haryana High Court Chandigarh. Few Rors have been judges also but the strength is miniscule. A list extracted from REA directory-2011 is as below;

| S. No | Name S/Sh/Ms | Service type | From | Posting Status | Remarks |
|---|---|---|---|---|---|
| 1 | Amarjit Singh | Sub-Judge | Kunjpura, Karnal | Palwal –FBD | |
| 2 | Isha Samdhyan | CJ cum JMIC | Chuhad Majra, Karnal | HCS(Judiciary) | |
| 3 | Kamal Singh | ADA | Kot Mohalla, Karnal | DTO office Ambala | |
| 4 | Kuldeep Singh | HCS-Judicial | Dherdu, Kaithal | CJ cum JM Pehowa | |
| 5 | Mange Ram | ADA | Chuhad Majra, Karnal | District Court | |
| 6 | Rajesh Kumar | Dy DA | Shamgadh, Karnal | SP office Panipat | |
| 7 | Ravinder Singh | ADA, CHD | Kutail, Karnal | Fin Rev Commissioner | |
| 8 | Sandeep Chauhan | JID (Judge) | Barani, Karnal | Judiciary | |
| 9 | Sat Prakash | Dy DA | Shamgadh, Karnal | Dist. Court KKR | |
| 10 | Sumer Singh Arya | Dist. Attorney | Panghala, Karnal | HSIDC, CHD | |

| 11 | Surender Kumar | Judge | Kurana, Panipat | UK- Judiciary | |
|----|----------------|-------|-----------------|---------------|---|
| 12 | Vijay Pal Singh | ADGC (Criminal) | PandoKhedi, UP | Dt Court Saharanpur | |
| 13 | Vijay Singh | CJM | Umari KKR | Court Yamunanagar | |
| 14 | Virender Singh | Session Judge | Kunjpura, Karnal | Retrd – Yamunanagar | |

**(k) Para-military Services:** There are about 100 personnel in BSF, CRPF etc. in officer & lower cadre from the Ror community.

Sh Satyavan Khanchi from Ahar, who joined as Asst Comndt in 1993, is DIG. Sh Suresh Taya, is Comndt, and Sh Balkar Singh Mehla, & Sh Suresh Malik are Dy Comndt/2IC. There are quite a few Sub Inspectors i/c 2 couple Sub Inspectors.

**(l) Police; Law & order Services:** Pre-Independence there were few Rors as constable only. Post-Independence there were couple of, even there were 3 from my village i/c 1 as Asst Sub Inspector by 1965, but none beyond SHO level. The scenario changed in the late 20th century as lot of persons from the community started appearing for direct recruitment for Sub Inspector or Assistant sub-Inspector post in Haryana, UP, and in UT: Chandigarh & Delhi. Sh Nihal Singh from Lohari is said to be the 1st officer of SP level, now retired. There were about 700 personnel under various categories in police services as per data of REA-2011Directory. Now it might have reached to 1000 numbers. Out of this more than 375 are Sub Inspector/Inspector/SHO etc, one each SP/DSP/ASP and 3 Jail wardens.

Not aware of the highest rank achieved by any Ror in Chandigarh UT police, in Delhi UT police Sh Kali Ram Malik starting his career as ASI achieved the highest rank of ACP. There are couple of officers working in CBI, CVC etc at middle management level either from Police services or on deputation or as direct recruitment.

Now the glass ceiling has been broken by one Ms Ritu Khokhar, from Bhadad village, dist. Panipat, the 1st IPS officer through Civil Services-2018. Mr Ashok Chauhan, of Amin (Kurukshetra), upgraded from HPCS to IPS is the 1st officer from community in state police department. Ms Swati Chaudhary d/o Sh Sadhu Ram from Bahlolpur (UP), 1st girl from the community, who stood 3rd in UP-PCS 2016, is a Deputy SP in UP.

**(m) Mass Media & related Services:** The mass media; Electronic (Radio/ TV) or print (News-papers) or social media; webcasting, etc., the most potent means of dissemination of information, education, or entertainment from one to many. In Electronic media in Engineering wing only two Rors namely Mr Dila Ram from Taraodi and Mr Ishwar Singh Mehla (myself) from Gudha (Kohand) & in the News wing only one; Mr Ajeet Singh of Indian Information Services from Harsinghpura were there. In news agency PTI, the only Ror is Mr Vijay Dabur from Amargadh in charge PTI Bureau Chandigarh. Though Media has immense potential for employment but it appears to be not preferred by Rors, as even including employee of lower level there are hardly approx. 25 persons only from the community.

**(n)Transport, Aviation and Marine Services:** Transport sector encompasses surface, air, and water, e.g., Roadways, Railways, Aviation, & Marine. In Roadways there about 150 employees but mostly of driver & conductor category only. In Railway there are about 20 employees including Mr Bipin Kumar IES; Chief Mechanical Engineer; from Gandevada (UP), Sh Maman Singh from Kurana Chief Material Manager, 2 Assistant Divisional Engineer (Sh Harpal Singh; Rasina; Sh Randhir Singh Grak; Badsalu),1 Senior Engineer, 2 Junior Engineer, 1 Station Master (Sh Vinod Kumar; Rasina), and 1 Assistant SM (Sh Balwan Singh; Sandhir). As on date there are hardly 2 to 3 in Merchant Navy, one among them is Mr Nishant Chaudhary s/o Sh Kishan Singh, Chief Officer, from village Kaarkhana, settled in Karnal and recently one Mr Amit Dahiya Ror originally from Gudha, settled in Karnal, is a commercial Pilot with Indigo airlines, in civil aviation.

**(o) Public, and corporate sector Services:** Both these sectors are big employer of manpower be it core service sectors or in IT and software, which has a major share now a days. In the late 20$^{th}$ century with the opening of MBA stream, lot of youth from commerce, science or Engineering stream studied it. Many MBAs through campus placements are working in public sector banks or PSUs, and many through GATE joined fortune 500 company like IOC, ONGC, NFL, and EIL etc. As on date about 800 personnel from the community are working in these sectors. Also, few are working in pvt banks and corporates even at the level of Director & Coo, VP, and General Managers in India and even Overseas. Now they are almost in all type of services & working in govt/public or private sectors within India or Overseas. A list of few, partly extracted from REA-2011 directory, is as below;

| A list of Rors officers/executives working in Public, and corporate sector Services | | | | |
|---|---|---|---|---|
| S. No | Name | Post & Org | Village | Presently/ Remarks |
| 1 | Dhir Singh | GM, NFL Noida | Prem Kheda-KNL | Park View Apts Noida |
| 2 | Jagdish Bodla | Divisional Sales Manager, Dow Agro | Pabnawa-Kaithal | Sector 23 A, Gurugram |
| 3 | Jasmer Singh | Group Manager, ST Microelectronics | Kutail/Sec-9 KNL | Jalvayu Vihar G Noida |
| 4 | Jogi Ram | Divisional Engineer Telcom, KKR | Buchi-Kaithal | Gurdev Nagar KKR |
| 5 | Karam Singh Taya | Xen Marketing Board CHD | Rasina-Kaithal | Sec 14 Panchkula |
| 6 | Krishan Lal Khainchi | GM, Tirupati Sugar Ltd, Champaran Bihar | Shera-Panipat | Sec-5, KKR |
| 7 | Rajbir Singh Taya | Manager Area, NFL Shimla | Rasina-Kaithal | Sec-7, Karnal |
| 8 | Rajender Singh | Director-RA, R&D Ranbaxy GGm | Staundi-KNL | Dwarka-ND |
| 9 | Roshan Lal Tamak | Business Head -Olam Agro-GGm | Pabnawa-Kaithal | Mayur Vihar Ph-1 ND |
| 10 | Sanjay Dabur | V. President-Strategic Unit Sharaf Energy Dubai | Amargadh-NLK | UAE-Dubai |
| 11 | Satya Vir Singh Mahla | Dy GM (Seeds) Nagarjun Fertilisers ltd | Mohana-Sonipat | Prabhat Nagar HYD |
| 12 | Sohan Lal | Chief Manager Marketing NFL NOIDA | Karsa-Dod KNL | Zirakpur-Pb |
| 13 | Poonam Dabur | CEO:The Greater Change | Jamba-Chandigadh | UAE-Dubai |

**(p) Self-Employment and Business Occupations:** Now-a-days, instead of seeking employment, persons from Ror community also have become entrepreneurs & employment providers and have their own business ventures in IT and other sectors. Almost in every town in the district where Ror Community inhabits, lot of Ror entrepreneurs are running schools & others institutes for teaching or academies, including overseas in Perth Australia. In Kaithal, Kurukshetra, and Nilokheri there are lot of Rors who are into Aadhat business (commission agents) in APMC market.

* * * * *

# Chapter-13. Rors: The Way forward

## 13.1 Basis of Caste Status

The main parameter for deciding the social status or standing of a caste, is its political standing/space it occupies in the area of its habitat whether present or past. Then, extended basis of the status is; occupation, & within a common occupation political prominence and social standing. The latter being partly regulated by a set of very arbitrary rules which are peculiar to Indian caste system. It is neither tautology nor false logic to say that social standing is dependent upon caste & caste upon social standing, as the two depends upon each other in different senses. The rise in social scale accompanies increased political importance and is followed by a rise in caste status; while the fall in grade of caste, is accompanied by loss of social standing. (Ref; Para 337, Panjab castes; D. Ibbetson, page 5-6)

## 13.2 Caste Status Parameters

As stated in the Karnal District Gazetteer by Denzil Ibbetson, settlement report of Mr Douie, & ASI report 1871-72 of Mr A Cunningham, Rors are a martial race/caste having befitting status equal to that of Jats, & Gujars, and also Rajputs as they are one of them only. They are landowning minor dominant caste, and have all the qualities & traits of a martial tribe. Main factors which reflect the status of a caste Vis-a-Vis similar rank castes are as herein.

(a) **Ranking in Varna System:** This is the first & foremost important index of the caste status, as devised by Manu, the great law maker & writer of Manusmriti, which categorises Hindus, the followers of Sanatan Dharma in four Varnas & their life cycles further in four phases. There is no such intricate, logical, well thought of classification and detailed law book on the human life on the earth. As per this classification Rors falls under Kshatriyas Varna.

(b) **Physical Features:** Physical features are the best indicator of a race, tribe & the caste. The scientific tools to determine physical features of a race/tribe are; shape of the Head, the Nose, the Face, and the physical stature of its people. As per these, Rors are well-built, tall, fine stalwart men with imposing stature of much the same stamp as other kshatriyas martial race like Rajput, Jats etc. (Ref; Karnal dist. Gazetteer 1883-84, pp 96-97 Ch. 1- A; Population)

**(c) Social intercourse:** Broadly no superior caste will eat or drink from the hands or vessels of an inferior one. All food is divided into *pakki roti;* fried with *ghee: kachchi roti; not fried.* Jats, Gujars, Rors, Rahbaris & Ahirs eat/drink without any scruples. Brahmins & Rajputs will not eat from anyone below a Jat, Gujar or Ror; these three tribes do not eat or drink with any of the menial or lower castes. (ibid88-89)

**(d) Hukka Smoking sharing:** "In North India, Hukka smoking sharing custom is a parameter of caste status as castes, which share a single Hukka, are of equal status." (Ref; Gazette of India Part 1 Delhi p-508). Karnal dist. Gazetteer of 1883-84, (pp-25), Ch-1; People, & also para; 358 of 1881 Census report on social intercourse among various castes states; Except Brahmin & Taga, each caste will smoke from a pipe with a brass bowl, taking out the stem & using his hand with the fingers closed instead, from the same people with whom they eat pakki roti; but they will not drink/smoke from earthen vessels or use the same stem-pipe, except with those whose kachchi roti they eat. Jats, Gujars, Rors, Rahbaris & Ahirs eat, smoke and drink in common without any scruples.

**(e) Similarities of Social Customs:** Jats, Gujar, and Rors have similar or almost same customs, rituals, and related ceremonies in respect of following social activities. Hence are of equal stature or standing.

**(i) Marriages & related ceremonies:** Jats marry at about 5 to 7 years old; Rors & Gujars at 12 to14; Rajputs at 15 to 16 or even older. Foster relation-ship is equivalent to blood relationship as a bar to marriage. Any number of wives may be married, but a second wife is seldom taken unless the first is childless. A sister of first wife may be married or any relation in the same degree; but not one above or below. Brahmin fixes an auspicious day for all castes mentioned above and decides how many ceremonial *Oiling (baan)* the boy is to undergo. (ibid51 to 59)

**(ii) Karewa/Remarriage of widows**: Except *Rajputs, Brahmin & Tagas, who do not allow Karewa,* a widow of other castes can remarry. In Karewa, on the death of a man, his younger brother has the first claim to the widow, then his elder brother, and after them other relations in the same degree; though *Karewa* cannot be performed while the girl is a minor, as her consent is necessary. But it has been extended so that a man may marry a widow whom he could not have married as a virgin, the only restriction being that she is not of his own clan. Thus, a Gujar may marry a Jat or Ror widow of any clan but his own. (True, & even I know a case where a Brahman widow married a Ror) (ibid60-61)

**(iii) Division of tribes; endogamy and exogamy:** The internal organization of the tribe is much more important as it has bearing upon its social relations.

The tribe as a whole is strictly endogamous; i.e., no Jat can, in the first instance, marry a Gujar or a Ror, or anyone but a Jat & so on. But every tribe is divided into clans or gotra; and these clans are strictly exogamous & it is true for a Rajput, or a Gujar or a Ror, or a Jat. (ibid86)

**(f) Political Importance & Social standing:** On political & artificial basis of a caste: 'Panjab castes': Denzil Ibbetson, (pp; 5-6), states, "Social standing of a caste, depends on the political importance, whether present or past, whereas actual calling of everyday life is same for all castes. There is wide distinction between dominant & subject tribes; and a tribe which has acquired political independence in one part of the country, will enjoy a position in the ranks of caste which is denied to it in tracts where it is in subordinate position."

## 13.3 Problems ailing the Ror community

As seen from above, the most important parameters of a caste ranking are; its social status & political standing. Ror caste is lacking in the latter most. In addition to it, there are many other ailments. The apex body of Rors, has perhaps proved a behemoth crumbling under its own prejudices, inefficient & archaic working, and mismanagement? On analysing the ground realities, followings appear to be the most relevant causes ailing the caste;

**(a) No structured Organisational body:** Absence of an organised structured body like Khap of Jaat, among Rors, for directing, regulating, and monitoring the affairs of the community to its last member for enhancing & strengthening its political power & social standing, is perhaps the main cause of sorry state of affairs. Though the elders of the community envisaged and established Ror Mahasabha way back in 1958 for this purpose, but it lacks the structured organisational mechanism by way of an Aakhil Bhartiya Ror Mahasabha at apex level, state level Mahasabha, district/tehsil level Sabhas, sub-tehsil/block level Sabha, village & Paana level committees, including Sabhas in Metros like Delhi & NCR & in other cities of northern India, where thousands of Rors inhabit, to take care of the cause of the community up to its last member.

**(b) No communication with who's who of the community:** There is complete disconnect, almost No communication & interaction by the apex body with various who's who of the community like; acclaimed Academicians, professionals, retired bureaucrats, Military Veterans etc for seeking their suggestions & views either informally or formally for discussing developmental plans of the community. Also, there is no interaction by the apex body with common Ror youths for ascertaining their aspirations & feedbacks, except mandatory meetings of its executives & collegium members. So, everyone from the community feels disconnected from it, with no interest in its activities. Surprisingly this apex body even does not have a regular means for dissemination of information like; news bulletin or periodicals, to inform its masses in general & its members in particular for the developments & happenings in the caste on various matters. Even, it does not have a functional website or such facility in the age of IT & social media.

(c) **No Think Tank for Political Strategy:** As stated in Ch-10 para 10.4, on political standing of Rors, till 2022; there had been15 legislators; one MLC from 1937 to 1946 & 14 MLAs from 1957 to 2022 from the Ror community. But in this period of 75 years there was only once, a cabinet minister, a Speaker of Vidhan Sabha, two minister of state and once a Deputy Speaker. So, there is no substantial space of this community in the political pie of the state as few insignificant ministries were insufficient to catapult the community to a respectable political and socio-economical level to create the stature. The stalwarts who were MLA 3~4 times, played role on local political canvass of the state only but never on state-wide stage, forget the national level role as there is no MP from the community till date. The executive body of the Mahasabha and other sundry umbrella associations are rudderless, disjointed from main cause & appears to be collection of heterogenous groups for name's sake. So, a "Think Tank", for preparing political strategy in particular, is the dire need of the hour for the community.

(d) **Neglect of Elite & Veterans of the caste:** There are plenty of self-made high-ranking elite officers in civil and military, specialised in their field who are national & international experts, but are completely neglected by the apex Ror body. Had they been tapped off as resource person by associating them in some committee as advisors, or in the Ror institutes, it would have catapulted the career & employment statistics of the community youths? These professionals, who have manned & managed professional departments in govts, defence, and corporate sectors could have been immensely beneficial, had the apex body taken their services & assigned some role for utilizing their expertise for the upliftment of the community in educational/vocational discipline.

(e) **Absence of career counselling for youths:** Though, Ror Employee Association is there for this purpose, but how far it has helped the needy youths of the community, is not known as there is no data either on Ror Mahasabha or REA website on the outcomes of its counselling or other programs. In the absence of performance outcome in public domain there appears to be no significant support or help to the needy youths of the community by this body in career counselling, coaching or financial help through scholarships etc for the marginal but bright youths. Every year more than 100s Ror boys/girls secure more than 90 % marks in their 10th/12th exams but hardly 10 % go for professional education to secure executive career & remaining 90 % end up in non-professional education & lower-level non-executive jobs, as the present state level employment status data shows.

**(f) Rors living in Metro cities are disconnected:** Rors, especially working in central govt, military, & corporate sectors, are growing almost fully disconnected from the community, as apex body does not have any type of communication either in print or electronic, with its most productive class living in metros & other cities away from the main hub of the community. Being in Delhi since 1986, I have been observing, how the welfare body of the communities like; Jat, Rajput, Baniya, Saini, even Kumhar, Jhinwar etc keep regular communication through notices in print media, with their Samaj for social gathering, meetings on reforms needed in the customs & rituals for marriages etc, facilitation of meritorious 10th/12th class students & professionals, annual Mangal Milan for interaction between eligible boys & girls of the community in the presence of their parents.

**(g) No Vision for Marginal Community Members:** There are lot of meritorious youths in the community who are financially weak and cannot afford their further education in spite of first-class marks, without financial help and consequently are deprived of good employment. Most of the time parents of such wards, to continue their education further, seek loan from the market on high interest rates by pledging their assets. So, to take care of such cases Ror apex body must have a committee to search & identify such youths, who are meritorious in study but economically weak & unable to afford higher education, for extending financial help by way of full finance as per the requirements. This should include the sportspersons also for sports equipment, & the training expenses etc as parents of such players pledge their assets to ensure the cost of training & kits etc of their wards.

**(h) No Holistic Development Plans for Community:** Since its inception, the apex body, perhaps never had deliberations on the need of short & long-term plans for the all-round socio-economic development of the community. To achieve the befitting status for the caste in academics, scientific, technical, Medical, defence, sports, and in other services, the apex body must have a committee which should prepare, short and long-term plan & strategy to train & prepare employable youths as per their aptitude, from the community.

**(i) No Alliances Policy:** Caste lacks social life strategy in tune with the time. In present times the girls of the service class Ror parents with professional qualifications have become highly mobile with first class highly paid pan-India jobs, even other than that of their parent's residence including overseas living independently. This has led to a serious problem of suitable alliances for such girls from the community. The apex body of the community from nineties should have put in place some concise policy for facilitating suitable alliances for such cases from the community. Consequent to the absence of such policy, so many educated girls have been lost to other castes, as such girls in the absence of compatible alliance from the community go for inter-caste marriage. It can happen in modern times sometimes, and it should be acceptable, but it happening frequently, is great loss to the community as so many families from the community, could have been benefitted by these highly placed educated earning girls.

**(j) Literate Ror hesitant to reveal Caste Name:** Rors in All India Civil, Military, & other allied services are hesitant to reveal their caste name apprehending lest it not be construed as a low caste. So they tell either similar to Rajputs or Jat or simply Agrarian caste. This complex, service class Rors suffer due to not knowing the social status & origin of their caste vis-a-vis the social status & origin of similar placed castes. So there is need to dispel such misconceptions.

**(k) No uniformity in using Surnames:** There is no uniformity in using Surnames/Titles, as is normally followed even in well-known castes. There was no problem till sixties, when much Rors were not in services as even affixing surname that time was not in vogue also. But afterwards every community started using surnames & when Rors especially who were in service faced this, they were caught unaware.

In the absence of a strategy & guidelines from the apex body, someone used his gotr, someone village name, someone Chaudhary, & some other neutral title like Verma etc. Consequently, it became free for all & community became identity less from the social stature and inter-caste relation point of view.

**(l) Apparent Taunting Sayings:** Leave aside the common Ror, even a writer of the Ror history, wrote in his book that, "the Rors are jeered at by the people of other caste by Sayings such as, "Kahin ki int kahin ka Roda, Bhanumati ne kunba Joda, Ror Handi Fod etc, which is true in real life.

**(m) No Visual History or foot prints:** History is a tale of what has or may have happened in the past. Also, it is the study of the past; specially the people. Monumental history includes memorials, historical buildings, Charitable Hospitals, Dharmshalas, Pios, Educational institutes, and other permanent structures which keep on telling the story of the creators for centuries. Ror caste though stated to be a martial caste but does not have any such material, except as in ASI report 1871-72 Vol-IV of Raja Ror, to establish its pre-existence as there are no other footprints in monuments anywhere in any form including in written before in the census & district gazetteers by Britishers or the People's history by words of mouth by elders and Bhaats of the Ror Samaj.

**(n) Alienation of Remote villages;** As written in para 10.2, Ch-10, there were lot of Ror villages in the beginning of 20<sup>th</sup> century which were located away from the main Ror community hub of Karnal, Kaithal, Kurukshetra, Panipat etc, in the areas like Ambala, Ludhiana, Mathura, Bulandshahr, Delhi, Rohtak, Palwal, Sirsa, & Elnabad, including Fatehabad & Varanasi etc. Over the period being far-away from the main hub, they got disconnected from the main group, and when they faced difficulty in marriages of their wards & other social intercourses, they started marrying with equal status caste e.g., Kurmi, Jats, Ahirs, etc. Also, they adopted their social customs & thus amalgamated fully. However, it appears that they have adopted Ror as their surname but enrolled in the dominant or caste of those area.

**(o) No Mentoring & Mentee relationship;** As explained in para 13.2 (f) the social status and political standing of a caste is most important for its rank/ stature in the society. Normally, it is seen that politicians who are in position of authority, handhold the capable officers of their caste by getting them appointed on deputation to the decision-making, and man power recruiting key positions in various departments under their domain. They in turn then help in providing employment to the suitable youths of their community in various positions. This handholding is like, 'Mentoring & Mentee relationship' in any profession/ institute. This is lacking to the maximum extent among the Ror community. Every community does it & flourishes by this kinship, including the established & advanced ones.

**(p) Neglect & Omission of Ror Community in Govt documents:** It is observed that pre-independence dist. gazetteers, more or less were a true picture of the area wise principal castes & their social set up etc, and has ample description about Rors. But the post-independence revised Gazetteers of; Rohtak (except Jwara; Mohana & Tihad villages are not even mentioned in gazetteers),

Yamunanagar, Jind, Muzaffarnagar, & Bijnor etc. have no description of Rors. This non-inclusion of Ror caste continued in the dist. Gazetteers prepared post creation of new districts also. This way, already a small & less known Ror community, was relegated to oblivion while describing the principal tribes of that districts by the concerned authorities. Even all new district Gazetteers have included Aroras & Khatris etc., who came post partition in this part of India, but not the existing, landowning minor dominant tribe, and a martial caste Ror, inhabiting the heartland of Karnal, Kaithal & Kurukshetra districts since centuries.

**(q) Fission/Fragmentation in the caste:** True to Hindi idiom," Kangali Mae Aata Geela," lot of factions has taken root in the Ror community on account of some vested interests, with political ambitions. Consequently, a caste already struggling with identity crises, has been pushed to the wall as some calls, Ror originated from Maratha, some says Jat, & some says from Aroras? Tragedy is, each faction takes endorsement from few elites of the community to further their interest & publish a book. These factionalisms; a sort of self-destruction mode, have led to the degeneration of caste stature & it's standing further. The caste now has been become a case of jeer & ridicule by every other caste.

**(r) No Scientifically Authenticated History of origin:** Though history of origin of almost every caste is ambiguous & embroiled with contradictions & impossibilities, but of Ror it is starker as till date even there are no concerted efforts for getting written the chronologically history of the origin of the caste, by scientific authenticated means, through historians/Sociologists/ Anthropologists working in state/central universities who has written history of other castes.

## 13.4 Solutions and way outs for ailments

The ailments plaguing the community has arisen from the lack of continual guidance by the apex body, not keeping pace with changing times and the poor awareness about own caste vis-a-vis other castes as Rors, specially educated lot, do not carry their caste on their sleeve as others do. Multiplicity of views on the origin of Ror caste, even though it is true for all other castes also, have further messed up & confused the already ambiguous matter shrouded in haze. Had there been an unanimously accepted rationale view or the dictate for the most beneficial & heralded view about the origin of the caste & the uniform adoption of the same by unanimous acceptance from all the major group leaders of the caste, this state of confusion, still persisting, should not have been there. Some solutions to come out of this state of helplessness, confusion, and to remove ailments are summarised below.

**(a) Re-engineer Apex Body structure:** Any institution, if it involves its member up to last level, then only it can act, direct & function smoothly, otherwise there are chances of malfunctioning and completely ineffective outcomes. The present organisational setup of Ror Maha Sabha is outdated, & ineffective as it has not been able to catapult the caste to the befitting social & political level by addressing the problems ailing it. So, the dire need is to re-engineer the present organisational set up, to an organisational structure for reaching to the last level. Therefore, Ror Mahasabha need to change its aims & objectives and the functioning for its extending its reach to the last member by having committee up to Paana level for connecting, and percolation of its views and actions to the last member of the community at the grass root level for implementation.

**(b) Need for Regular Community News Bulletins:** Any institution/ community is alive only when it has regular communication & interaction with its executives & masses. So, the Apex body must have regular & periodical meetings with its members to take up the community upliftment schemes & welfare measures. Also, it should have monthly online news bulletin and periodicals for disseminating the welfare & developmental works done by it, other happenings in the community to keep its members, even residing in remote locations, abreast of current events. Apex body should put all records & public related information on line & seek feedbacks on its working & activities.

**(c) Think-tank for Political Strategy:** It is a disgusting state of affairs that Ror caste does not have a Member of Parliament till date even though 4 candidates from the community had contested election in the past but due to divided loyalty between all & sundry political parties for their self-goal instead of unitedly with a single entity, disgruntled and dissenting attitude of some, none could make it to the winning position. Consequently, a caste boasting with the epithet of '*Ror Raja*,' since 1947 is without a MP. So, the possible way out is to have a think tank to work out strategy & have political consensus under the umbrella body, even for each MLA election select only one candidate for each assembly segment and full support for a single candidate for MP election even without any party affiliation.

**(d) Resources Cell of Experts & Veterans;** Apex body of the community or the REA should have a resource cell and prepare data bank of all the high-ranking serving and retired professionals of the community, across all service sectors including private sector, who have manned and managed professional departments in their field. Their expertise as per the requirements should be utilized for guiding the youths to make better career in various fields. Their services can be utilized as consultants/advisors in the executive committee/ governing bodies of various institutions or for establishing and operating new institutions. These veterans & experts with decades of experience under their belt are the most precious resource and must be utilized for advancement & upliftment of the community.

**(e) Career counselling & mapping of Employment Opportunities**: REA, every year prepares list of the meritorious 10th & 12th class children of the community for scholarships & perhaps also do career counselling etc. But efforts towards their career counselling, appears to be wanting as plenty of them being 1st timers from the peasant family background, not having correct prospective of various services ends up in insignificant careers. In the year 2020, there were whopping 144 meritorious students (49 class 12th, & 95 class 10th), who had secured above 90 % which if translates to class 1 jobs, have the potential to change the profile of the community exponentially. With this trend in earlier years also at least 100s of students might have secured above 90%, & had even 50% of these numbers been translated to class I/II services, it had the put community to a higher social level. But the ground reality appears to be starkly different as share of Rors in class-1 jobs under Haryana Govt as on Dec 2017, is pathetic 28 officers only. If we include central & Military services, at the most it may be 200. It means there is a serious deficiency in career selection due to unawareness of job's prospective by these aspirants. Hence inevitable need is of career counselling for 10th & 12th meritorious students by REA or a committee of community experts/veterans.

In addition. mapping & preparing report for field-wise employment avenues/opportunities in each dept to direct the youths accordingly, by coaching or training them is another dire need & a must. Find out unrepresented service fields by the community and prepare strategy accordingly to have presence of the community members in it. So, the directory of the Ror employees, accordingly is required to be prepared in the format of officers, executives & officials and other categories/ranks like the Haryana govt has prepared category & caste-wise list, as it can be operated for working out the long-term & short-term strategy for increasing the employment opportunity.

**(f) Cell for Metro/City dwelling Rors**: A cell need to be created in HQ of Sabha for coordinating & connecting with community members working in the central govt, military, public & corporate sectors and staying in Delhi NCR & other pan-India cities. This way it will be helpful in bringing this caste force in the mainstream with the apex body of their Samaj facilitating social gathering, updated political awareness, facilitation of meritorious 10th & 12th class students & professionals of all fields, annual Mangal Milan interaction of eligible boys & girls of the community and to encourage more interest & brotherhood feeling among community members.

**(g) Financial Help for Marginal community youths:** REA perhaps due to funds constraint, is not taking care of full education expenditure of professional courses like Engineering & Medical, of the economically weaker candidates from the shortlisted list of meritorious 10th &12th students. In the absence of non-availability of finance such youths end up in the lower insignificant jobs. So, to take care of such cases there should be a search committee for shortlisting such youths, who are bright in study but economically unable to afford higher education due to financial constraints, for extending financial help, or even making available full finance as per the requirement of the course. This should include aspiring sportspersons also who are not able to afford costly sports equipment, kits and trainings, and other expenses of the training centres.

**(h) Developmental Plans for Community Youths:** For all-round development of youths & their employments in civil and military sectors, the only way out is well thought developmental plan under the stewardship of experts & veterans. The committee should prepare short term (annual) and long term (say five yearly) plan & strategy to prepare employable youths as per their aptitude from the community. This can be achieved by having own educational institutes or through already existing established by govt or private bodies. There are lot of experts in the community, who will be able to provide guidance and expertise to run community institutes smoothly & successfully.

**(i) To hold annual Mangal Milan:** Unlike earlier times, wherein girls were not studying beyond school level, alliances were decided through Nais or relatives as the Rors were mainly village centric & majority were engaged in agrarian activities only. Now the female wards of lot of high-profile service class Rors, living in metros, also highly paid pan-India jobs, are staying in places far away from their parent's residence in a casteless social environment, including overseas living independently, with their peer groups. This has led to a serious problem of finding suitable alliances for such wards from the community, as they had least opportunity of mixing & interacting with the community members & also in the absence of this have a low view of the own community, but had ample opportunity to mix up with the boys of other communities in schools & working places. So, arranging annual Mangal Milan's for such eligible youths is inevitable to enable them to have alliance match from the community in the first place before they think of opting for inter-caste marriages. As everyone is aware inter-caste marriage is full loss to the community as it is deprived off of a well-educated and capable double livelihood earner, children career & home maker women of the calibre.

**(j) Instil confidence in Ror Masses:** Ror caste is hardly known outside its core region, in the absence of liberal use of the caste name by its public figures, politicians, highly placed Civil & Military officers, gold medallists' & even Khel Ratna recipient sportspersons of national & international fame. So, the apex body should interact with all such persons periodically & impress upon them to use caste name liberally & frequently, without any hesitancy to instil confidence in all Rors on any platform as & when caste name is needed to be mentioned.

**(k) Uniform policy for affixing Surname:** Usually, it is observed that the Rors in their offices, due to their physical features, body stamp, language & Kshatriya traits are assumed to be Jat or Rajput, more the former ones, due to the tone of their speech being from Haryana/UP or UK. Apex body should deliberate for adopting a uniform surname policy which should be followed by all without any variation instead of using clan/village name, surname/got or neutral surnames like Varma, Chaudhary etc. Even a uniform title can be; 'Raud,' 'Rore', 'Rode' or 'Rodvanshi' or even the already prevalent & in use, 'Ror' like Rajput, Raghuvanshi, Sharma, Gupta, Arora, Khatri, Yaduvanshi, etc., for few generations till it get ingrained in the psyche of the masses that there is a martial caste by such name.

**(l) Educate Rors for Taunting Proverbs:** The taunting proverb like, *"Kahin ki int khin ka Roda, Bhanumati ne Kunba Joda"*: "कहीं की ईंट, कहीं का रोड़ा, भानुमती ने कुनबा जोड़ा," are part of the social canvass of the society and should be taken as normal way of social-life. As seen in chapter 3; castes in proverbs; each caste is identified by plenty of proverbs and sayings about it. In almost each caste like; Jat, Rajput, Gujar, Baniya, Brahmin etc there are much more demeaning & taunting proverbs & sayings than about the Rors. So why the Rors should feel offended from theses proverbs if other's do not even with the meaner proverbs? So, we should accept these proverbs & sayings, which are part of social-life canvas without malice and feel proud of our caste.

**(m) Create visual History and permanent foot prints:** History is preserved in many forms, permanent landmarks like; Dharmshalas, Charitable dispensaries, Water halts or Piao's, schools etc created by a community, are one type & are the living history of any community for the times to come. So, one must create permanent land marks at prominent locations in religious towns, & tourist places etc where people from all walks of life visit regularly. So, Ror Mahasabha should create landmarks for living history like construction of Dharmshalas, opening of Educational Institutes, Charitable dispensaries etc at historical & religious places in Haryana and the places like capital Delhi NCR, holy places Pehowa, Haridwar, Prayagraj, including Ayodhya, Nashik, Rameswaram etc.

**(n) Task Force for Alienated Rors:** Ror Mahasabha, the apex body should make concerted efforts by creating a task force to locate all the alienated (alag-thalag) & lost Rors by undertaking a special campaign, which will study the ground conditions, for future remedial measures also, as to why they switched caste or adopted other caste and the possibility of bringing them back to the Ror caste fold. *Few such cases originally said to be from Sindh Aror(a) are from Prayagraj, Kaushambi, Fatehpur, RaiBreilly, Chitrkoot, Pratapgadh etc dist of UP, where in Prayagraj (approx 100 villages in Karachhana, Meja, Sahson & Sadar tehsils), & Kaushambi dist (approx-100 villages in Chail & Sirathu tehsil), and in Fatehpur dist- approx - 84 villages in Khaga tehsil are inhabited by* **Singh Ror & Sengar Ror** *as* **Kshtriya Ror.**

*Another case is of* **Ror** *- Bakisiya & Nagraka villages of Jhansi dist.*

*Also another case is of Rajput family located in* **Shimla** *in Bundelkhand region. (Matter courtesy; Advocate Kunwar Sameer Singh Ror (Brijendra Singh)- Muradpur).*

*However* **Rors** *living in Ellenabad dist Sirsa Haryana, who are now part of an influential caste still use* **Ror** *as their surname in remembrance of their original caste.*

**(o) Assess Ror Employees for Handholding & Scroll:** There is an inevitable need for keeping the track as to how many Rors are employed in the govt jobs (Central & state), private and in corporate sectors. Also, it is needed in order to assess the education, economical & social status of the caste including to shortlist the persons for handholding/deputation etc. This data should be prepared as being done by govt statistical departments category-wise to assess the services/fields remaining unrepresented & take necessary remedial measures for improvements. While collecting the data, veterans in each discipline/group, who have attained highest rank/post earlier not achieved by any other Rors in that group for preparing scroll just like the honour roll of the classes kept by schools, also need to be noted. This function can be easily undertaken by the Ror Employees Association. This can be used for seeking proportionate jobs & other welfare favours from the govts in proportion to the community population also.

**(p) Monitoring of community related Govt documents:** As explained in Ch-5, Sec 5.4 some district Gazetteers, conspicuously have missed the Ror caste from the chapter on principal community of that district. These being the official referral documents of Govt for all purposes in future, and such matter not coming into the knowledge is a serious lackadaisical attitude & the gross negligence. There are thousands of Rors Govt employee at various levels in the state govt and it is really surprising that no one from the so many officials appear to have read or come across these documents and pointed out the lapses of omitting the Ror caste. So, there is a dire need of a watch dog body in the community apex body for monitoring such matters.

**(q) No fragmentation of the caste:** Enough is enough now, there should be brakes on, 'free for all' field to link the caste by prejudiced ideology of one's likings with a motive, without any scientific research. Such motivated prejudiced fragmentation of already less known caste is suicidal. So, apex body, by creating a chair for commissioning to write the authenticated history on the origin of the Ror caste, should also issue a dictate directing it's all members to abstain from further fragmenting the caste by connecting it to any other caste/community, without their concurrence.

**(r) A chair in university for study on The Ror Caste:** To find out the real causes leading to the origin, and the developments in the journey of the formation of the Ror caste as well to set aside all hazy, untrue versions going on all around, the apex body of the caste must have a scientifically researched authenticated history in place. This will put to rest all the hearsays, half-truths, prejudiced assumptions, and motivated connections with one or the other caste. So, a chair should be got created for sponsoring PhD programmes on the subject of origin & development of Ror caste and in particular on its size and the reason of its inhabiting certain locations in the heartland of Haryana, from the History departments of Kurukshetra University, or PU Chandigadh or Delhi University or other reputed university etc.

* * * * *

# Chapter-14. Rors: Gots, Habitats, and Traits

## 14.1 Ror Vanshavali

Below super division of Jaati is Vansh. Main vansh are; Suryavanshi, & Chandervanshi. Secondary vansh are; Agnivanshi or Agnikula, Naagbansi, Rajvanshi, Raghuvanshi, & Yaduvanshi. The history of Vansh is recorded in Vanshavali. Smaller division below vansh is Kul (Clan), Shakha or Khap. Each vansh consists of several Clans, which claim direct patrilineage from a remote but common male ancestor who supposedly belonged to that Vansh. Ror caste is said to have evolved out of 17 Kulas or Royal races out of 36 (ref; Col Tod's Annals & Antiques of Rajasthan). These17 kulas are; Chauhan, Khatti, Dabiya, Bala, Pramara, Solanki, Rathore, Gohil, Jat, Dhaiya, Sengar, Tomar, Bargujar, Mohila, Kushwaha, Atri (not part of 36 races?) & Bhatti. (Ref; pp-64/65 of Major Keshwar). But Dr. Surender Kadiyan says, Ror caste has evolved out of 13 Rajput vansh viz; Dahiya, Guchchhle, Rode, Guhilot, Panwar, Bhatti, Chauhan, Tomar, Kushwaha or Kachhwaha, Drupad, Khokhra, Pundir, & Madhad. (Ref; p-21&22 of his book; Ror Udbhav & Vikas).

As propounded by Bhaats, Ror vansh starts after lapse of 26 generations from Yayati vansh King Dushyant (Durdaan) of Prayagraj, from 28th generation King Ruru (3182 BCE). Hence the Ror Vansh tree is;

28. Ruru, 29. Taalam Dev, 30. Batihotr, 31. Sahdev, 32. Parurikh, 33. Mukan Dev; (Talan Dev & Devapi; contemporary 2 warriors of Mahabharat), 34. Mal Dev, 35. Ajay Dev, 36. VijayDev, 37. Sarang Dev, 38. Jujur Dev, 39. Raj Dev, 40. Bhanvarrikh, 41. Indrajit, 42. AnadiDev, 43. NarDev, 44. Hridhyarikh, 45. Mahenderrikh, 46. Sugadh, 47. BaalDev, 48. BaalanDev, 49. Chandramani, 50. Hariman, 51.Chintaman, 52. Devman, 53. Abhayman, 54. Shambhun, 55. Rishiman, 56. Chavalman, 57. Dharma Sen, 58. Tisman, 59. Indraman, 60. Samrat Dhaj or Raj Ror, 61. Kunuk, 62. Rudak, 63. Hadak, 64. Devanik, 65. Ahinik, 66. Paripat, 67. Bal Shah, 68. Vijay Bhan, 69. Khangan, 70. Brahdarth, 71. Haransh, 72. Brahdath, 73. Ishman, 74. Shridhar, 75. Mohari, 76. Prashanket, 77. Amirvan, 78. Maha Sen, 79. Brahghol, 80. HariKirt, 81. Som, 82. Mitrvaan, 83. Pushyapat, 84. Sudav, 85. Bidirakh, 86. Nahak Maan, 87. Mangal Mitra, 88. Surat, 89. Pushapkarket, 90. Antarket, 91. Sutjay, 92. Brahdhvaj, 93. Bahook, 94. Kanshjayi, 95. Kagnish, 96. Kapish, 97. Sumantra, 98. Linglaav, 99. Manas Jit, 100. Sunderket, 101. Dadrod(r) (ref pp 89 to 92, Ror Etihas ki ek Jhalak; Dr Rajpal; & pp-18 to 19; Rode Vansh Ka 5000. Varsh ka Etihas; Sh Ram Das)

*Sh Ram Das Rode in his book, 'Rod Vansh ka 5000 Varsh ka Etihas', says, up to 620AD, Ror or Rore, Arore, Rohad, Rode, Roda or Rora had a common history & lineage.* Incidentally Ror Dynasty ruled between 450 BCE to 489 CE.

## 14.2 Gotra & Brahmanical Gotra

The word Gotra means a family lineage, the descendants from a common ancestor. Brahmanical Gotras emanates from seven Hindu Rishis, though it is not clear whether it is as of a carnal or spiritual father. Many of the founders of these gotras occur among ancient genealogies of the pre-historic Rajput dynasties. *The Rajas in question being not merely namesake, but distinctly stated to be the actual founder of the gotra; and even the priestly classes, like the menials owe their tribal divisions to the great families to whom their ancestors were attached.* Whatever the origin, Brahmanical gotras among Brahmins are absolutely hereditary. Gotra is wider than tribe, as new tribes & clans can be & are constantly being formed, but no new Brahmanical Gotra is possible. *Brahmanical gotras, extends far beyond the body of Brahmins; as the theory of the Hindu religion is that every Hindu, whatever be his caste, belongs to someone or other of them.* Gotras thus defined is used on the occasion of marriage, Sankalpa, & similar formal ceremonies. (Ref; p-353, "Races, Castes, & Tribes", Panjab census 1881; Denzil Ibbetson)

## 14.3 Villages & Towns Ror Inhabit

The locations or villages & towns inhabited by Rors in 3 states, 11 districts, & 28 Tehsils of Haryana, UP, & UK alphabetically along with major surname found in them are listed below. (During service & post-retirements lot of Rors have settled in cities where they were working. As such they are in good numbers in Delhi & NCR including Chandigarh UT and other towns or cities. The wards of such parents, also have mostly secured jobs in these/other pan-India cities and have settled in such places, which can be deemed habitation of such people of the caste presently.)

**1. Haryana:1. Dist. Karnal: 1. Asandh tehsil**; 1. Asandh*; Mixed, 2. Bahri; Chulhan, 3. Baal-Rangdan; Kandhol, Thaula, 4. Bhambharhedi; Balda, Bhakoru, Jhojhru, Taya, Turan, 5. Chochada; Malgas, 6. Chor-Karsa; Kainwal, Kharngad, 7. Gangatehadi; Turan, 8. Jauli; Turan, 9. KaulKheda; Turan, 10. Lalaine; Dabda, Golhan, 11. Mund; Deendayal, Danker, Mad, Rojda, Salar, 12. Panghala; Kenwal, Kharngad, Khokhar, Turan, 13. Popda; Turan, 14. Rahda; Rojda, Garaak, 15. Rangruti-Kheda; Chauhan, 16. Salwan; Samdhyan, 17. Uplani; Kandhol, Mehla. **2. Gharaunda Tehsil;** 1. Alipur Khalsa; Dumyan/Domain, 2. Bastada; Chulhan, Ghadtan, Hurda, Raitan, Turan, 3. Budhanpur; Dumyan, Gora/Gore, 4. Dingar

Majra; Gulia, Lather, 5. Faridpur; Kainwal, Suhra, 6. Gharaunda*; Mixed, 7. Gudha; Dahiya, Kainwal, Mehla, Rojda, 8. Harsingh Pura; Domain/Dumyan, Kandhol, 9. Jhinwarhedi; Beniwal, Turan, 10. Kaimla; Dhankar/Dhankhad, Mehla, Pawar, 11. Kalhedi; Jood, 12. Kalram; Gulia, Kaltangadiya, 13. Kharkaali; Kandhol, Kharngad, 14. Panaudi; Mehla, Nosraan, Thardak, 15. Pundri; Dumyan, Kharngad, Memain, 16. Staundi; Beniwal, Chopda, Dhakla, Dhankhad, Lather, Sagwal, Rojda. (Progressive Total 17+16 =33 no) **3. Indri Tehsil**; 1. Bibipur; Khokhar, 2. Battan-Khedi; Battan, 3. Gorgadh; Kanyra, Lather, Mehla, 4. Gudha (Indri); Taya, 5. Gumto; Battan, Dabda, Mehla, 6. Halwana; Thardak, Mehla, 7. Indri*; Mixed, 8. Kamaalpur Rodan; Kalyan, Khasbar, Laharwal, Mehla, Singariya, Zood, 9. Nangla Rodan; Balda, Chopda, Danker, Dabda, Jood, Khokhar, Lather, 10. Shekhpura; Beniwal, Dabda, Kalyaniya, 11. Samora; Chopda, Mehla, Taya. (Progressive Total 33+11=44 no) 4. **Karnal Tehsil**; 1. Amupur; Bataan, Dudyan, Khenchi, Zood, 2. Baldi; Garaak, Khanchi, 3. Baraas; Dabda, Bhukna, 4. Bastali; Dandal, 5. Bazida-Jattan; Khenchi, Rana, 6. Bazida-Rodan; Bhukna, Singariya, 7. Beed-Majra; Bodla, 8. Dacchar; Jandsalaar, 9. Dadupur-Rodan; Battan, Dodain, Dabda, Jandsalaar, Machhran, Nadiyal, Taya, 10. Daniyalpur; Gheed, 11. Dhakwala -Rodan; Chopda, 12. Gohida; Taya, 13. Gyondar*; Mixed, 14. Gullarpur; Garaak, 15. Guniyana; Balda, Kharngad, Machhran, Thardak, 16. Jyani; Kalyan, Kanyan, Khokhar, Rojda, 17. Hathlana; Jaandsalaar, 18. Hemada; Deendayal, 19. Jundla*; Mixed, 20. Kachhwa; Jaandsalaar, 21. Kalaampura; Khokhra, 22. Karnal; Dabda, Dankra, Hurda, Jhakla, Kaltangadiya, Kharngad, Lather, Sirdha, Thaula, 23. Katlahedi; Kadiyan, 24. Kuchchpura; Mehla, Machhran, 25. Kunjpura; Atri, Bhau, Dabda, Khokhar, Mehla, Moman, 26. Kutail; Kalyan, Kaltangadiya, Kharngad, Kandhol, 27. Manjura; Kadiyan, Machhran, Salyan, Thardak, 28. Mahmadpur; Mehla, Kalyaniya, Dahiya, 29. Mughal Majra; Bhakoru, 30. Nali Khurd; Khokhar, 31. Nasirpur; Chuchan 32. Neval; Atri, Memain, Kharngad, Kadiyan Lorkan, Thardak, 33. Nissang; Hurda, Machhran, 34. Phusgarh; Kharngad, 35. Picholia; Jood, 36. Prem Kheda; Garaak, 37. Peont; Dhanyan, 38. Rasulpur Kalan; Memain, 39. Rasulpur-Khurd; Memain, 40. Rindal; Kharngad, 41. Rukanpur; Chopda, 42. Sambhali; Jaglan, Sandyan, 43. Savant; Deendayal, Geed, Graak, Kanyan, Malgas, Mehla, Salaar, Turan, 44. Shahpur; Chauhan, Kadiyan, Kanyra, Kaltangadiya, Kharngad, 45. Sarfabad Majra; Badsar, Golia, Kainwal, Rojda, Lorkan, 46. Shekhpura Bangar; Dabda, Davne, Kalyan, Kharngad, Maniyal, 47. Shekhpura Jagir 48. Shubhri; Ruhlyan. (Progressive Total 44+48= 92 no) 5. **Nilokheri Tehsil**; 1. Aibla; Dandal, Jhojhru, Bhakla, Bodla, 2. Abeli; Jhojhru, Bhakla, 3. Amargadh; Dabda (Dabur), Dudhiyan, Rojda, Salar, 4. Anjanthali; Dhanyan, 5. Arjahedi; Laharwal, 6. Badsalu; Laharwal, Mehla, Salar, 7. Bakipur; Dankra, Kanyra, 8. Baraana; Balda, Jhojhru, 9. Barani; Chauhan, Khanchi, 10. Badeda; Jhakla, Nadan, Salar, 11. Badthal; Dabda, Thardak, Turan, Ruhlyan, 12. Bhaini-kalan; Golhan, Lather, Mehla, 13. Bhaini-Khurd; Samdhyan, Turan, Mehla, 14. Bhukhapuri; Kanyra, 15. Brahman-Majra; Khanchi,

16. Butana; Dhankhad, Salar, 17. Dabarthala; Golhan, 18. Dadupur-Khurd; Keshwar, Turan, 19. Gholpura; Gholia, 20. Gitapur; Thardak, 21. Hebatpur; Kainwal, 22. Jamba; Huda, Kalyan, Samdhyan, 23. Jhanjhadi; Jhakla, Khokhar, 24. Kamaalpur; Singariya, 25. Karsa-Dod; Kainsa, Ruhlyan, 26. Khajambda; Kenwal, Jood, 27. Koyar; Baau/Bahu, Golia, Mehla, 28. Latheron; Lather, 29. Majra-Rodan; Bhakoru, Mehla, 30. Manak Majra; Battan, Bhukna, Chulyan, Kanger, Keshwar, 31. Mohadi (Jagir); Mehla, Samdhyan, 32. Nadana; Chauhan, 33. Nigdu; Bhakhna, 34. Nilokheri*, Mix, 35. Padvala; Beniwal, Gadtan, Lather, 36. Panjokhara; Dhanker, 37. Raipur Rodan; Chauhan, 38. Ramana; Dhankhad, 39. Sambhi; Balda, 40. Sandir; Kadiyan, Khasbar, 41. Shamgadh; Bhau, Beniwal, Khasbar, Khenchi, Laharwal, Turka, Jhojhru, 42. Shekhpura; Kalyaniya, Kharngad, 43. Sidpur; Mehla, Jaandsalaar, Raitan, 44. Sikri; Jaandsalaar, 45. Sovat; Dandal, Jaandsalaar, Kalyan, Malgas, 46. Shollo; Deendayal, 47. Sultanpur; Chauhan, Chopda, Golhan, Salar, 48. Sundarpur; Kadiyan, 49. Taraodi; Dabda, Ghoal (Gulia), Khasbar, Khokhar, 50. Tigri; Golhan, 51. Yunispur; Kainwal. (Progressive Total; 92+51=143 no)

**2. Dist. Kurukshetra: 1. Pehowa Tehsil;** 1. Daserpur; Mehla, 2. Gadhi Rodan; Kandhol, 3. Kamoda; Graak, 4. Khanpur Rodan; Mehla, Raitan, 5. Lohar Majra; Bhakoru, 6. Maigdo; not known? 7. Mustapur; Golhan 8. Pehowa*; Mixed, 9. Seharda Dera; Mehla.(PT152no)

**2. ThanesarTehsil;** 1. Alampur; Taya, 2. Amin; Chauhan, 3. BeedAmin; Chauhan, 4. ChanderbhanPur; Chauhan, 5. Dyalpur; Bataan, Chauhan, Dabda, 6. Fatuhpur; Bhukna, Kalyan, Ruhlyan, 7. Haripur; Kharngad, 8. Ishakpur; Thardak, Turka, 9. Jhirbadi; Mola, 10. Jyotisar; Mehla, 11. Khaspur; Jhojhru, Sandyan, 12. Khedi-Ramnagar; Battan, Kalyan, 13. Kunwar- Khedi; Hurda, 14. Kurukshetra*; Mixed, 15. Mathana; Battan, Chauhan, Kalyan, Garaak, Kanyra, Mola, Salar, Raitan, 16. Mirzapur; Chopda, Hurda, Kharngad, Mehla, 17. Narkatari; Chopda, Kadiyan, 18. Palwal; Mehla, Sadyan, 19. Pindarsi; Mehla, 20. Pipli*; Mixed, 21. Ramgadh; Battan, Taya, 22. Ratgal; Chauhan, Gadtan, 23. Salarpur; Turka, 24. Snehadi; Turka, 25. Samani; Bhuran, 26. Thanesar *; Mixed, 27. Umari; Mola. (DT36 no) (PT179 no)

**3. Dist. Kaithal: 1. Fatehpur Pundri Tehsil;** 1. Aanhu; Dabda, Mehla, 2. Ahmadpur; Mehla, Taya, Raitan, 3. Baakal; Garaak, 4. Bandrana; Kaltangadiya, Thardak, 5. Barsana; Bataan, 6. Bhana; Sirdha, 7. Buchchi; Kalyaniya, Ruhlyan, 8. Chuhad-Majra; Samdhyan, 9. Dadwana; Bodla, 10. Deeg; Golhan, 11. Dherdu; Golhan, 12. Fatehpur; Gadtan, Gora, 13. Habadi; Balda, 14. Jadaula; Mehla, 15. Jamba; Kalyan, 1 6. Jathedi; Thardak, 17. Kaul; Beniwal, Sagwal, 18. Khedi-Matarva; Ghadtan, 19. Khedi-Sakra; Taya, 20. Madud; Tamak, 21. Mohna; Kangra, 22. Munerhedi; Khinchi, Mehla, 23. Pabla; Balda, 24. Pabnava; Bodla, Tamak, 25. Pai; Bhukna, Jood, 26; Pharal; Jhrotiya, Khasbar, 27. Pundri (Fatehpur); Golhan, Kainwal, Kharngad, 28. Ramana-Ramani; Dhankhad, 29. Rasina; Taya, 30. Ravan-Kheda; not known, 31. Sakra; Kanyra, Taya, 32. Saanch; Balda, Dabda, Mehla, Kaliya, Kaltangadiya, 33. Sangrauli; Dankra, Dhadhan, Kandhol, Mehla, 34. Sirsal; Turan, 35. Tyontha; Dhadhan,

Kalyan, Kharngad, Keshwar. **2. Kaithal Tehsil;** 1. Baalu; Badsar, 2. Dhand; Mehla, Rojda, 3. Harsaula; Chulhan, 4. Kaichhana; Could not be ascertained? 5. Kaithal*; Mixed, 6. Kalayat; Chulhan, 7. Khanoda; Dankra, Kanyra, 8. Khedi Sikandar; Kandhol, 9. Mundadi; Chuchan, Dhadhan, Gora, Jood, 10. Rajaund; Kaltangadiya, Chulhan, 11. Sajuma; not known? 12. Shayot; Gora, (DT 47 no) (P T 226 no)

**4. Dist. Panipat 1. Israna Tehsil;** 1. Ahar; Dumyan, Khasbar, Khanchi, Khokher, Singariya, 2. Balaana; Tamak, 3. Chhichhdana; Memain, Turan, 4. Israna*; Mixed, 5. Khalila; Kandhol, Khenchi, 6. Kurana; Jaglan, Madh.**2. PanipatTehsil;** 1. Alupur; Dumyan, Ghadtan, Kandhol, Kharngad, 2. Barana; Balda, Jhojhru, 3. Badoli; Nosraan, 4. Bhadad; Kalyaniya, Khokhar, 5. Kalkha; Kalyan, 6. Khandra; Dhanyan, Chopda, 7. Khukhdana; Kaliya, Kandhol, Tamak, 8. Luhari; Rojda, Sagwal, 9. Madlauda*; Mixed, 10. Nain; Mehla, Tamak, 11. Oasari; Jhojhru, 12. Palhedi; Dumyan, 13. Panipat*; mixed, 14. Shera; Ghiyad, Khanchi, 15. ShimlaMolana; Samdhyan, 16. Sutana; Dahlan, Kainwal, Tamak, 17. Thirana; Khanchi, Taya, 18. Untla; Ghadtan, Khasbar(DT24 no) (PT 250 no)

**5. Dist. Sonipat: 1. Gohana Tehsil;** 1. Jwara; Dhanyan, Ghughan, 2. Gohana*; Mixed, 3. Tihad; Mehla. **2. Sonipat Tehsil;** 1. Mohana; Khasbar (Keshwar), Mehla, 2. Sonipat*; Mixed. (DT 5 no) (PT 255 no)

**6. Dist. Yamunanagar: 1. Jagadhri Tehsil;** 1. Budiyon; Could not be ascertained? 2. Jagadhri; Laharwal, 3. Ror Chhappar; Could not be ascertained? 4. Vaterali; Could not be ascertained? 5. Yamunanagar*; Mixed. **2. Radaur Tehsil;** 1. Gumthala Rao; Dumyan, Dhankhad (2 families-1 Kaimla; 1 Baraana) (DT 6 no) (PT 261 no)

**7. Dist. Jind: 1. Safidon Tehsil;** 1. Aahlan; Turan, Sirdha, 2. Ainchra Khurd; Jaglan, Khasbar, 3. Deedwada; Balda, 4. Dhathrat (Seharda); Balda, Chhadkan, 5. Kaarkhana; Madh, Khanchi, Mehla, Jaglan, Dhankhad, 6. Malsari-Kheda; Madh, 7. Morkhi; Madh, 8. Pillu- Kheda*; Mixed, 9. Ritauli; Turan, Sirdha.10. Safidon*; Mixed (DT 10 no) (PT 271 no)

**Uttarakhand: 8. Dist. Haridwar: 1. Haridwar Tehsil;** 1. Daluwala Grunt; Khokhar, 2. Haridwar*; Mixed, 3. Kaluwas; Rana (1 family), 4. Manubass Grunt; Beniwal. **2. Roorkee Tehsil;** 1. Belda; Balda, Balyan, Chopda, Dumyan, Ghadtan, Ghiyad, Jhakla, Jood, Khanchi, Khokhar, Maniyal, Mehla, Thaula, 2. Beldi; Beniwal, Chopda, Ghiyad, Khinchi, 3. Bharapur; Beniwal, Ghiyad, Thaula, 4. Bhauri; Beniwal, Ghiyad, Thaula, 5. Dariyapur; Geed, 6. Rahmatpur; Ghiyad, Thaula, 7. Ranghadwala; Beniwal, Ghiyad, Laharwal, Mehla, 8. Roorkee*; Mixed, 9. Sohalpur Gada; Kharngad, Thaula. (DT 13 no) (PT 284 no)

**Uttar Pradesh: 9. Dist. Bijnor: 1. Bijnor Tehsil;** 1. Bijnor*; mixed, 2. Dharam Pura; Chopda 3. Ravli; Ghiyad, Kharngad, Mehla, Taya, Thardak 2. **Chandpur Tehsil;** 1. Bhogpur; Balda, Ghiyad, 2. Gadarpura; Chopda, 3. Mansapur; Ghiyad (DT 6 no) (PT 290 no)

**10 Dist. Muzaffarnagar; 1. Kairana Tehsil;** 1. Datheda; Battan, Golhan, Sirdha, 2. Dera Sakra; Bhukna, Golhan, Kanyan, Mehla, Taya, 3. Kairana; Badsar, Thardak **2. Khatauli Tehsil;** 1. Dudhali; Kadiyan. 3. **Muzaffarnagar Teh.** 1. Gadhi; Dabda, Kandhol, 2. Gosgadh; Sagwal, khokhar, Raitan, Domyan, 3. Gyana-Majra; Bod, Chhadkan, Dabdal, Jhojhru, Kadiyan, Mehla, Thaula, 4. Luhari; Beniwal, Bhakoru, Jaglan, Jhojhru, Kadiyan, Mehla, 5. Nanuta*; Mixed, 6. Tanda; Jaglan. **4. Shamli Tehsil;** 1. Ahmadpur; Taya, 2. Gandevada; Mehla, 3. Hasanpur; Jaglan, Danker, 4. Jalalabad; Bhawaniwal, 5. Janipur; Chopda, 6. Khanpur; Beniwal, Raitan, Samdhan, Thardak, 7. Kuan Kheda; Hurda, 8. Kutubgadh; Guchchhle, Kadiyan, Kharngad, Turan, 9. Nagla-Rodan; Hurde, Memain, Salar, Rojda, 10. Shamli*; Mixed, 11. Thana Bhawan*; Mixed. (DT 21 no) (PT 311 no)

**11. Dist. Saharanpur; 1. Deoband Tehsil;** 1. Divalhedi; Dankra, Kalyaniya, Khokhar, Mehla, 2. Gangoh*; Mixed. **2. Nakur Tehsil;** 1. Bahlolpur; Jhojhru, Kalyan, Kalyaniya, 2. Chaupura; Ghadtan, Kalyan, Kanyan, 3. Dhulawli; Mehla, 4. Kalsi; Ghiyad, 5. Khalidpur; Dodain, Khokhar, 6. Peer Majra; Ghiyad, Guchchhle, 7. Ramraya Khedi; Garaak **3. Rampur Maniharan Teh;** 1. Bhaisrau ; Beniwal, Jhakla, 2. Bhojpur; Beniwal, Guchchhle, Balda, Ghiyad, Thaula, 3. Chaura; Guchchhle, Ghadtan, 4. Jaidpura; Mehla, Kaltangadiya, 5. KuanKheda; Ghadtan, 6. Pando-Khedi; Guchchhle, Kaltangadiya, Mehla. **4. Saharanpur Tehsil;** 1. Badoli; Beniwal, Kalyaniya, 2. Lakhnaur; Batan, Beniwal, Ghadtan, 3. Saharanpur*; Mixed, 4. Saidpura/Sidpura; Kalyaniya, 5. Wazidpur/Bazidpur; Ghiyad, Raitan. (DT 20 no) (PT 331 no)

**12. Towns/Metro locations;** 1. Ambala Cantt, 2. Chandigarh,3. Panchkula, 4.Mohali, 5. Zirakpur, 6. Delhi, 7.Ghaziabad, 8. Faridabad, 9 Noida, 10. G Noida, 11. Gurugram, 12. Hisar, 13. Jind, 14. Rohtak. (PT 345 no)

**Originally villages inhabited by Rors come out to be 305.** If 26 nearby **urban locations**, where Ror settled in late 20th century, are included then total it becomes **305+26=331. If 14 Metro & cities,** where Rors settled post-retirement in 21st century due to education /job etc of their wards are included then inhabitations become **331+14 =345.**

So, the figure of **350 villages** inhabited by Rors as recorded in '**People of India**', series on **Haryana** - ref Ch-7, para 7.6, **is on higher side.**

**NB;** 1 *For firm & final number of locations, Ror Apex body should get checked through their resources.* 2.* Asterisk; Ror are not native but settled due to job etc. 3. Broad source for village names; is map by Mr Zile Singh Chauhan of Raipur Rodan. 4. Gotr wrote to be residing in various villages in above para & tabulation of next para,might have some errors on account of duplicate entries due to unconfirmed sources.

**5. Correction in tabulation of next para 14.4;** sr no 9 & 35 Delete Gosgadh village & reduce total numbers to 19 & 7 respectively.

## 14.4 Ror Surname alphabetically Village-wise

To assess each gotra size, alphabetically Gotra & villages inhabited by the people of that got are tabulated below.

| | | | Table showing Alphabetically Got/Surnames of Rors along with the village inhabited | |
|---|---|---|---|---|
| S. No | English/ | Hindi | Found in Villages | No |
| 1 | Atri (Bohiyan) | अत्री | Neval, Kunjpura | 2 |
| 2 | Baau/Bhosle | बाऊ/भाऊ | Hathlana, Koyar, Kunjpura, Neval, Shamgadh | 5 |
| 3 | Badsar | बडसर | Baalu, Bastada, Datheda, Gadhi Hasanpur, Hathlana, Jhinwarhedi, Kalhedi, Kaimla, Kairana, Karnal, Kuchchpura, Sharfabad Majra, Mirzapur, Neval, | 14 |
| 4 | Balda/Balde | बालदा/बालदे | Baal Ranghdan, Baraana, Belda, Bhambharhedi, Bhojpur, Dhathrat, Guniyana, Habdi, Khalidpur, Nagla Rodan, Pabla, Rasina, Saanch, Sambhi, Shera | 15 |
| 5 | Ballan/Balyan | बालान/ बाल्याण | Belda | 1 |
| 6 | Battan | बताण | Barsana, Battan Khedi, Bazida Rodan, Brahman Majra, Chhichhdana, Dabarthala, Dadupur Rodan, Datheda, Dera Sakra, Dyalpur, Gholpura, Gudha (Kohand), Gumton, Hathlana, Khandra, Khedi-Ramnagar, Kuchchpura, Kunjpura, Lakhnaur, Manak Majra, Manjura, Nagla Rodan, Nali Khurd, Nissing, Pyont, Shekhpura Jagir, Yunispur | 27 |
| 7 | Bhakla | भाकला | Abela, Abeli, Kutail | 3 |
| 8 | Bhakoru | भकोरू | Aahun, Baraana, Bomberhedi, Gumthala Rao, Kunjpura, Lohar Majra, Luhari, Staundi | 8 |
| 9 | Beniwal/ Bhawaniwal | बेनीवाल/ भवानीवाल | Bakdoli, Beladi, Bhaisrau, Bhauri, Bhojpur, Gosgadh, Jalalabad, Jhinwarhedi, Kaul, Khanpur (UP), Lakhnaur, Manuwas, Nangla-Rodan, Luhari, Padvala, Ranghadwala, Shekhpura, Staundi, Sutana, Shamgadh | 20 |
| 10 | Bhukna | भूकणा/ | Aibla Jagir, Aibli, Bazida Rodan, Fatuhpur, Majra Rodan, Manak Majra, Nigdu, Pabnava | 8 |
| 11 | Bhuran | भुराण | Samaani | 1 |
| 12 | Bod | बोद | Gyana Majra | 1 |
| 13 | Bodla/Bodle | बोदला, बोदले | Aibla Jagir, Beed-Majra, Dadwana, Pabnava | 4 |
| 14 | Chauhan/ Dalpate | चौहाण/ दलपते | Amin, Baal Ranghdan, Badthal, Balaana, Barani Khalsa, Beed-Amin, ChanderBhanpur, Dyalpur, Gholpura, Hebatpur, Kamoda, Karnal, Mathana, Mohadi Jagir, Nadana, Nali Khurd, Nasirpur, Panjokhara, Raipur-Rodan, Ratgal, Sanehedi Khalsa, Shahpur, Shamgadh, Sultanpur, Yunispur | 25 |
| 15 | Chhachhra | छाछरा | Chhichhdana, Dhakwala | 2 |
| 16 | Chhakdan/ | छकडाण/ | Dhathrath, Gyana Majra (Also written as Chhaukar) | 2 |

| | | | | |
|---|---|---|---|---|
| 17 | Chopda | चोपड़ा | Brahman Majra, Belda, Beldi, Dabarthala, Dhakwala, Gorgadh, Gholpura, Jhinwarhedi, Khandra, Majra Rodan, Mirzapur, Nagla Rodan, Nasirpur, Rukanpur, Samora, Shahpur, Staundi, Sultanpur | 18 |
| 18 | Chuchan | चूचाण | Mundadi, Nasirpur, Sidpur (Also called as Chuchayan चूचायण) | 3 |
| 19 | Chuhlan/ Chuliyan | चुहलाण/ चुलियाण | Bahri, Bastada, Bataan Khedi, Habdi, Harsola, Kaithal, Kalayat, Manak Majra, Panghala, Rajaund. (Chuliyan Chulyan or Chulhaan चुल्याण or चुलहाण) | 10 |
| 20 | Dabda/Dabur | दाबड़ा/डाबर | Aahun, Amargadh/Kala-Majra, Badthal, Baldi, Bhambharhedi, Baraas, Beri-Khedi, Dadupur Rodan, Dyalpur, Gadhi Hasanpur, Gumton, Kalaampura, Karnal, Kunjpura, Lalaine, Nagla Rodan, Samaani, Saanch, Shahpur, Shekhpura Banger & Jagir, Sikri, Sirsal, Staundi, Taraodi | 24 |
| 21 | Dabdal | डबदाल | Baraana, Bahlolpur, Bhambharhedi, Gyana Majra, Kunjpura, Luhari, Shamgadh | 7 |
| 22 | Dadan | ददाण | Mundadi, Sangrauli, Staundi, Tyontha (Also called as Dhadhan ढढाण) | 4 |
| 23 | Dahiya | दहिया | Gudha, Gharaunda*, Kurana*, Khukhdana*, Mahmadpur* (*all shifted from Gudha) | 5 |
| 24 | Dahlan | दहलाण | Habdi, Sutana | 2 |
| 25 | Dandaal | दंदाल | Abela, Abeli, Bastali, Hemanda, Solu-Majra, | 5 |
| 26 | Davne | दावणे | Shekhpura | 1 |
| 27 | Deendayal | दीनदयाल | Aibla Jagir, Bastali, Haibatpur, Hemda, Mund, Munerhedi, Savant, Shollo, Shamgadh | 9 |
| 28 | Dhandaan | ढंढाण | Chhichhdana, Khanpur Rodan, Mundadi, Sangrauli, Staundi, Tanda, | 6 |
| 29 | Dhakla | ढाकला | Faridpur, Kalhedi, Staundi | 3 |
| 30 | Dhankar/er | ढाँकर/डाखर | Anjanthali, Butaana, Dayalpur, Kaimla, Karnal, Khandra, Mund, Nagla Rodan, Panjokhara, Staundi | 9 |
| 31 | Dhankhad | धनखड़ | Butaana, Gumthala Rao, Kaimla, Karnal, Panjokhara, Ramana | 6 |
| 32 | Dhanyan | धनयाण | Anjanthali, Jwara, Khandra, Pyont | 4 |
| 33 | Domyan/ Domain/ | डोमयाण/ डोमैण/ | Ahar, Alipur Khalsa, Belda, Budhanpur, Gosgadh, Harsinghpura, Nali Khurd, Palhedi, Pundri (KNL) (Also called & written as Dumyan डूमयाण Dumiyan डूमयाण) | 10 |
| 34 | Dudyan/ Dodain | दुदयान/दूदाण | Ainchra, Dadupur-Rodan, Pundri | 3 |
| 35 | Doodman | डूडमाण | Ahar, Alipur, Budhanpur, Gosgadh, Harsinghpura, Khalila, Palhedi, Pundri | 8 |
| 36 | Dudyan/ Dudhiyan | दुदयान/ दुधियान | Aahun, Amargadh (Kala Majra), Amupur, Bazida Rodan, Deed, Khalidpur, Tyontha | 6 |
| 37 | Gadtan | घड़ताण | Alupur, Bastada, Bastali, Belda, Chaura, Dera Sakra, Fatehpur, Jhinwarhedi, Kamaalpur Rodan, Khedi Matarva, Lakhnaur, Manjura, Mirzapur, Padvala, Pundri, Ratgal, Ritauli, Sanehedi Khalsa, Untla | 19 |
| 38 | Ghiyad/Geed | घीयड़/घीड़ | Bhambharhedi, Bazidpur, Belda, Beldi, Bhauri, Bhojpur, Daluwala, Datheda, Daniyalpur, Dariyapur Dayalpur, Guniyana, Jyani, Kalsi, Karnal, Majra Rodan, Mansapur, Pabla, Rahmatpur, Ranghadwala, Rasulpur Khurd, Ravli, Savant, Shahpur, Shera | 24 |

| 39 | Ghughan | घूघण | Jwara. (Also called as Gugyan गुग्याण) | 1 |
|---|---|---|---|---|
| 40 | Golhan/Gollan | गोल्हण/गोल्लण | Baldi, Bhaini Kalan, Dabarthala, Datheda, Dayalpur, Deeg, Dera Sakra, Dherdu, Kalhedi, Lalaine, Nagla Rodan, Pai (Gate), Pundri, Sirsal, Sultanpur, Mustapur/Murtjapur, Tigri | 17 |
| 41 | Gora/Gore | गोरा/गोरे | Barana, Budhanpur, Fatehpur, Kamaalpur, Mund, Mundadi, Rahmatpur, Sirsal, Shayot | 9 |
| 42 | Graak | ग्राक | Anjanthali, Baldi, Baakal, Badsalu, Chochada, Dhathrath, Gullarpur, Hathlana, Kamoda, Mathana, Mohadi Jagir, Nissing, Prem-Kheda, Phusgadh, Pindarsi, Rahda, Ramraj Khedi, Savant | 18 |
| 43 | Guchchhla/e | गुच्छला/गुच्छले | Badsalu, Bhojpur, Chaura, PandoKhedi, Kutubgadh, Manuwas, Sohalpur (or Guchchhle) | 7 |
| 44 | Gulia/Gholia | गुलिया/घोलिया | Badsalu, Bataan Khedi, Dinger Majra, Gholpura, Gyondar, Kalram, Koyar, Sharfabad Majra, Taraodi or गोलिया | 9 |
| 45 | Hurda/Huda | हुरडा/हुड्डा | Bastada, Balaana, Butana, Jamba, Kalaampura, Kamaalpur-Bakdoli, Karnal, Kuan Khedi, Mirzapur, Naagal, Nissang, Sharfabad Majra | 12 |
| 46 | Jaglan/Jogran | जागलान | Ainchra, Hasanpur, Kurana, Luhari, Mirzapur, Rasina, Sambhli, Tanda, Untla (जोगरान) | 9 |
| 47 | Jandsalaar | जांडसलार | Dacchar, Dadupur-Rodan, Hathlana, Shekhpura (Bangar), Sikri, Nagla Rodan, Sidpur, Sovat | 8 |
| 48 | Jhakla | झाकला | Badeda, Bhaisrau, Belda, Jhanjhadi, Karnal | 5 |
| 49 | Jhrotiya | झरोटिया | Pharal | 1 |
| 50 | Jhojhru | झोझरू | Aibla, Aibli, Bahlolpur, Baraana, Bomberhedi, GyanaMajra, Khaspur, Kunjpura, Luhari, Oasari, Shamgadh | 11 |
| 51 | Kadiyan | कादियान | Dudhali, Gyna Majra, Kalhedi, Katlahedi, Khanpur, Kutubgadh, Luhari, Manjura, Mirzapur, Narkatari, Neval, Pabnava, Sandir, Sundarpur | 14 |
| 52 | Kaandal | कन्दाल | Dadupur Khurd, Latheron, Majra | 3 |
| 53 | Kainwal/Kahanwal | केनवाल/कहनवाल | Ahar, Amin, Badsalu, Beed-Majra, Bhojpur Rodan, Chor-Karsa, Faridpur, Gudha, Hebatpur, Kaimla, Khajambda, Kanwar Khedi, Khanoda, Khawaja Ahmadpur, Kutubgadh, Nagla Rodan, Pabnava, Palwal, Panghala, Panjokhara, Pundri, Sidpur, Sutana, Sharfabad Majra, Shekhpura Jagir, Tigri, Yunispur. | 27 |
| 54 | Kainsa/Kapsa | कैंसा/केपसा | Bukhapuri, Karsa Dod, Khandra, Mathana, Shahpur, Shekhpura Jagir | 6 |
| 55 | Kaira/Kayra | कैरा/कायरा | Gorgadh, Khedi-Sakra, Koyar, Sakra | 4 |
| 56 | Kaltagra | कलतगरा | Bandrana, Jundla, Karnal, Kutail, Pando-Khedi, Saanch, Shahpur | 7 |
| 57 | Kaliya* | कालिया | Khukhdana, Saanch (* an offshoot from Kaltagadiya or Kalntagadiya?) | 2 |
| 58 | Kalntagadiya | कलंतगड़िया | Bandrana, Brahman Majra, Jaidpura, Jundla, Karnal, Kalram, Kutail, Pando-Khedi, Rajaund, Saanch, Shahpur or कतलागड़िया | 11 |
| 59 | Kalyan/Kalyaniya | कल्याण/कल्याणीया | Ahmadpur (Shamli), Bahlolpur, Baldi, Bandrana, Barani, Bhadaud, Bhauri, Buchchi, Chaupura, Chhichhdana, Datheda, Dhalawli, Divalhedi, Jyani, Kalkha, Kamaalpur Rodan, Kutail, Mahmadpur, Mathana, Saanch, Sidpur, Sikri, Shekhpura Bangar. | 23 |

| 60 | Kandhol | कंधोल/kandol | Alupur, Baal Ranghdan, Gadhi Rodan, Harsinghpura, Khalila Majra, Kharkaali, Khandra, Khukhdana, Khedi, Kutail, Sangrauli, Uplani, (Also spelt as Khandol) | 12 |
|---|---|---|---|---|
| 61 | Kangar/ Kangra | कंगर/कांगरा | Bakipur, Brahman Majra, Divalhedi, Gumton, Karnal, Khanoda, Khedi Ramnagar, Hasanpur, Manak Majra, Mohna, Sangrauli, Yunispur | 12 |
| 62 | Kanyan | कन्यान | Amargadh, Buchchi, Bahlolpur, Dayalpur, Dera Sakra, Fatuhpur, Jamba (Kaithal), Jyani, Khedi Matarva, Khedi-Ramnagar, Kuchchpura, Kunjpura, Mathana, Nain, Savant, Shamgadh, Sidpura (UP), Tyontha | 18 |
| 63 | Kanyra/ Kaynra | कांयरा/कायंरा | Bhukhapuri, Gorgadh, Koyar, Mathana, Sakra, Shahpura, | 6 |
| 64 | Khasbar/ Kheswar | खसबर/केशवर | Ahar, Ainchra, Alupur, Baal Ranghdan, Dadupur-Khurd, Gullarpur, Jundla, Kamaalpur Rodan, Manak Majra, Mohana, Mohna, Mundadi, Nain, Narkatari, Pharal, Pundri, Sandhir, Shamgadh, Tanda, Tyontha | 21 |
| 65 | Kanchi/ Khinchi/ Khenchi | खिंची/खैंची | Ahar, Beldi, Belada, Beladi, Barana, Barani Khalsa, Brahman Majra, Bazida Jattan, Khalila Majra, Khandra, Munerhedi, Shamgadh, Shera | 13 |
| 66 | Kharngad | खरंगड़ | Alupur, Baldi, Gunyana, Haripur, Karnal, Chor-Karsa, Guniyana, Khedi-Sikandar, Kutail, Kharkaali, Kutubgadh, Majra Rodan, Mirzapur, Mundadi, Munerhedi, Neval, Panghala, Pundri, Phusgadh, Ramgadh, Ranghadwala, Ravli, Rindal, Shekhpura Jagir, Tyontha, Shahpur, Sohalpur | 27 |
| 67 | Khokhar/ Khokher | खोखर | Ahar, Belda, Bhadaud, Bibipur Jatan, Daluwala, Divalhedi, Gosgadh, Habdi, Indri, Jhanjhadi, Jyani, Kalaampura, Karnal, Khalidpur, Kunjpura, Kutail, Mahmadpur, Manjura, Mirzapur, Nagla Rodan, Nali Khurd, Nasirpur, Panghala, Sikri, Sohalpur | 26 |
| 68 | Kunkaan | कुकॉण | Bhambharhedi, Shamgadh | 2 |
| 69 | Ladkyan/ Lodkan/ Lorkan | लड़क्यान/ लोड़कान | Belada, Beladi, Bhaisrau, Bhojpur Rodan, Chaupura, Dhalawli, Lakhnaur, Manuwas, Nagla Rodan, Neval, Padwal, Pandoli, Ranghadwala, Sharfabad Majra, Tanda लड़कान | 15 |
| 70 | Laharwal | लहरवाल/ लहरवान | Arjahedi, Badsalu, Jagadhari, Kamaalpur, Ranghadwala, Shamgadh | 6 |
| 71 | Lambad/ Lamba | लंबड़/लाम्बा | Baraana Karnal & Panipat (Lambra/लाम्बरा) | 2 |
| 72 | Lather | लाठर | Amargadh, Baal Ranghdan, Badthal, Bhambharhedi, Bhauri, Gorgadh, DingerMajra, Karnal, Nangla Rodan, Padvala, Phusgadh, Shamgadh, Staundi, Yunispur | 14 |
| 73 | Madh/ Madhotra | मड/मढोत्रा | Chhichhdana, Dathrat, Kamaalpur, Kaarkhana, Khandra, Kurana, Malsari-Kheda, Morkhi, Mund, Shimla Molana, Untla | 11 |
| 74 | Machhran | मछराण | Dadupur Rodan, Guniyana, Hathlana, Kuchchpura, Nissang, Manjura | 6 |
| 75 | Malgas | मलगस | Chochada, Popdan, Savant | 3 |
| 76 | Maniyal | मणियाल | Belda, Beldi, Bhauri, Daluwala Rodan, Luhari, Manubass, Ranghadwala, Shekhpura, Sutana | 9 |

| No. | Surname | | Villages | Count |
|---|---|---|---|---|
| 77 | Masaaniya | मसाणिया | Dadupur khurd, Naagal | 2 |
| 78 | Mehla/ Mahla/Mahle (*Mepla misspelt Mehla?*) | मेहला/महला /महले/माहले (Ibbetson report no; 55 says Mepla surname Rors are found in Ambala, Jagadhari, Naraingadh) | Aahun, Ahmadpur (Shamli), Anjanthali, Badsalu, Bastada, Baldi, Bhaini Kalan & Khurd, Bhauri, Belda, Bibipur Jattan, Duserpur, Dayalpur, Dera Sakra, Dhalawli, Divalhedi, Gandevada, Gorgadh, Gudha, Gumton, Gyana Majra, Hathlana, Jadaula, Jaidpura, Jhirbadi, Jyotisar, Kaarkhana, Kaimla, Kamaalpur Rodan, Khanpur Rodan, Khedi Matarva, Koyar, Kuchchpura, Kutubgadh, Mahmadpur, Majra Rodan, Mirzapur, Mohana, Mohadi jagir, Mundadi, Munerhedi, Nain, Palwal, Panaudi, PandoKhedi, Panjokhara, Pindarsi, Ranghadwala, Ravli, Rod Majra, Sambhi, Savant, Saanch, Samora, Sangrauli, Shahpur, Seharda Dera, Shekhpura (Bangar), Shera, Sidpura, Sohalpur, Tanda, Tihad, Untla, Uplani, Yunispur. | 66 |
| 79 | Memain | मेमैण | Chhichhdana, Dhakwala, Kunjpura, Neval, Pundri, Pabla, Rasulpur, | 7 |
| 80 | Mokkal | मोक्कल | Bahlolpur, Jhinwarhedi | 2 |
| 81 | Mola | मोला | Jhirbadi, Mathana, Umri | 3 |
| 82 | Mota | मोटा | Baraana, Bahlolpur, Bhambharhedi, GyanaMajra, Kunjpura, Luhari, Shamgadh | 7 |
| 83 | Moman | मोमण | Kunjpura, Naagal, Rasulpur, Pundri | 4 |
| 84 | Mule/Mulyan | मुले/मलयाण | Bastada, Jhirbadi, Umari | 3 |
| 85 | Nadaan | नाडान/ Nadiyal | Budheda, Bhaiswal, Dadupur Rodan, Karnal, Mirzapur, Pabla, Salarpur | 7 |
| 86 | Nosraan | नौसराण | Badoli (Bhartoli), Kurana, Panaudi | 3 |
| 87 | Pawar/ Panwar | पवार/पंवार | Jhanjhadi, Kaimla | 2 |
| 88 | Raitan/ Rahtan | रायताण/ रहताण | Ahmadpur (Shamli; UP), Badthal, Bastada, Bazida Rodan, Bazidpur, Beldi, Khanpur, Mathana, Sidpur | 9 |
| 89 | Rana | राणा | Belada, Bhaisrau, Bazida Jattan, Chander Bhanpur | 4 |
| 90 | Rorvanshi | रोड़वंशी | Daserpur, Kaluwas, Majra | 2 |
| 91 | Rojda | रोजड़ा | Amin, Bataan Khedi, Beed Majra, Dhand, Gudha, Jyani, Kamoda, Khedi Ramnagar, Kunjpura, Luhari, Mund, Nagla, Nanu Khedi, Rahda, Sharfabad Majra, Staundi | 16 |
| 92 | Ruhlaan | रुहलाण/ रुल्हण | Badthal, Buchchi, Fatuhpur, Karnal, Karsa-Dod, Shubhri (also as; Ruhlyan/रुहल्याण) | 6 |
| 93 | Sagwal | सगवाल (सागवान) | Dabarthala, Gohida, Gosgadh, Hebatpur, Jhinwarhedi, Kaul, Luhari, Mathana, Mohadi Jagir, Neval, Pabla, Ritauli, Shahpur, Shekhpura Jagir, Staundi, Thana Bhawan | 16 |
| 94 | Salyan | सल्याण | Manjura | 1 |
| 95 | Salaar | सलार | Amargadh, Badsalu, Budheda, Butana, Kachhwa, Mathana, Mund, Nagla Rodan (UP), Savant, Sultanpur | 10 |
| 96 | Samdhyan | समध्याण | Bhaini Khurd, Bhambharhedi, Beed Majra, Chuhad Majra, Guniyana, Jamba, Khanpur, Luhari, Mirzapur, Mohadi, Salwan, Shimla Molana (or Samdan समदान) | 12 |

| 97 | Sadyan | साड्याण | Khanpur, Khaspur, Palwal, Sambhli, Snehadi; (Sandyan/Sandhan/ संधान) | 5 |
|---|---|---|---|---|
| 98 | Singariya | सिंगरिया | Ahar, Bazida Rodan, Balaana, Jhanjhadi, Kamaalpur Rodan, Kunjpura, (Singra/सिंगरा) | 6 |
| 99 | Sirda/Sirdha | सिरदा/सिरड़ा | Bhana, Datheda, Hathlana, Karnal, Kunjpura, Ritauli also as; सिरड़ | 6 |
| 100 | Surha | सुरहा | Faridpur, Jamba, Kurana, Manjura | 4 |
| 101 | Tamak | तमक/टमक | Amin, Balaana, Gholpura, Kanwar Khedi, Khukhdana, Madud, Nain, Pabnava, Shera, Sutana, Yunispur as; टामक/तामक | 11 |
| 102 | Taya | ताया/टाया | Ahmadpur, Alampur, Baraana, Bhauri, Bastali, Bhambharhedi, Dadupur Rodan, Dera Sakra, Gudha (Indri), Hebatpur, Kalaampura, Khedi-Sakra, Rasina, Ranghadwala, Ravli, Sakra, Samora, Saanch, Shamgadh, Staundi | 19 |
| 103 | Thardak | थरड़क/ठरड़क | Aahun, Anjanthali, Badthal, Bandrana, Beed Majra, Dayalpur, Dera Sakra, Dinger Majra, Geetapur, Guniyana, Halwana, Jyani, Jathedi, Kaimla, Kairana, Kanwar Khedi, Khanpur, Manjura, Mathana, Nali Khurd, Neval, Pabla, Pai, Panaudi, Panjokhara, Ravli, Sangrauli, Shahpur, Shamgadh, Shekhpura Jagir, Tigri, Tyontha | 32 |
| 104 | Thaula | ठौला/ठौल्ला | Chhichhdana, Dhakwala, Sohalpur | 3 |
| 105 | Tholla | थौला/थौल्ला, | Baal Rangdan, Bhauri, Belda, Bhojpur, GyanaMajra, Karnal, Rahmat Pur, Ranghadwala, Sohalpur | 9 |
| 106 | Turan | टूर्न/तुरान | Aahlan, Badsalu, Badthal, Bastada, Bhaini Kalan, Bhambharhedi, Chhichhdana, Deed, Gangatehadi, Jauli, JhinwariKheda, KaulKheda, Khandra, Khanpur Rodan, Kuchchpura, Kutubgadh, Majra Rodan, Nagla Rodan, Nain, Panghala, Phusgadh, Popda, Pundri, Ritauli, Shamgadh, Sidpur, Sirsal, Savant | 28 |
| 107 | Turka | तुर्का/तुर्क | Baldi, Sanehedi Khalsa, Ishakpur, Salarpur, Shamgadh | 5 |
| 108 | Zood/Jood | जूड़ | Aalampur, Baldi, Belda, Kalhedi, Khajambda, Khanpur Rodan, Mundadi, Nagla Rodan, Pai, Picholia, Ramana-Ramani | 11 |

**NB;** These numbers are not firm & final number as total *gots* as per Dr Surinder Kadiyan is 86+76=162, as explained in the para below.

## 14.5 Ror Gotras category

Surnames, perhaps evolved as a way to sort people into groups by occupation or place of origin or clan affiliation or from a famous patronym. Dr. Kadiyan (ref; his book pp18-22), divides Ror gots into two categories of main 86; well-known and established & 76 lesser known, stated to be not fully known, & where these are found. So, in all, there are 86+76=162 gotras/surnames/sub-caste. Census-1891: Punjab & its Feudatories, Part-III, during British time also had recorded 169 sub-castes (Surnames) of Rors. (Ref; page-930/982 census-1981 report; Ch -6, Section, 6.4(c) also).

**Main**; 1. Atri(Bohiyan), 2. Kandhol(Khandol), 3. Kanyan, 4. Kaltagadiya(Kalntgada), 5. Kalyan(Kilgiya), 6. Kahanwal, 7. Kadiyan, 8. Kangar(Kaankar), 9. Kayra(Kapra), 10. Kaliya, 11. Kayasa/Kainsa, 12. Kharngad, 13. Khasbar (Keshwar), 14. Khanchi/Khichi/Khinchi, 15. Khokhra/Khokhre, 16. Graak, 17. Gora/Gore, 18. Golhan (Gollen, Guliyan), 19. Guchchhla (Guchchhle), 20. Ghadtan, 21. Ghiyad (Geed/Gheed), 22. Ghughan (Ghughyan), 23. Chulhan (Chulyan), 24. Chuchan, 25. Chopda, 26. Chauhan (Dopla/Bachhas), 27. Chhadkan (Chhakdan), 28. Chhachhra, 29. Chhokar, 30. Janjar, 31. Jaglan (Jogran), 32. Jaandsalaar, 33. Jood (Zood), 34. Jhakla/Jhankla, 35. Jhojhru, 36. Tamak/Taamak, 37. Taya, 38. Turan, 39. Thardak, 40. Taula/Thaula, 41. Dhakla, 42. Dhankar, 43. Dhandhan(Dandan), 44. Dumyan (Domain), 45. Turka (Turk/Turke), 46. Dandaal (Dandayal/Dadaal/Dadiyan), 47. Dahiya (Dahia/Dahe), 48. Dabda (Dabur), 49. Dudyan (Durdan/Dhanyan/Dhumaan), 50. Nadayan (Nudyan), 51. Nosran, 52. Badsar (Badsir), 53. Bataan, 54. Balda/Balde, 55. Baliyan (Balyaan), 56. Bod (Budh), 57. Bodla, 58. Beniwal (Bhawaniwal), 59. Bhakuru (Bakhoru), 60. Bhankla (Bhakle), 61. Bhukna (Bhukhne), 62. Bhuran (Bharan), 63. Bhogra, 64. Machhran, 65. Mad/Madh, 66. Memain(Mamaniya/Mamyan), 67. Malgas, 68. Mehla(Mahla), 69. Moman, 70. Mola, 71. Rana, 72. Raitan(Ratyan), 73. Ruhlyan, 74. Rabda, 75. Rojda, 76. Laharwal(Laharwan), 77. Lather, 78. Lambad(Lamda), 79. Sandhan, 80. Sagwal, 81. Sandyan, 82. Singariya, 83. Sirdha (Sirda), 84. Surha (Surra), 85. Salyan (Sulyan), 86. Hurda (Hurde);

**Lessor known**; 1. Kalatiya, 2. Kandal, 3. Kanhad, 4. Kasiye, 5. Kukyan, 6. Kilgiya, 7. Keniwal, 8. Khangad, 9. Khndhadhe, 10. Khadgad, 11. Khadiyan, 12. Khindra, 13. Khudal, 14. Gantgadiye, 15. Gugain, 16. Gholiya, 17. Chutkalyan, 18. Chunchar, 19. Chokre, 20. Choter, 21. Chotle, 22. Jotle, 23. Jandwal, 24. Jodiya, 25. Jola, 26. Jhrotiye, 27. Jhukru, 28. Taankar, 29. Toon, 30. Dudhan, 31. Thadak, 32. Daadyan, 33. Dogra, 34. Dharkle, 35. Tahe, 36. Dankhad, 37. Dalpate, 38. Dahlaan, 39. Daabdaal, 40. Dujaan, 41. Dhankla, 42. Nadyan, 43. Naasit, 44. Naahaniya, 45. Padihaar, 46. Puniya, 47. Bakhore, 48. Bachchas, 49. Barsad, 50. Bagadi, 51. Buvaniya, 52. Bokla/Bokle, 53. Bogi, 54. Bochye, 55. Bhawaniwal, 56. Bhukra/Bhukre, 57. Bhujaak, 58. Mod/More, 59. Maniyaal, 60. Yola, 61. Rahatvaan, 62. Rugyaan, 63. Rode, 64. Lachhiwada, 65. Lodkaan, 66. Valiyaan, 67. Vaarge, 68. Sarhad, 69. Saaman, 70. Siswal, 71. Shishlaan, 72. Haldaan, 73. Hathiyariya, 74. Hukke, 75. Huraj, 76. Hulke.

**NB**; *Though Dr Kadiyan gotra count is almost equal to as in Punjab census-1891, but for firm & final total, and whether main or secondary & the criteria for it, the apex Ror body should get it verified through their independent sources for freezing the name & number.*

## 14.6 Ror surnames Common with other Castes

The fact many clans have same surname in different caste is explained as; say, a Bachhas Rajput, married a Gujar woman; her offspring will be Gujars, but their descendants became Bachhas clans of Gujars. This sort of tradition is proof of descent through females, which once was the rule in India & probably all over the world. *So, it is rash to attribute all such traditions merely to a desire to claim descent from a Rajput ancestor.* Actually, some Rajput clans have sprang from Bhaat, or Brahmin or Carpenter fathers and Rajput women. Presently the offspring of a mixed marriage carry the caste of the father, but pure blood will not intermarry with them, so it becomes a different caste. This also accounts for many clans in different castes bearing the same name. (Ref; Karnal Dist. Gazetteer; 1883-84, p-87)

This explains the reason for same surnames in various castes e.g., Rajputs, Jats, Gujars, Rors, Ahirs, Punjabis and even in Marathas with some variation in pronunciation and spelling like Mehla: Mahle; Balda: Balde; Bodla: Bodle; Dabda: Dabhade; Chauhan: Chavan; and many more. Such common surnames found across castes are tabulated below as redrawn from the part Table-XIII Appendix to Imperial table, (ref para 6.6 chapter-6).

| S No | Ror Surname | Ahir | Fakir | Gujar | Jat | Arora/Khatri | Maratha | Rajput |
|---|---|---|---|---|---|---|---|---|
| | **Ror Surnames found in other castes/Tribes**** | | | | | | | |
| 1 | Atri | | | | Yes | | Yes | Yes |
| 2 | Baau* | | | | | | Yes | |
| 3 | Balda*/Balde | | | | | | Yes | |
| 4 | Bodla*/Bodle | | Yes | | | | Yes | |
| 5 | Chauhan*/Chavan | Yes | | | Yes | | | Yes |
| 6 | Chopda | Yes | | | Yes | Yes | | Yes |
| 7 | Dahia*/Dahe | Yes | | | Yes | | | |
| 8 | Dabda*/Dabhade | Yes | | | | | Yes | Yes |
| 9 | Dandaal* | | | | | | | Yes |
| 10 | Dhankhad | | | | Yes | | | |
| 11 | Gohlan* | | | | | | | Yes |
| 12 | Gulia* | Yes | | | Yes | | | |
| 13 | Jaglan* | | | | Yes | | | |
| 14 | Kadian*/Kade | | | | Yes | | | |
| 15 | Kandal* | Yes | | | | | | |
| 16 | Kangar | Yes | | | | | | |
| 17 | Khanchi* | | Yes | | | | | Yes |
| 18 | Khokhar* | | Yes | | Yes | Yes | Yes | Yes |
| 19 | Lambad* | Yes | | | Yes | Yes | | |
| 20 | Lather | | | | Yes | | | |
| 21 | Mehla*/Mahle | Yes | | | Yes | | Yes | Yes |

| | | | | | | | | |
|---|---|---|---|---|---|---|---|---|
| 22 | Malik | | | Yes | Yes | Yes | | |
| 23 | Mor(e)* | | | | Yes | | Yes | |
| 24 | Nain | | | | Yes | | | Yes |
| 25 | Rana*/Rane | | | Yes | Yes | | | Yes |
| 26 | Rawal | | | Yes | | Yes | | Yes |
| 27 | Rode | | | | | Yes | | |
| 28 | Ror */Rod | | | | Yes | | | Yes |
| 29 | Sagwal* | | | | Yes | | | Yes |
| 30 | Taya | | | | | | | Yes |
| 31 | Turan* | | | | Yes | | | Yes |
| Total | | 9 | 3 | 3 | 19 | 5 | 8 | 16 |

Legend: * All versions of spelling e.g., Bhau, Balde, Bodle, Chavan Dahiya, Dabur, Dabda, Dabhade, Deendayal, Gholia, Golhan, Jogran, Kadiyan, Kade, Kaindal, Khenchi, Khinchi, Khokhra, Lamba, Mahal, Mahla, Mahale, Mohil, Mohila, Mohile, Rane, Rod, Raur, Rore, Rour, Sangwan, Tuar etc.

** Any discrepancy in commonality is inadvertent only & not by any prejudice. NB: 1. Some minor tribes, which have sub-caste/gots similar to Rors; 1. Awan; Mehla Sub-caste, 2. Fakir has Bodla & Khokhar, 3. Sunar has Khichi & Khokhar, & 4. Some Minors have Bodla, Dabar, Mahla, Rode etc.

## 14.8  Rors Vs Maratha Traits

People of India are identified by attributes like; physical features, ethnicity, social, linguistic, & cultural traits. The tabulation below compares the traits of Rors Vs Marathas in order to evaluate the similarities between these two races.

| Comparison of physical, cultural and other traits of Rors & Marathas | | | |
|---|---|---|---|
| Parameters of Traits | Rors | Marathas | Remarks |
| 1.Caste Composition | Standalone, & minor landowning | Group of caste*Kshatriya, Agrarian | *Kunbi, & Non-Kunbi, |
| 2. Caste Type & status | Regional level | National Level | Peasant, Sutar, Mahar |
| 3. Ethnicity | North-western | Western-Konkani | |
| 4. Racially | Indo-Aryan | Scytho-Dravidian | |
| 5. Linguistically | Hindi-Haryanvi | Marathi & Konkani | |
| 6.Physical(a) Indefinite-Built | Medium & Strong, | Stout & strong, | |
| Posture/Stature/ Height | Upright & Manly, Medium to Tall | Upright & Manly, Average to Medium | |
| Color & texture of skin | Whitish to Dark Brown | Brown to Dusky dark | |

| | | | |
|---|---|---|---|
| Color of Eyes | Dark Brown | Dark Brown & Grey-Konkani region | |
| Form of Face | Long, well defined | Medium, fully developed & round | |
| (b)Definite -Shape of Head | Long, proportioned | Medium to short tending to round | |
| Shape of Forehead | Broad & flat | Medium & flat | |
| Shape of Nose | Long & sharp | Medium/short & tending to flat | |
| Shape of Face | Long, sharp features | Medium broad, sharp features | |
| 7.Behaviour Aspect -Nature | Peaceful, Dormant & Docile | Aggressive & overpowering | |
| Type of Character | Non-tenacious, straight forward & Scrupulous dealings, but scheming & secretive, conformity behaviour, lacks determination | Tenacity of character, Guerrilla Methods of warfare, Unscrupulous dealings, Genius for scheming/intrigue & individuality of Character | Spirited, courage, & resolve Character Individuality; determined; uniqueness |
| 8. Language | Hindi-Haryanvi, UP effect in east | Marathi & Konkani | |
| 9.Social Division | Gotra/clans | Kunbis, Non-Kunbis | |
| Culture | Typical; North with Punjabi effect | Typ. Marathi Territorial & South effect | |
| No of Gots & Vansh | 162 & 13* | 96 & 22 | *As per Maj Keshwar 17 |
| Social Intercourse | Equal; Jat, Ahir, Gujar, Rahbari | Kunbis are higher than all others | |
| Succession laws | Equal, Chundavand* | Equal, No other law | *(half-brother case) |
| 10.Cloth etc (a) Men | Dhoti-kurta-Pagdi, Bali in ears** | Dhoti-kurta-Topi, Bali in ears** | ** old timer or fashion |
| (b) women | Lehenga- Kurta, Pendal etc | Sari-Choli/Blouse, Mangalsutr | |
| 11. Food Habits | Veg*; majority averse to non-veg | Veg*; majority not averse to non-veg | Veg*; Vegetarians |
| Staple Diet | Roti, Dal Chawal, Milk, Mild spicy | Chapati, Bhaji, Rice Dal, Spicy Food | |
| Famous deserts/ sweet food | Churma, Kheer, Gulgale, Pude | Puran-Poli, Shrikhand, Modak | |

| 12.Marriage etc; Bhaat* | Yes | Yes | *Maternal parent's Laag |
|---|---|---|---|
| Village Exogamy | Observed strictly | Not practiced | |
| Clan/Caste | Exogamy/Endogamous | Same, with exception of cross-cousin | |
| Cross-cousin | Not allowed at all | Allowed including i/c Mama, Bua | |
| With Deceased wife's sister | Allowed | Allowed | |
| Marriage-Got avoided | 4; Both parents & grand mothers | Yes; cross-cousins* marriage allowed | * Bua & Mama Children |
| Satta/Watta (Exchange) | Yes, | Yes, (Few Maratha castes in villages) | Not by educated in both |
| Identification Mark; (a) Bride | Wear Paper Mauri on forehead | Wear pearl bead Mala* on forehead | *Called Mundavalya |
| (b)Bride Groom | Lofty Mod on head secured by Pagdi or Pagdi with a crown | Wear pearl bead Mala* on forehead (Mundavalya) & a Pagdi with crown | |
| Identification Mark; | Mod/Pagdi & Crown, No Sword | Pagdi with crown & Carry Sword | |
| No of marriage permitted | Monogamous | Were Polygamous in 18th century | |
| Widow re-marriage/ Karewa | Yes, Permitted in a particular way | No, not permitted | |
| Family Relationship* names | Maa & Baap, Dada & Dadi, Bhai & Bahan | Aai & Baba, Ajoba & Aji, Bhau & Bahin | Only 5 similar out of 42, i.e., 12 % similarities |
| 13. Religious Symbol | No sacred thread (Janeu) | Wear sacred thread (Janeu) | |
| 14. Gots/clans | 162 | 96 | |

NB* Out of 42 names of relationships only 5 names i.e.; Mama, Mami, Nanand, Sasu (spouse's mother), & Sadhu (husband of wife's sister) are same.

**Linguistic, Social, Cultural, and Marriage rituals similarities?** Dr Vasant More, in order to prove his point that Rods (as he spelled) of Haryana are Maratha only, has shown similarities in r.o. linguistic, social, cultural & Marriage rituals between Rors & Marathas (Ref. his book Rod Maratha; Ch-7; pp 56 to 63/89). These similarities are analysed in detail in the paragraph below.

## (a) Linguistic Comparison भाषा;

My analysis; 1. Headgear फ़टका, खंडका, or पगड़ी, 2. Male's Baithak & animal keeping place called बाड़ा, & 3. Door or door Leaf कवाड़; Not only Rors, but all other castes in rural Haryana & Northern part call these by the same name only. 4. Door Latch अडणा; A device for keeping doors secured & closed from inside. Not correct as no Ror calls it by this name. Instead, it is called Sliding latch or Musla. 5. Earthen Pitcher गडा or घड़ा, 6. Ladoo लाड्डू, 7. Buffalo महैंस, 8. Hare ससा, 9. Neck मुंडी, 10. Smart श्याणा बुद्धिमान, 11. When कदी or कधी means when, 12. Stop थाम्बले, & 13. Noon दुपहर or दपर; Not only Rors, but every caste in rural in Haryana, in general, uses all these words.14. Defame कुचेष्टा या मज़ाक या बदनामी, 15. Information माहिती या जानकारी के लिए शब्द; No such word were ever/are in use, linguistically or in slang, by Rors in their day-to-day talks. 16. घणा in हिंदी कोल्हू के लिए & मराठी घाणा; Not correct as no Ror (रोड़) use or has ever used such word for कोल्हू. In Haryana & Ror Lingua-franca घणा means more quantity, ज्यादा. But घाण; Ror & other castes use it to denote the quantity of sugarcane fed to कोल्हू crushing-wheels. 17. राम-राम in Hindi & Haryana, & मराठी भी; is a greeting among Hindus, when they meet, & not only by Rors but it is spoken all over Haryana.18. जाना; Dr More says that in हिंदी it is आटा चक्की, & in मराठी it means– जात. So, again he is not correct as for रोड़ it means to go, जाना. 19. गोधड़ी Quilt; हिंदी में गुदड़ी, मराठी में गोधड़ी; रोड़ calls it गुदड़ी, wrong comparison. 20. शिका: in हिंदी it is छींका, & he says रोड़ call it शिका & in मराठी it is शिंके. Here also he is not correct as Ror call it छींका. 21. काठी: is a मराठी शब्द: रोड़ इसे लाठी कहते है, and not काठी. 22. परात: It is परात for सभी. 23. पाहुणा: मराठी, हिंदी अतिथि, Ror रोड़ of Haryana call it बटेऊ & not पाहुणा, Only in UP they call it so. 24. गालना: In हिंदी it is to pour i.e., डालना, in मराठी it is घालणे, but Ror रोड़ call it घालणा or डालदे. 25. धार काढणे; to milk cow/buffalo; रोड़ call it धार काढले, Dr More says मराठी भी call it same. 26. Simplton; साधा-भोला; In हिंदी it is सीधा-सादा, in मराठी it is साधा- भोला; रोड़ call it सीधा -सादा or साधा-भोला. 27.Wall भिंत; मराठी & रोड़ भिंत. In हिंदी it is दीवार. Above analysis shows hardly 10% similarity in spoken words in day-to-day life by Marathas & Rors of Haryana, establishing Rors are not Marathas.

## (b) Mariage Rituals Comparison;

Pointwise analysed as; 1. साटा प्रथा Exchange of Brides; This exchange of bride directly or sometimes indirectly between two families are prevalent & common among not only Rors & Marathas but Aroras, Jats, Dohri Rajputs of Jammu Hills Gurdaspur (ref; census-1901, pp-321, p386/486) also including Karewa i.e., Widow re-marriage. 2. भंडारे का मुखिया मामा In-charge of Marriage sweets Store; Since maternal uncle (brother of Bride/Groom mother), contribute appreciable finance & in bride/groom cloths in the marriage in the form of Bhaat & being from a different village, not having any inclination of extending favour to anyone of the village of her sister in-laws place, is the best choice, and it is similar system in all caste of Haryana & Northern India & not in Rors & Marathas only. 3.मीणाई के लाइड्डू special Ladoos for Maternal Party welcome; These are oversized Ladoos and specially made for the maternal party. As explained under previous point it is prevalent in all caste of Haryana & Northern India & not in Rors & Marathas only. 4. मंगल स्नान या बान बिठाणा The Oiling of Groom or Bride is given by the married women of the clan in 5,7,9, or 11 numbers while singing baan songs. Dr More says since concerned song contains the words like; Tata pani-e-Samudra ka, so & so…son of so & so…. is being given bath, and as there is no ocean near Haryana, and the ocean of Konkan region has warm water, so the Rors being Maratha only have this tradition. This is bizarre & illogical as all caste of Haryana & Northern India have this tradition & not only Rors. So far as Tata Pani is concerned it may be of Jai Samud Lake of Mewar as it being a closed lake has warm waters and Rors are stated to have come from Chitore after migration. Also, as the Rajputs of Mewad were bulwark & flag bearer of Hindu resistance to Mughal invaders, their traditions were followed by all Hindus of this side of Bharatvarsh. 5.सोबड़ा जाना Bride's Male accompany, and 6. विवाह मंडप में वधू को मामा द्वारा लाना to bring Bride for phere in marriage mandap; Not only Rors, but every agrarian caste including backwards & menial in Haryana & Northern India, in general, in villages have this tradition. So, the analysis shows that not only Rors but all caste of Haryana follows these marriage rituals, and as it cannot be construed that Ror are Marathas.

**(c) Similarities in festivals Celebration** त्यौहार मनाने में समानता; Statements that Marathas do not celebrate Raksha Bandhan & celebrates Govardhan Puja, like Rors, and as such Rors are Marathas, is again illogical as lot of castes, being agrarian, in Northern India celebrate Govardhan Puja more enthusiastically than Diwali. So far as not celebrating Raksha Bandhan in Medieval period, it may be due to their affinity with Rajputs ancestry etc, but now everyone celebrates it. Further uncanny simile of Bhai Dooj Khotli, it may be mentioned that not only Rors, but all communities of North & Middle India celebrate Bhai-Dooj and send Khotli for their married sisters & daughters.

**(d) Some misc. Quotes;** (1). Big Maratha or Long Live or Chhatrapati ke Jay बड़ा मराठा या छत्रपति की जय, & (2). Crying for Victory or जय रोया; I have not ever heard Rors saying this epithet or sobriquet except being said so & propagated through the sinister motivated campaign of 2002. This is totally false & concocted and there are no such sayings among Rors. Yes, Ror womenfolk abuse or express their indignation & bad-wish against their husbands, when upset or not happy in general with the saying, 'भाई रोया',

(cry for your brother or curse be on your brother) or other saying to menfolk like नाश पिट्या (wish You be doomed?).

So, from the above paras it can be deduced that no broad/major social, linguistic, cultural or marriage ritual similarities exists between Rors & Marthas, and all are motivated canards by one concerned party for political gain.

* * * * *

# Chapter-15. Rors; Connect the Dots

## 15.1 History of Ror community

The phrase that, "Historians and Intellectuals may forget but people won't forget as it perpetuates through, 'the words of the mouth,' from generation to generation seems to be true for the history of the origin of The Ror caste." If we, closely observe & examine the facts on the origin of the other castes like; Rajputs, Jats, & Gujars, etc, we will find that there also, are conflicting, varying, & ambiguous. And same is true with the origin of the Ror caste.

However, such ambiguities & difficulties should not lead to dejection but it should provide a challenge to find the solution as its very inquisitive subject matter to delve upon. So, the efforts of those who have tried to pen the history of the origin of the Ror Caste are commendable. Therefore, need is to have a group of veterans, literate & expert to eliminate the farce ones and come out with the authenticated certified version (s) of the history of the origin of the Ror caste.

## 15.2 Wrap-up from the Past on Rors

Rors had been addressed by all communities with the epithet of, 'ROR RAJA' or 'CHAUDHARY.' Almost all Rors had been saying this to themselves, as heard from the mouth of their ancestors that;

> They are believed to have come from Dilli–Badli Jhajjar to Haryana.
> They initially occupied 84 (Chaurasi) locations in the South-West of Thanesar (Kurukshetra).
> They dug the Brahm Sarovar at Kurukshetra as a party of Royal Pilgrimage sometime after 1707. This may be the reason few historians link them (tauntingly) to Ods, a special caste still in north, expert in digging canals?
> There were 72 Rors employed as 'caretakers & security Guards' in the cavalry of Marathas at Bhau-Samaana while Maratha Army camped in the pre-third battle of Panipat recce mission up to Lahore/Peshawar.
> On their settlement in the present locations, almost all are unanimous & recall that their great grandfathers had come from so & so village to inhabit the present villages. But about the dates even educated lots are horribly wild. About livelihood & occupation, most say that their great grandfathers had a *"Lainda" flock of 100 buffaloes* and a *"Chauna" of 100*

*cows*. Also, they were having best *bullocks of Nagore breed*; most envied of by everyone in rural north India.

> From pastoral life, Rors became full-fledged agriculturists in early 20th century when the water of Western Yamuna and other canals of East Punjab were made available by then Government. (Ref write-up of col Ram Chander)

> There were 4 Ror 'Lambardars' in Thanesar, 2 Ror Lambardars in Karnal, 2 Ror Lambardars in Dathrat and 6 prominent principal family out of 23 in Karnal, and many other villages also (See Karnal Annals also for Lambardars).

> Rors had been proudly addressing each other as "Chaudhry Saheb." And it is to state that all peasantry class in Mewar, especially around Udaipur are called *Chaudhary*. These Chaudharies between 1572 & 1583, after Scorched Earthed Policy of Maharana Pratap moved out of Mewar & migrated to places towards Malwa, Nagore, Jodhpur, Bikaner etc and further, the heartland of Haryana. (Ref; Maharanas; by Omendra Ratnu pp-195)

## 15.3 Rors: Few Peculiarities & Folklores

1. People sarcastically (satirically) call Rors as the 37th caste and also the people who had lifted horses' dung; as caretaker of horses of the Maratha cavalry during recce for 3rd battle of Panipat.

2. Their conversation with each other is laced with **'Ra' and 'Ri'** a typical Rajasthani slang particularly of Mewar region.

3. 'Chaurasi' area South-West of Kurukshetra had been their original strong-hold; perhaps it's even now?

4. A folk-tale from elders: Heard from the generation born in 1900 AD, *"Bhains Charae Malwa, Dhar kaadi Ajmer, kheer Banai Agra, kha Jaye Bikaner"*. Indore in MP is the center of Malwa region. Means these geographical areas were of the interest to forefathers of Rors, who may be a pastoral, farmers, soldiers, feudal or rulers?

5. Ror women, sing a song of tragic historical event around 1500-1600, about the daughter & daughter-in-law of Rawal Chanda, ruler of Mewar. Daughter-in-law of Chanda Rawal tells the son of a Mughal, who had caught the hand of Chanda Rawal's daughter for a bride, to leave her for the honour of Chanda Rawal. Daughter-in-law offered herself to become his bride. But son of Mughal did not relent and took

her by force & lodged her in a military camp, where the Chanda Rawal's daughter burnt herself alive in the tent.

6. On the auspicious occasions, '*Sati*' is glorified in the first song. There are 'Satis' by different names in major villages. Women sing 'Devi' song highlighting that 'Devi' temple is on a high hill (Aravalis?) and tiring for them to climb.

7. Rors had been boasting of their exceptional pair of bullocks as good as '*Nagore*'. Nagore in Marwar near Jodhpur had excellent bullocks. If you recollect Chapter-4 of this book, has a proverb on this.

8. On close observation, 'Ror Gotras', subject to research for arriving at final percentage; nearly 50% of Ror *gots* matches with Jats of Haryana & Rajasthan, 40% with Rajputs & balance 10% may be with Marathas & others. (Ref; Point for research for Ror Raja Itihas; by Col Ram Chander (retd); VSM)

## 15.4 Dots which need to be connected

As read, there are many postulations on the origin theory of the Rors; written, as well as oral, but no monumental & authenticated written history by any Historian as to who are Rors? From where they came? Who were they? Also, why, and how could they occupy the most fertile heartland of Haryana along the oldest & ancient land route for the traders of all the times to foreign lands of central Asia etc. Similarly, in UP also, they are found in the most fertile Ganga doab region situated between two most revered rivers of the land. So, to find out the truth & authentic writeup on the history of origin many loose ends, labyrinth of maize, are required to be straightened, half-truths fact checked and finally the dots need to be connected. There are umpteen such dots scattered here and there, having lot of material & points to be connected for gleaning the history of origin of the Rors, as described in next para.

### (a) Is Rajput Vansh precursor of Ror caste?

There are strong indications & revelations that Rors have originated from 13 or 17 kula (to be furthered researched for firm & final number) of Rajputs viz; 1. Bhatti, 2. Chauhan, 3. Dahia, 4. Guchchhle, 5. Guhila/Grahilot, 6. Jat, 7. Kachhwaha, 8. Khichi, 9. Khokhra, 10. Mohil/Mohilas, 11. Madhad, 12. Panwar, 13. Pundir, 14. Rathore, 15. Ror/Rode, 16. Tomar/Tuar, & 17. Sengar. This needs detailed research in mission mode by a group of subject experts from the Ror community, to be appointed by Apex Ror body (?) etc, in association with some commissioned historians of the Rajasthan in general and Chitore in particular including the detailed study of the Annals & Antiquity of Rajasthan of Col James Tod.

**(b) The dots of Karewa custom in Rors**

Such customs are adopted when the population of males in a race reduces due to war or other fatal causalities from enemy encounters. Later, over the time, such practices become regular custom. As is believed history of Rorvansh takes a turn when the most famous of the race Raja Dhaj (grandson of Tisman) abducts Saurath; a damsel from Saurashtra & is forced to abandon his capital after heavy casualties of his soldiers in the fight with her kins. This is said to be the starting of Karewa custom among Rors as lot of young Ror women had become widows after the above fight. Similar anecdote is, "The Chauhans of Delhi district also had taken to widow marriage as they had lost lot of their valiant soldiers & generals in various battles including at Tarawadi in 1192." (Ref; Delhi district Gazetteer & Panjab Castes; Denzil Ibbetson; pp-135). Due to this, they were no longer recognised by their fellow Rajputs. Like that Rors also had taken to Karewa system, which can be construed to be originated from Rajputs. There are plenty of Chauhan, Khichi/Khanchi, Mehla or Mohila & other Rajput clans in the present Ror caste. Few other martial caste like Jat, Rajputs of Himachal, including Arora/Khatris also, follow Karewa.

**(c) The dots of; Pitron ke Gahne custom in Rors**

It is to state that each Ror family keeps Gahne, in a niche above the main entrance door of their home; Oblations (offerings of; Bura, cloth, & money (coins) in two or three (as per pitr) earthen pots, for some ancestor(s), who was issueless, or had met unnatural or violent death, as a sign of veneration, remembrance, penance & also as a shield for protecting the house members from all unnatural deaths, illness or vicissitudes. The oblations in these pots are changed twice a year; in Chaitra/Baisakh, & in Kartik month after the Rabbi & Kharif crops. This custom is not confined to Mewar, but there is a deified (Devata) Putra in every Rajput family; the one who has met a violent death and same is, true for each Ror family, who also follow this custom of Pitrideva.

This custom & practice is followed by Rors exactly as Guhila Rajputs, progeny of Bappa Rawal of Mewar had been doing. Initially, a son of Bappa Rawal was worshipped, but after the enshrinement of Raghudeva, the 2nd son of Rana Lakha, & younger brother of Chonda, whose estates were Kelwara and Kawaria and who was assassinated in the act of putting the dress of honour sent by Rao Ranmall, the Rathore Rao of Jodhpur & maternal grand-father of the child Rana Mokal, who wanted to usurp Mewar & finish the lineage of Bappa Rawal. Raghudeva was so much beloved for his virtues, courage, and manly beauty, that his murder became martyrdom, and obtained for him the divine honours, and a place amongst the Di Patres (Pitrideva) of Mewar. His image was on every hearth, and was daily worshipped with the Penates (Kuldevta). Twice in the year his altar used to receive public homage from every Sisodia, from the Rana to the serf. On the 8th day of the Dussehra, or ' military festival,' when the levies are mustered at the Chaugan, and on the 10th of Chait his altars are purified, and his image is washed and placed thereon. Women pray for the safety of their children; husbands, that their wives may be faithful & fruitful. (Ref; pp-324-26, p-396-98/676; Annals of Mewar part-IV of Book; Annals of Rajasthan by col Tod; Edited by W Crooke)

### (d) The dots of; Raja Ror of Kagarol, or of Bhainsror or of Banera?

The fort of Raja Ror, at Bhainsror, in Southern Rajasthan is said to have come up in 200 BC and also the Kagarol (Kaga Ror) ruins near present-day Agra have been said to have a similar time-line for another branch of Ror Raja. The coins found in the Agra circle by A Cunningham, CSI of ASI, seem to indicate a close relationship between the Ror rulers of the area & the rulers of Hastinapur and Indraprastha. The coins are said to be of 3rd century CE as seen from general style of the coins & the type of Sanskrit used. Raja Ror of Kagarol has already been described in details in ASI report 1871-72 Vol-IV (ref; sec; 5.5 Raja Ror) and it appears to have existed around Agra side, then a part of Rajasthan.

There is another, a 3rd Raja Rorji around 1700 AD, and even today there are 10 villages around Banera named after his ten sons. The Banera (between Chittorgarh & Udaipur) was the seat of the followers of Shakti Singh (the estranged brother of Maharana Pratap, who had aligned with Akbar), who as head of Banera was given the title of Raja by Delhi Durbar. *(Are Ror descendants of Shakti Singh, & is this the guilt, they suffer & are scared of revelation of this black spot on them?)*

Rajputs since ages have been naming their sons as Rorji/Ror Singh? There are lot of places in Rajasthan ending with Ror like; Bhainsror, (a fort of Ranas about 60 Kms from Chittorgarh), Behror near Alwar, Rorji ka Khera (about 50 Kms from Udaipur). It may also be stated here that, before the battle of Haldi Ghati, due to, *'scorched earth policy'* (stoppage of all agricultural activities), almost all Peasantry class (called Chaudhary), between 1572 & 1583 moved out of Mewar & migrated to places towards Malwa, Nagore, Jodhpur, Bikaner etc. (ref last para of section 15.2)

(After Haldi Ghati battle, Maharana Pratap stayed with Bhils in the jungles of Aravali & attained moksha in 1595 AD. Shakti Singh accepted the authority of Akbar and was awarded all privileges like that of the rulers of Jaipur, Jodhpur etc. After Rana Pratap his son Amra (Amar Singh) also accepted the authority of Mughals around 1615 AD, but he was excused not to present himself in Mughal Darbar like other rulers.)

Shakti Singh's descendants called Shaktawats ruled some places about 100 Kms around Udaipur/Chittorgarh like Mandalgarh, Bhainsror, Shahpura & Banera. Mughals had given the title of Raja to Shaktawat rulers. Around 1710 AD Rorji, (Ror Raja of Banera), along with other princes & Raja of Aamer came on pilgrimage to Kurukshetra and is said to have permanently settled around Kurukshetra along with all his accompanied and hence perhaps the name of the caste as 'Ror'. However, the factual position as to which Ror Raja or all the three of them are ancestors of Ror caste, needs detailed research for firm & final truth, as there is huge time period difference between first two & the third one.

### (e) The dots of; Keeping Jagga Bhaats/bards by Rajputs & Rors

Jagga Bhaats, the lineage keepers from Tunga, (a place 40 Kms on Jaipur-Agra Highway), records new marriages & births in the families in their books called, 'Pothis'. These Bhaats visit Rajputs of Northern Haryana & Western UP and also Rors. They had been visiting Ror villages for a long time. Traditionally they were given one Rupee & one Kg grains for their services. They have divided their "Jajmans" in the ratio of 2:1, i.e., two brothers go to Rajputs & one to Rors. They seem to have undisputable authentic records of 8-9 generations of nearly all the Ror villages.

The Jagga Bhaats, the genealogy recorder & keepers, perhaps may not be able to produce convincing chronological history of the Rors due to their limited resources, & understanding, but to discard them on this basis will amount to closing forever a vital historical resource of lineage records since generations. So, dots need to be connected by further research as to *why they (Jagga Bhaats) are common to Rors & Rajputs?*

**Bards or Jogi of Rors**: As with all martial races & in particularly Rajputs, Rors also have tradition of keeping Bards/wandering minstrel/songster. They sing tales of valour, bravery, tragedy, and benevolence of many of Rajput Ranas from Mewar like; Jauhar of Padmini, valour tales of Jaimal Patta, & Amar Singh Rathore etc or tales of bravery & sacrifice of Aalha & Uddal of Bundelkhand etc, in Ror Villages on annual visit for months together & were paid for that by kind & cash. In my village Gudha, the Jogi of Ahar (a citadel of Khanchi's, similar to Ahar near Udaipur), used to come. So, this also need further research as to why this tradition of *keeping bards is common to Rors & Rajputs?*

### (f) The dots of; Ror clan/gotras

The dots furnished below are on some of the Gotras of Rors (ref; material of research by Col Ram Chander (VSM), (retd), except wherever different reference is given). A concerted researcher is needed to establish the facts.

**Atri:** There are Atri Rajputs near Tunga village of Jagga Bhaats in Rajasthan, Atri Jats in Meerut, and of course Maratha Brahmins Atri (exact Aatre?). Rors of Kunjpura & nearby should delve to find out the connection?

**Bodla:** A small section of Wattu Rajputs of lower & middle Sutlej, who for some generations enjoyed a character for peculiar sanctity. They spread from Multan to Bahawalpur to Montgomery, then to Sirsa. They were credited with power of curing disease by exorcism; specially snake bite & hydrophobia; they are recognised wandering gharishthi saints. Bodla of Pabnava; called Fakir ke; need to delve? (A Glossary of Tribes and castes in Punjab & NWFP; Vol-I pp114-115)

**Hurda:** Hurda is now a tehsil/sub-division, earlier a state of Rajputs of Bhilwara district of Rajasthan. The people who ruled in Hurda, may be a clan of Ranas as it falls near Chittorgarh/Udaipur in Mewar.

**Mehla/Mahla:** Mohila or Mohil, an ancient ruling race, one of the 36 Royal races, ruled in 1440 villages of Nagore in Marwar Rajasthan. Rathors of Jodhpur defeated them around 1500 AD. After defeat they were degraded from rulers, & said to have merged with Jats & became farmers. (Ref; appendix 'D' Vol. II pp-1127 & 1144 of Rajasthan Annals-by Tod).

**Mahlan/Mehlawat:** Descendants of Shakti Singh called Shaktawats ruled some places about 100 Kms around Udaipur/Chittorgarh like Mandalgarh, Bhainsror Garh, Shahpura & Banera. Also, there are some branches of them called as Rajawat (Mahlan/Mehlawat) There are lot of Mahlan/Mehlawat in Delhi around Mahipalpur etc.

**Chauhan:** Chauhans the most valiant & bravest ruling Rajput race, in North India, disintegrated, and even converted to Islam after losing the battle of Taravadi in 1192. Chauhans of Delhi had started following Karewa after they lost most of their young men in the continuous battles. There are lot of Chauhans among Rors.

**Chopra:** About 30 kms on Sirsi road from Jaipur, there are 5 villages of Chopra Jats. Possibly some Chopra Jats had gone with Jai Singh of Jaipur to Kurukshetra in 1710 AD. Ethnically, as explained & accepted by Ibbetson, it is for certain that Ror Chopra's are not connected with Punjabi Khatri Chopra's, in any way.

**Khokhra and Dandhal:** Rathors of Kanauj or Gahadpur or Gadhipura, a Suryavanshi race originated from Kush s/o Bhagwan Raam, have 24 Sakha, among them which are similar to Ror got of Dhandal or Dandhal, Khokhra, Malavat, and Maholi (said to be later corrupted to Mehla) (ref pp-105 of Tod's annals). Up to 1820 AD they were shown as part of Rathors. Dandhal who write Deendayal as their gotra need to re-think & research further? (Ref; appendix E Volume I pp-106-Tod)

**Khichi:** A Chauhan clan, ruled in Malwa region, from the fort of Gagraun. After the capture of this fort around 1400 AD by a Muslim Sultan, Khinchi disintegrated & deserted the fort & surrounding habitations. Some of them had become Khichad Jats, some were forced by Muslims to be Butchers and degraded to Khatik. *Ancient seat of Khichi's, before Gagraun, was Ahar, 5 kms from Udaipur, now a mound under ASI control and a tourist historical site. Still largest village of Khichi/Khanchi Rors is Ahar in Panipat district* (ref; Tod's annals)

**Turan:** The last Tomar or Tuar Rajput King Anangpal, who established Delhi, passed it on to Prithviraj Chauhan his daughter's son as he had no male heir. Tomar name seems to have corrupted to Turan (?).

**Taya:** Tayas of Udaipur appears to had branched off from Ranas of Udaipur. Among Rors also, there are Tayas mostly in five villages of Kaithal district. Other gotras in these villages had merged with Tayas some 250 +years back.

**Sagwal:** Sagwara is a sub-division of Udaipur near Gujarat border. If Sagwal & Sangwan are similar, then there is an 84 villages 'Khap' of Sangwan Jats near Delhi/Rohtak. *Sagwal, either are Rajputs of Sagwara or Jats of Haryana.*

**Other Gotras:** Thola, Badsar, Dhankhad, Beniwal, Joon, Baliana, Lambah are Jats in Rajasthan & Haryana. Gohlan might be from Gohil; or Gahlan Jats of Haryana. (Ref; Point for research for Ror Raja Itihas; Col Ram Chander (VSM), (retd)

**(g) The dots; Rors were; (i) already inhabiting Haryana, and (ii) later settled astride GT Road by Marathas**

**(i) Rors were already inhabiting Haryana; (a)** The records of Sauram Khap Panchayat, since the time of Thanesar king Harshavardhan (rule 606 – 647 CE), have vivid descriptions of Rors warriors who took part in various battles against invaders from the north-west along with warriors of other castes, including in 1857 against British. Rode Vans ka 5000 Varsh ka Itihas by Sh Ram Das Rode also mentions the names of these Ror Yodhas who fought various battles (for names & events refer page 229 to 230, 237, & 241 to 253 of the book). Few such Ror warriors were ;(1) *Champat Ror* was one of the Dy Senapati o/o the four of 75000 Yodha's force for assisting Khilji's to defeat invading Moghuls in 1298 AD between Sirhind & Panipat. (2) In the Sabha called by Rana Kumbha (ruled 1433-1468) for a combined Hindu force at Chitore Gadh in 1523vs(1466AD) against invaders, *Ram Dyal Ror* was one out of the five Yodhas sent by Sarva Khap. (3) In 1526 VS (1469AD), *Hari Ram Kadiyan Rode,* was one of the Brahmchari Mandal consisting of seven Brahmchari Malla Yodhas for the protection of Hindu Women from Malechchas. (4) *Karam Chand Ror* was the Up Senapati of the 30000 Malla Yodha force prepared in 1598 AD (1655vs) in the meeting at Mathura for protection of Hindus. (5) *Tej Pal Rode* was one o/o the 2200 representatives of Sarva Khap Panchayat who facilitated in the coronation meeting of Shajahan at Agra in 1627 AD (1684vs). (6) The force of 38000 Malla Yodha & 12000 Cavalry created for defending insults to Hindus under Banda Bahadur chairmanship in 1707 AD (1764vs) at Gadh Mukteshwar consisted of all castes including Rors. (7) Ram Dayal Ror, as per the decision taken in Haridwar Sabha in 1419AD (1476vs), was one o/o five Malla Yodhas sent to train Vijayanagar army.

**(b)** Dr Himmat Singh Sinha, a prof of Eminence in Dept of Philosophy of Kurukshetra University, also corroborates, that Rors were already inhabiting in Haryana before the 3rd battle of Panipat, in one of his video of 2021 on The Quest YouTube channel email; thequestkurukshetra@gmail.com

**(c)** As already stated in para 6.10 chapter -10 of this book, Rors of Bijnor are said to have migrated to Bijnor some four century ago (~1491 AD) from a place called Fatehpur Pundri in the Karnal District. Half this village was owned by the Rors, and half by a colony of Sayyids. The Sayyid's quarrelled with the Rors, who were forced to emigrate under their leader Mahi Chand. (Ref; Tribes and Castes of North-Western Provinces & Oudh: Vol-IV, (pp-243 to 244) William Crooke.) But why it is not recorded in Ain-e-Akbari is a matter of further research?

**(ii) Rors were later settled astride GT Road by Marathas;** Marathas, between 1740-60, were in total domination of territories astride Grand Trunk Road from Delhi to Peshawar/Kabul. They had established a military camp of 5~10000 soldiers & 3~4000 horses at "Bahu-Samaana" on GT road for their military operation in Punjab & beyond. This is the period when Rors, already inhabiting in Haryana, came in contact Marathas. Marathas from the days of Shivaji' were staunch Hindus, so they must have been influenced by the strong Kshatriya traits of Rors, living nearby the pious Hindu teerth of Kurukshetra, and employed 72 Rors to look after their horses in Bahu-Samaana military camp.

Marathas, while fighting bitter battles with Muslims had developed strong anti-Muslim feelings, particularly against converted ones. They used to over-run Muslim settlements & settle Hindus in these. Between Delhi & Ambala, except few Mughal administrators stationed in Samalkha, Panipat, Karnal, Kurukshetra & Ambala, there could never come up big villages/towns because the Muslim armies were always on the move along GT road route. Marathas overran & destroyed all such Muslim posts, also attacked & banished Nawab of Kunjpura. Barring a few Muslim villages, most of the Muslim settlements, 30-40 kms astride G.T road, were destroyed. This is 20 years' time initially (1740-1760) when Rors in 15-30 strengths depending upon their past Rajasthan groupings, were made to settle 30 kms astride GT Road by Marathas. This support of Marathas made Rors stature higher, kept them united, and even Jats of Haryana, who could have overrun their villages, did not dare to do so. (Ref; Col Ram Chander material for research on Rors).

### (h) The Dots of; Nagore Jodi of Bullocks

There is a saying, about the Nagore bullocks in the villages inhabited by Rors, "Tere Pas Kaun Se Nagore ke Jodi Hai?" or "Dekh Lee Tere Nagore ke Jodi." तेरे पास कौन से नगोरी हैं? Or देख ली तेरे नगोरी की जोड़ी? The bullocks of Nagore are of special breed and well built & envy in the villages. Hence the best bullocks in the village were always addressed by Nagore Jodi. Nagore cattle fair, still is very famous for Bullocks, Cows, Camels, etc. Mohilas (corrupted to Mehlas) before they were evicted by Rathors of Marwad, were inhabiting 1440 villages in Nagore estate.

### (i) The dots of; Power Centres of Rors

Every Ror progeny believe that their ancestors had come from Badli (Jhajjar), on south-west of Delhi. Now big question, staring in the blank is where is Badalgadh & Khatkangari & what position they hold with respect to Kagarol or Khagrol or Kasaundigadh or Rori Shankar of Sindh in Rors history? These dots need to be connected in order to trace the time line & path of the movements of Raja Ror or Ror caste. Dr Rajpal Singh, in the 3rd chapter of his book 'Etihas ki Ek Jhalak,' describes in details, all possible seats of the Powers of Rors, where they dwelled and flourished (pp-14 to38). Referring Bhaats, the seats of power of Rors, starting with Raja Ruru of Khatkangari (Gujrat) near Palan Pur, then Mukun Dev (s.no 48) who established Badli, & Raja Dhaj (s.no 60), who established Rori Shankar in Sindh, have been examined in details. As per the artifacts, coins found from the archaeological remains of Rodvanshi Rajas from nearby places of Agra; Tisman (s.no 58), Dhaj (s.no 60), & Khangan (s.no 69), had very good relations including matrimonial with the Rajas of Mathura, Virat Nagar, and Indraprastha. He says may be Khedagadh or Kasaundigadh, (52 Gadhis) is Khatkanagari? Further, referring Bhaats, he says, 7 brothers with their sons out of 9 sons of Dadror (s.no 101), had inhabited Badli, who had fled towards Kurukshetra after tiff over Dola with Qutbudin. Badalgadh, a fort, also called Lodhi Khan ka Tilla, in the north-west of present fort in Sikandra, is said to be established by Baalan Dev (s.no 48) & up to Dadror (s.no 101); 54 Rodvanshi Raja ruled from here. But all these needs detailed research to establish the facts. If we take the postulation that Rors have sprang from Rajputs, then their seats of power were Mandalgarh, Bhainsror Garh, Shahpura and Banera etc also. (ref section 15.5)

### (j) The dots of; Why Rors are not recorded in Ain-e-Akbari?

As per Ain-e-Akbari, (ref. sect 5.3. (1) ch; 5); principal castes of Pargana Karnal are stated to be Rangad & Chauhans, and of Pargana Panipat; Afghans, Gujars & Rangad; Tagas in Ganaur; Afghan & Jats in Sonepat; Jats in Gohana; Rajputs, Rangads & Jats in Safidon; Rangads in Pundri; Rangads & Jats in Habari; Rangads & Tagas in Indri. A tribal distribution map in the Settlement Report of Panipat Tehsil & Karnal Pargana, at the time of Ain-e-Akbari (1590AD), prepared by Ibbetson shows that the then Afghans held large part of the lower Khadar and also formerly held part of Bangar, now occupied by Gujars. At present there is only one Afghan village, besides part of the city of Panipat. There was total disappearance of Afghans, due to changes in the course of the Jamna River, and it is noticed that they have been replaced very largely by Gujars. Afghans had left their Bangar villages for the more productive & easy working Khadar soil, which became available by the change of course by the Jamna River. But in the intermediate parts of Khadar the people have only been settled for some eight (8) generations, which, @ Indian estimate of 25 years a generation, would bring their first 'arrival well this side of the date of the Ain-e-Akbari i.e., by 1600 AD."

Gujars, who were intimately connected with Rajputs, were settled by them in portion of their territory & they originally held the area about Naraina, Sutana and Nain, *were largely replaced by Jats & Rors*; while the Gujars has spread over parts of the Khadar formerly occupied by Afghans. *Rors are chiefly to be found in the Indri Nardak and the adjoining tract of Kaithal. Pai village, which belonged to Mandhars Rajputs, Habari to the east was a Chauhan village, and Mundri, which was a Tunwar village are now Ror villages. Tunwars who held Korana, Pharal and Rasulpur, in which they had a large fort, but now are Ror villages.* (Ref; Karnal dist. Gazetteer pp-81 to 83)

It is interesting to mention that even Jats are not mentioned as a prominent caste of the tract in Akbar's time, as they probably gained footing during breaking up of the Mughal dynasty, when they became an important element in the politics of the time. (Ref; sec 5.3.(1) on Jats of Karnal dist.) If one look back and refer to last para of the section 15.2 of this chapter, it is reiterated that, due to '*Scorched Earth Policy*' of Maharana Pratap, wherein all agricultural activities in the plains of Mewad were banned in order not to make food, fodder & other eatable available to Akbar forces, almost all Peasantry class (called Chaudhary & incidentally all, Rors proudly address each other as "Chaudhary Saheb"), between 1572 & 1583 moved out of Mewar & migrated to places towards Malwa, Nagore, Jodhpur, Bikaner etc and further it may be to Karnal, the heartland of Haryana. (Ref; Maharanas; by Omendra Ratnu pp-195, Prabhat Prakashan) So, from the above it is evident & amply clear why Rors are not recorded in the of Ain-e-Akbari of 1590 AD.

Also, extract from the records of Sarva Khap Panchayat Sauram (Muzaffarnagar), penned by Master Nihal Singh Arya, Pracharak, (resident of Jessore Khedi Rohtak / WZ-8 Hari Singh Park, Naya Multan Nagar Delhi-56) with the consent of Mahamantri Kabul Singh ji (page- 271-72,276 & 347), which were made available to Sh Surat Singh of Bastada for handing over to Ror Mahasabha Karnal on 18/20-6-1981, clearly show the Rors were inhabiting Haryana from the times (7th Century) of Raja Harshvardhan of Thanesar. The details has already been elaborated in section g(i) (a), (b), & (c) above. Why the Rors are not mentioned in the Ain-e-Akbari of 1590 AD, is a matter of research to establish the truth, as even the tribal distribution map of Ibbetson in his Settlement Report of Panipat Tehsil & Karnal Pargana, also states Rors came to this area after the period of Ain-e-Akbari.

**(k) The dots of; Are Ror from the Aror of Sind?**

There is another belief as heard from the elders that Rors are from the Aror and the main city Rori or Rohri of Sindh. As per Wikipedia open-source there are 165 Hindu Empire & Dynasties starting with Gopala Dynasty from1400 to 841 BC, then Pundravardhan Kingdom 1280 to 345 BCE, *the 27th dynasty in this list of 165 dynasties is the **Ror Dynasty, period 450 to 489 CE** with capital at Rori (presently Pakistan).* The tweeter handle of Govt of Pakistan @pid_gov states (verbatim), "Aror was the ancient capital of Sindh, originally ruled by Ror Dynasty." In 711AD, Aror was captured by the army of Md bin Kasim. Historians recorded the city's name as Al-Rur, Al-Ruhr, and Al-Ror. Another tweeter handle from Pakistan @aaftab_khaskhelion 4/5/2020 states (verbatim), "The Rai Dynasty was a Buddhist Kingdom that ruled Sindh from 524 to 632 AD. This was the 1st Sindhi Kingdom established in over 800 years; the last being the Ror Dynasty. # RajaDahirIsNationalHero. The one-page attachment to this handle (page-159) title, 'Ra Khengar' (book title unknown) in its 2nd para says (verbatim); "In Sindh Land is the country of Pawur, of which **Ror Pawur** was raja. A daughter was born to him under the Mool Constellation (Nakshtra). The astrologer said to Raja Ror, that whosoever married a girl born in such a time will lose his throne. The Raja was very sorry when, he heard this, so he sent his daughter away into the forest, where a potter named Hurmuteeo, found her & brought her up. She was so beautiful that the Lakha Phoolanaee sent an embassy to demand her in marriage. The potter said that he must ask his caste fellows before he gave away his daughter.

Lakha threatened him with violence; and the potter, therefore, fled and went to Mujeywuree, in Soreth, where he lived with his family." This is another story & different than that of Sorath where the same name damsel was abducted by Raja Ror of Kagarol? So, the matter needs detailed research as to which is real Sorath i.e., the Soreth of Sindh, who is daughter of Raja Ror Pawur or the Sorath of Gir Nagar/Kathiawad Gujrat, which is said to be have been abducted by Raja Ror of Kagarol from Banjaras, a well-known folklore & Swang. (a stage enacted famous story of the bygone era, similar to Jatras of eastern Indian region.)

There is another story on the end of **Sindh Rule of Rawar or Ror Dynasty**, which has been extracted from the Chachnama (account of Sindh campaign of Muslim Invaders), & given in the book Astyamev Jayte (pp-226 by Sh Abhijit Joag; Bhishma Prakashan), wherein it is stated that in a single campaign during the first wave of invasion by Muslim Invaders, Md Kasim finished the rule of Rawar dynasty. This Rawar or Ror dynasty, as recorded in the Census of India 1901; Vol.17, Punjab; its feudatories & the North-West Frontier Province, under Para16 (pp-310; page; 373/486), on Khojas of Jhang, was one sub-divisions out of the 10 sub-divisions of Khojas (are mainly Khatris converted to Islam, who had hitherto preserved their original from Hindus divisions). May be this is the shame & guilt which lead to the loss of self-esteem among them, which they recovered a bit when they got fillip from Marathas while they were settled astride GT Road by them as a trusted ally since Rajputs, Sikhs, Jat & Gujars were sceptical of Marathas presence in North India.

### (l) The dots of; Marriage related Songs of Rors?

During Baan ceremony of marriage related ceremonies among Rors, ubton (a concoction or paste for skin enhancing) are applied on the body of the to be groom/ bride, by married relative womenfolk of the clan accompanied with the song in the background, "*Tatta Pani ye Samudra ka*, (Though proponent of Maratha theory says it is Konkan Sea, but in fact it is Jai Samudra, sea of victory, a massive lake of circumference about 30 miles created by two natural buttresses making it a water body like sea, near Udaipur, by Rana Jai Singh, who ruled Mewar between 1681-98 & it benefited the cultivation, especially in r.o. the crop of rice, which requires perpetual irrigation), Beta Nahaey ye ....followed by the name of Grandfather, father, Taau, Chacha,& other close relations. Similarly, for Bhaat, mother of the bride/groom to be, goes to her parent's place with Gud etc for inviting them to marriage. This invitation at maternal place in the night as well as the reception of Maternal relatives on the Manda day of the marriage at the bride/groom place, a 1ˢᵗ event & pre-cursor for the start of the other functions of the marriage, is accompanied with songs by the ladies, which also reflects of the surroundings resembling to hills & hillocks of Mewar area. However, since there is no recorded history of Rors migration from Rajputana, except words of mouth from the ancestors, or other indirect inferences, detailed research is needed to establish the factual position.

## 15.5 Overview on Rors; as by Col Ram Chander

An extract on Ror Raja: from the material sketched by Col Ram Chander, VSM (retd), who gleaned it from the Annals & Antiquity of Rajasthan; (col James Todd), & from his own memoirs and as heard from elders, is as below.

**Who are Rors & Seat of Powers?** So far there is convincingly no proof available in written as to who are Rors. Rajputs since ages have been naming their sons as Rorji/ Ror Singh. Bhainsror, Behror near Alwar, Rorji ka Khera (50 Kms from Udaipur on the road to Chittorgarh), are named 'Ror' as suffix. Like this there are many places. Also, there used to be a sect of Rajputs called *Rehad*; during Muslim invasions (1100-1300) they were defeated & melted away, but later resurfaced as Chaudhry's; now called as "Rar" Jats; 'Mirdhas' of Jodhpur/Nagaur. Another item, Col Ram Chander, states for the detailed study is; after the battle of Haldi Ghati in 1576 AD, Rana Pratap's estranged brother, Shakti Singh, accepted the authority of Akbar & was awarded all privileges like that of the rulers of Jaipur, Jodhpur etc. After Rana Pratap, his son Amra (Amar Singh) also accepted the authority of Mughals, in1615, though he was exempted not to present himself in Mughal Darbar like other rulers.

Shakti Singh's descendants & his other Rajputs followers called Shaktawats, ruled few places some 100 Kms around Udaipur/Chittorgarh like Mandalgarh, Bhainsror Garh, Shahpura and Banera. Mughals had given the title of Raja to Shaktawat rulers. This Rorji also called Ror Raja, who ruled Banera, had ten villages named after his ten sons and they do write Ror with their villages. So, researchers have to devote time on this riddle of Ror Raja.

Bhainsror Garh an impregnable fort of 2$^{nd}$ century BC, positioned strategically between two rivers, the Chambal and Bamani, had passed through the hands of several clans before becoming the seat of a premier of noble of Mewar, the large region around Udaipur and Princely State of the Sisodia clan.

This fort at Bhainsror in Southern Rajasthan perhaps came up in the 2$^{nd}$ century BC & the Kagarol (Kaga Ror) ruins near present-day Agra also point to a similar time-line *for another branch of Rors who ruled from there.*

**Digging Kurukshetra Brahm Sarovar;** Elderly Ror say that they had been hearing from their ancestors that Rors had dug the Kurukshetra Brahm Sarovar. Jagga Bhat Deshraj of Tunga, also confirmed that Rors had done yajna at Kurukshetra, but they are ignorant about date and period.

In 1710, Aurangzeb's widow wife, & also wife of Bahadur shah, both Rajputni, desired to go on pilgrimage to Kurukshetra. Ajit Singh of Jodhpur, Jai Singh of Jaipur, and rulers of Bundi & Banera were summoned to Delhi for accompanying them on pilgrimage to Kurukshetra. These

Rajput chieftains collected Rajput soldiers/workers of different gotras and Jats (Chaudhry's called at that time, even now also in Western and South-Western parts of Rajasthan) as camp workers, to go to Kurukshetra via Delhi. The rulers camped on the banks of Yamuna, present day ISBT. The workers possibly camped in nearby Badli village. From Badli village, the Mughal and Hindu Rajas' caravan moved to Kurukshetra. On reaching Kurukshetra, Royals stayed in their camps near present day Sanehat tank, whereas Rajput soldiers/workers and Chaudhry workers perhaps camped in 84 'Sirkis' South West of Kurukshetra.

Appendix-A of Col. Todd's book, 'Annals and antiquities of Rajasthan vol.-II, page-1016, throws light on the requirement of digging Kurukshetra Sarovar. As the digging under the supervision of Hindu Rajput chieftain (Ror Raja) took longer period, perhaps more workers were mustered from the villages between Delhi & Kurukshetra, who on the completion of mission, might have stayed back in Kurukshetra along with Rajput soldiers/workers. The soldiers-worker & Chaudhry workers from Rajasthan even after completion of the mission perhaps stayed back, on the persuasion of Ror Raja as there were no permanent dwellings those days & people could settle anywhere.

**Ror 37th Royal Race/Caste?** If we accept the above line of thinking, Ror Raja, perhaps, might have told all those, who had come with their families, for digging of Kurukshetra Sarovar that he would create 37th royal race of them if they stayed with him in this pious Hindu religious place. Rajput soldiers & Jat workers (Chaudhary) must have preferred to stay with Ror Raja. Since 7th/8th century, when Rajputs were created out of Hindu warrior races to 18th century up to the fall of Mughal empire, Bharat was ruled by 36 ruling royal races (ref; Col. Tod's book vol-1). Now-a-days 36 castes loosely are used to denote tradesmen like blacksmith, goldsmith, cobblers, & so on, farming communities like Jats, Gurjjar, Ahir & so on, businessmen like Baniyas and priests like Brahmins. But in actual if we survey castes all over India, number of castes will run into thousands. In medieval India, all above mentioned castes were in support of ruler & did not have much importance as on today. The caste which mattered were the rulers?

Though Ror Raja's ambition of creating 37th Royal Race/Caste never took off, but rather disappeared, however, his followers, calling themselves Rors did remain united initially in 84 'Sirkis' in the Dak jungles South-West of Kurukshetra (closer to Kurukshetra Sarovar). Marriages among them did not pose any problem because they had come from so many different gotras. Subsequently, with the passage of time & their pastoral life-style, they expanded East & West of Kurukshetra. Today their agricultural proficiency is a history.

**Possibly Ror Raja is of Rana Descent?** Ranas, Udaipur rulers (that includes of Banera also) for the last 600 years were called as Rawals, Gohil's, now Sisodias, in that order. So, it means, Ror Raja was a Gohil. The word Gohil might have corrupted to Gohila (or Gula) as Rors are sarcastically addressed by other castes of the region.

**Ror and Martha Interaction**: Marathas & Rors, astride present national highway, between 1740-1760 had intense interaction. Marathas might have merged with Rors after the third battle of Panipat. Researchers must identify Maratha gotras in Rors supported scientifically. Dabra in Rors, may be such gotr. I understand Ranas of Bazida Jattan may be Rane of Maharashtra (100% Maratha martial gotra). They are also doing well in business now a days. (As per me (the author of this book), possibility of mixing Maratha in Rors, if any at all, is before the battle rather than after the battle.)

**Rors as brand Marathas?** Maratha is the best brand amongst Martial communities in India. Marathas, Kunbi or non-Kunbi, rich or poor, gets respect in India. Some people amongst Rors not only claim that all Rors are Marathas, but they want to bulldoze and force their unresearched belief by aggressive posture, may be perhaps for political motives. Anything without logic & reasoning does not last for long. After reading this paper, Maratha advocates amongst Rors should cool down and become reasonable. Col Ram Chander advice to Maratha brand, is to invite Jagga Bhaats who are a link between the past and the present with hardly any fee and restore their activities honourably.

**Territorial area of Rors**: It is clear that Rors were in small area south of Kurukshetra and as everyone is aware, being pastoral community used to go to Himalaya foothills for animal grazing in summers (I had heard about such annual practices of going to hills in summer with live stock by able bodied males, from my Father also, as grass was abundantly available there even in summer, who used to return after the onset of Monsoon as grass used to become available again in the plains for live-stocks). During lawlessness period, due to raids of Sikh misiles, some people must have settled down in present day UP.

**Why did Rajput Rors not merge with Rajputs of Karnal?** In the days between 1710-1740, the food, dress, & social life of Rajputs, due to their matrimonial alliances with Muslims, had become almost like Muslims. Rajputs of Rajasthan, although more in numbers, but they also had given their daughters to Muslims, but still they considered them superiors to the Rajputs of Haryana. After 1950 only Rajasthan Rajputs started taking daughters of Haryana Rajputs and even today with few exceptions, do not want to marry their daughters to Haryana Rajputs. This complex must have forced Rors, who had come from Rajputana, for not merging with Haryana Rajputs.

**Conclusion;** *Majority of the Rors are either Rajputs or Jats,* which are sought after & respectable brands. However, Col Ram Chander said that may be, some Maharashtrians after the third battle of Panipat in 1761 had merged with Jats, Brahmins and also Rors. This percentage in Rors like other communities could be a minuscule only. Some people perhaps due to political ambitions & social brand want to give all Rors a new brand of Marathas but that would be far from truth and untenable (author view also is, that it is far from physical, ethnical & social behaviour point of view).

✳ ✳ ✳ ✳ ✳

## Summary

Among 168-updated from 165-ref para 15.4(k)- Hindu Kingdom / Dynasties starting with Amvastha 3500-315 BC, & ending with Dogra Dynasty in 1952 CE, **Ror Dynasty at 27th place, ruled 450 BC to 489 CE from Rori Sindh.** DNA theory also corroborates it.

Trail of Rors start with Independent Rajanya Gana of Mahabharat times which under Magadh Ganrajya of Chandragupt Maurya merged into a single identity. This merger perhaps lead Rajanya Gana to change to **Rorwal or Rodwal or Ror?** Rohdyadi Gana of Acharya Panini's Ashtadhyayi (500BC) and Krodyadi & Rohdyadi Gana of Acharya Patanjali's Vayakaran (200BC) appear to be same Gana which inhabited Kuru Pradesh, Karnal, Kaithal & Panipat, the same places where Rors inhabit presently.

Lineage of Ror vansh, as propounded by Bhaats also, starts after lapse of 26 generations from Yayati vansh King Dushyant (Durdaan) of Prayagraj, from 28th generation King Ruru (3182 BCE), and ends with Dadrod(r) at sr no-101 (para 14.1 of this book

Sindh Rule of Ror Dynasty gets strength from a reference, gleaned from Chachnama (accounts of Sindh campaign of Muslim Invaders), and also given in the book Astyamev Jayte (pp-226 by Sh Abhijit Joag; Bhishma Prakashan), which states Muslim invader Kasim finished the rule of Rawar (Ror ?) dynasty- ref Para 16 pp-310; page; 373/486, Census of India 1901; Vol.17, Punjab; its feudatories & NWFP).

The Kagarol fort & 52 Gadhi near Agra, was ruled by Ror Dynasty, a Kshatriya Race & a tribe of Rajputs, from 2nd century BC (ref- ASI report 1871-72 vol-iv). The coins, ruins & artefacts found in the Agra circle related to Rodvanshi Raja Tisman, Dhaj, & Khangar indicates a close relationship between Ror rulers with the rulers of Hastinapur, Mathura, Bairath (Viraat Nagar) & Indraprastha. Also in similar time-line another branch of Ror Dynasty ruled from Bhainsrorgadh, a strategic fort located in Southern Rajasthan i/c smaller forts at Bahror, Kahror, Khichror etc.

After Sorath episode Raja Ror & his kins from these seat of power are said to have fled towards Lucknow, Bundelkhand & places like Badalgadh, Khatkanagri, and Badli in Jhajjar area (Haryana). With Qutbudin episode over Dola they are said to have fled from Badli towards places where they are presently in Karnal dist & other places in Haryana and UP.

It is corroborated from the facts that Rors were inhabiting the south-west of Haryana, from the times of Raja Harshavardhan of Thanesar (ref ; records of

Sauram Khap Panchayat), as described in 'Rode Vansh ka 5000 Varsh Ka Itihas' book by Sh Ram Das Rode. Dr H S Sinha, a prof of Eminence of Kurukshetra University also corroborate it..

But Rors were lying low due to some unknown political mishaps /reasons. These Rors came into prominence again in 1740, when they came in contact with Marathas for supporting them during their recce operation of the North-west before the 3$^{rd}$ Battle of Panipat, and were firmly settled astride GT Road. Hence, the reason why Rors are not recorded in the Ain-e-Akbari of 1590 AD? It is interesting to note even Jats are not mentioned as a prominent caste of the tract in Akbar's time, as they also probably gained firm footings during the breaking up of the Mughal dynasty, when they became an important element in the politics of the time. (Ref; sec 5.3.(2) - Jats of Karnal dist.)

Rors were categorised Minor Dominant Tribe (13 nos) at no.2 after Rajputs etc, in the 17 types of caste category system, devised by Ibbetson, in the census report of 1881 (ref; sec-6.3(a)(3) ch-6). (Other 12 castes/tribes are; Karral, Gakkhar, Awan, Khattar, Khokhar, Kharral, Daudpotra, Dogar, Taga, Meo, Khanzada, & Gujar tribes). But in the census report of 1891, (ibid sec-6.4(a) Rors are placed on higher pedestal i.e., at par with the Rajputs, in the 1$^{st}$ category under 'Agriculture & Pastoral', classification, and, as 1$^{st}$ group, in Military & Dominant caste categories, out of 4 group of castes devised on functional basis by Herbert Risley. The 1$^{st}$ group of Military & Dominant, as shown in Abstract 84, consists of 20 castes. (In addition to Rors, 19 other castes are; Awan, Daudpotra, Dhund, Dogar, Dogra, Gakkhar, Gorkha, Gujar, Jat, Kahut, Karral, Khanzada, Kharral, Khattar, Khokhar, Maratha, Meo, Mughal, & Rajputs).

Census 1891 recorded Rors in 7 locations, and enumerated as having 169 Sub-castes (Surnames) (ibid sec 6.4(c)).

Incidentally Dr. Surendar Kadiyan (ref; his book pp18-22), also divides Rors into162 gots of two categories; main 86; well-known plus 76 lesser known. Surnames, perhaps evolved to group people by occupation or place of origin or clan affiliation or from a famous patronym. *But it is intriguing & surprising that the largest & the main Ror clan Mehla found in 66 villages (about 20 %), does not find mention in 'Panjab caste' by Denzil Ibbetson or even in Karnal district gazetteer? Is it a case of misspelling or Maipla & Mual later on came to be called as Mehla?*

Rors, retabulated as below, according to 1891 census, were inhabiting 14 districts; 7 in erstwhile Panjab (present Haryana, Punjab & west Pakistan) & 7 in erstwhile North-west Provinces & Oudh (Present UP & UK), and in 3 Native states (Patiala, Bahawalpur & Jind). Now they have vanished or might have adopted dominant caste on account of alienation (other reason also?) from the main Ror hub of Haryana heartland, western UP & UK as now there is none in 6 (six) districts of Indian states viz; Ambala, Hosiarpur, Dehradun, Mathura, Etawah, & Benares.

| Population & Distribution of Rors in Panjab, Native states, & North-western Province (UP&UK) as per Census of 1891 | | | | | | | | |
|---|---|---|---|---|---|---|---|---|
| S. No | Districts | Population | S. No | Districts | Population | S. No | Districts | Population |
| **Panjab (7 Dist. & 15 Tehsils*)** | | | | **Total** | **43086** | | | **43086** |
| 1. | Rohtak | 407 | 2. | Delhi | 728 | 3. | Karnal | 39814 |
| 4. | Ambala | 2093 | 5 | Hosiarpur | 10 | 6. | Montgomery | 32 |
| 7. | Lahore | 2 | | | | | | |
| **Native States (3)** | | | | **Total** | **126** | Mod | Total | **1318** |
| 1. | Patiala | 110 | 2. | Bahawalpur | 16 | 3. | Jind# | 1192# |
| **North-West Province (UP& UK) @** | | | | **Total** | **4,459** | | | **4,459** |
| 1. | Dehradun | 3 | 2. | Saharanpur | 3,320 | 3. | Muzaffarnagar | 475 |
| 4. | Mathura | 1 | 5. | Etawah | 5 | 6. | Bijnor | 614 |
| 7. | Benares | 41 | | | | | | |
| | | | **Grand** | **Total** | **47671** | | **Mod G Total** | **48863** |

NB; 1. * 15 Tehsil wise Break-up; **1 Rohtak** 407; 1Rohtak 8, 2. Gohana; 399: 2. **Delhi** 728; 1. Sonipat 727, 2. Ballabgadh 1. 3 **Karnal** 39814; 1. Karnal 19812; 2. Panipat 5610, Kaithal 14392, 4 **Ambala** 2093; 1. Ambala 67, 2. Jagadhari 71, 3. Naraingadh 12, 4. Pipli 1943: 5 **Hosiarpur** 10; 1. Dasuya 10: 6 **Montgomery** 32, 1. Gugaira 25, 2. Pakpathan 7: 7. **Lahore** 2; 1. Chunian 2

NB 2. # Jind native state as per 1881 census had **1048** Rors population (ref; Part Abstract no; 83; Minor Dominant Tribe of Eastern Plains) of section 3.3(1) of ch-3 of book; In 1891, with minimum10 % increase it can be taken as **1192**.

NB 3. @ Tehsil wise break-up of UP & UK, then NW Province.

The above figures of 48863, now after 130 years is estimated to be about 10 lakhs, inhabiting about 305 villages. If 26 urban locations & 14 cosmopolitans are included, then it comes out to be about 345; whereas, 'People of India', series on Haryana, some 20 years back stated that Ror inhabit 350 villages in Haryana, UP, and UK.

The Ror, spelt as; 'Rour', were counted as part of Arya Samaj Sect in addition to the caste like; Rajput, Gujar, Jat, Kambohs, Khatri, Sunar etc in census-1911. Pandit Hari Kishan Kaul, (census superintendent), wrote; "Rors claim a Rajput origin & their social status is same. Rors were largely Hindu, with only a smaller number being Sikh."

As is evident, Ror caste evolved from, 'Ror Dynasty,' and has archaeological evidence of being a Kshatriya Vansh. So, the question as to why the Ror caste is not registered with All India Kshatriya Mahasabha, is not correct & logical, as present-day All India Kshatriya Mahasabha is a body of Rajput caste only, but the people of Ror Dynasty, who were earlier a Rajput tribe, are now an independent Ror caste.

A heartening & matter of pride for all the Rors is that caste have two Padam Shree recipient(s), & a Khel Ratan recipient Mr Neeraj Chopda, & couple of Arjuna award recipient(s), many Olympians medallists, & CWG gold medallist. This indicates Ror caste is poised for higher echelons in social parlance among the agrarian land-owning dominant martial castes in the field of sports.

Another field in which Rors are growing with a visible shift in their socio-economic profile is **Ror Diaspora,** which has impacted the life of their families back home in the backdrop of dwindling land holdings, saturation of govt jobs, & slow growth of entrepreneurial ecosystem. Now it is a route of economic upliftment of households & aspirational segment for next generation of Rors. They are in almost every developed country in IT, Research & International Corporate world manning CEO, VP posts, in addition to normal service sectors.

Another matter of pride is **Ror Girls,** who are doing exceptionally well in almost all fields within country or abroad, and have made mark in their on right, be it civil services, Defense, IT, Medical, Academic, Corporate or Engineering field.

Rors though a martial community, but there are about 85 officers only in military, and top rank achieved till 2025 is Major General. Rors have not proved befitting martial character pre- or post-independence, as except few individuals who proved par excellence as Vir Chakra awardee in some caste regiments and few as sports persons.

Rors have achieved high academic success with maximum no of Ph.D, Scientist & Expert Advisers in agriculture field. One among them have also achieved Vice-chancellor post of a Horticulture university.

Similarly, one Sh Himmat Singh, an advocate by profession, & an Ad AG of Govt of Haryana is 1st from the community to become Chairman of Haryana Public Service Commission (HPSC), a body for recruiting class A&B officers etc.

There are lot of Rors in Engineering, Medical, IT, Corporate, & banking services but achievements are moderate as none have arisen to top Level post.

Their share in Haryana Govt services of various category is also mediocre with 1.11% vs-a-vs their population share of approx 2% (ref-sec 12.2(a)).

Their overall position is at 14$^{th}$ place out of 19 caste with 16$^{th}$ place in group A, & 14$^{th}$ place in group B posts.

In All India Services ie IAS & IPS etc also there is dearth of representation as on date there are minuscule Rors in these services.

Politically, Rors have done fairly well as there were MLC/MLA of the Ror community from Karnal district since 1936, but they are yet to have a MP either in Lok Sabha or Rajya Sabha, & a MLC/MLA in UP/UK.

Also, notwithstanding the availability of so many professional & other educational institutes of national repute situated in their citadel like RECK/NITK, Kurukshetra University, & Medical College at Karnal & Kurukshetra, NDRI at Karnal, Sainik School at Kunjpura, the community still is found wanted in achieving the excellence in education, leading them to the top posts? I do not see any lack of availability of opportunity in the form of institutes but lack of ecosystem, or perhaps killing instincts or the lack of soft-skills among the educated Rors & lastly perhaps a very important factor of political clout?

So it is high time the apex body & veterans of the community brainstorm to find out the solution, as to why they are not able to achieve the top notches, despite having excellent qualifications & antecedents?

Rors I feel, even more than in agriculture have made and also are making a good living by Animal husbandry, but still were/are not selling milk as a business venture. May be they have left or changed their martial character for some very serious reasons or may be they have a narrow easy going tribal mentality, who are not very keen to expand beyond reasonable means or might have fallen below redemption level in some social mishap or unknown battle or consequential level political strife which shook their confidence,& reputation to the core which still is buried deep in their psyche & DNA.

**Conclusion;** The Ror caste evolved from 'Ror Dynasty,' which ruled from 450 BC to 489 CE at Rori (Sindh), around present day Agra (Kagarol, Kassaundi or Bawan Gadhi), khatkanagari, Bahror & Bhainsrorgadh etc. Sometime in end of 12$^{th}$ / beginning of 13$^{th}$ century they ceased to be a sword of force & lost political clout. Later in 17$^{th}$ century Raja Ror of Banera (Udaipur) joined them. They were inhabiting various parts of Haryana since 7$^{th}$ century as recorded by Sauram Khap Panchayat, which has been corroborated by Dr H S Sinha, a professor of imminence of kurukshetra university.

Rors are independent clans of Rajput tribes from the time of Raja Ror & also few Rajputs associates from Rajasthan, who joined them in the end of 17/beginning of 18$^{th}$ century.

Also the nuptial practices of 'Satta & Karewa' followed by Ror community establishes them to be evolved from Rajput clans as even in present times, a group of Dohri Rajputs among 4 hypergamous groups of Rajputs of Jammu Hills exchanges brides i.e. practice Satta & widow remarriage as Rors do? (Ref; sec 6.5.2). Even the Chauhan Rajputs of Delhi, Karnal & Gaurwa Rajputs of Gurgaon, during 12 th century followed the practice of widow remarriage, karewa & satta as Rors do.

So far evolving of Rors;

**(a) Out of leftover Maratha soldiers** from the $3^{rd}$ battle of Panipat is concerned- there is no possibility as book 'Panipat and Marathas' page 274-300 by Dr Hari Ram Gupta' a Punjab university historians, & book by Shankar Purshotam Joshi in Marathi does not support any leftover Maratha in Haryana as Ror. Comparison of traits of Rors & Marathas (ref; sec 14.8), establishes minuscule commonality physically, ethnically, & culturally. Socially also, out of 42 family relationships, only 5 names are similar, a fundamental attribute for any race to be similar. The 'Ror Maratha,' though a befitting national brand, but it is far away from the truth and untenable as it fails the scrutiny tests in physical,& social sphere including on anthropological parameters.

Abstarct-84 Punjab census 1881 & 1891, distinctly records 40,731 & 43,212 Rors, and 242 & 262 Marathas separately, which clearly establishes that Rors have not evolved from leftover Maratha soldiers from the $3^{rd}$ battle of Panipat.

A redrawn part table from Imperial table XIII, (see sec 6.6 ch-6) of various castes having sub-caste or surname similar to Ror, Maratha caste do not figure in it. Few surname stated to be common, as given in the table at sec 14.6 of this book appears to be made to look similar due to peculiar Haryanvi speaking style. Dr Kadiyan in his book also stated that these have been made to look similar.

Even Gyaneshwar Chaubey, a prof of BHU, a member of DNA research group states that Rors do not have any genetic ancestry commonality with Marathas.

Yes, Rors in their existing locations in Hariyana came into prominence, when they were made to settle astride GT Road by Marathas for helping them during their pre-1761 Panipat battle recce. During this period, only Rors helped Marathas, though record not traceable, as all other Kshatriyas abstained from helping Marathas because of their own selfish motives of either seeking more share in the power of north India or fear of Marathas annihilation.

**(b) Are Rors evolved out of Jats?** Rors are fine stalwart men of very much same type as Jats, but Rors are more peaceful & less grasping in their habits than the Jats. So, Rors are readily admitted as tenants, whereas latter would be kept at arm's length. Socially Jats occupy a position which is shared by Rors, Gujars, & Ahirs; in fact, all four eat & smoke Hukka together. But few Jat tribes practice fraternal polyandry, no bar to marriage with women of the lowest caste, & take bride price, whereas Rors do not practice fraternal polyandry, practice bar to marriage with women of lower caste & bride-price. So, Rors may not have evolved from Jats. Rather it seems other way round, & few Ror clans appear to have adopted Jat caste, who now affix Ror or Rode with their name, in perpetuity or remembrance of their original caste.

**(c) Are Ror Arora?** Notwithstanding the similar story of origin of the caste; 'after their encounter with Parsuram, is highly unlikely, as Aroras are of inferior physique, while Rors are robust, & of martial physique, and both ethnically are not same. Denzil Ibbetson says, "The Aroras are often called Roras in the east of Panjab; yet I can hardly believe that the fine, frank & stalwart Ror is of the same origin as the Arora. They also differ in marriage practices & rituals, and other traits of inter-personal social intercourse & linguistically significantly.

Finally, all the speculations on the history of origin of the Ror caste can be laid to rest ;

**(a)** If there is scientifically researched & authenticated history document penned by historians of repute in association with Ror historians under the patronship of Ror Apex Body, as a commissioned project, otherwise it will remain an enigma only.

**(b)** This document should include detailed researched description of all power centers of the Raja Ror lineage like Rori Shankar, Al Ror, Kagarol, Bawan Gadhi, Badalgadh, Khatkanagari, Bhainsrorgadh, Bahror, Badli (Jhajjar) etc.

**(c)** Also it should have a chapter about Sorath episode, which is said to be a reason for the downfall of Raja Ror clan, including the reasons & circumstances leading to the migrations of Rors initially from Sindh (Aror), then Kagarol & Badli etc.

Another important matter, the group during their research should study all the alienated branches of Raja Ror clan / caste inhabiting in diverse regions as stated elsewhere in this book & in particular in section 13.4 (n) of ch-13, and the books penned by other writers in particular by Sh Ram Das Rode, for assessing all India spread of Ror caste.

**(d)** Also as explained in the Explanatory Notes of this book it is imperative to select a most acceptable spelling for the caste which is less prone to misspelling & sounding dignified with no ambiguity i/c no chance of even inadvertent possibility of wrong spelling of the caste name. Enumerators / Govt staff in British census & various govt documents have used 9 variant of Ror caste spelling; viz **Raur, Raud, Roar, Rod, Rode, Rohad, Rora, Rore, Rour,** & now also people are using different spellings as per their idiosyncrasy. Hence, in my view; a most appropriate out of - **Rode /Rodes or Raud (रोड़) or Rohd or Rohad (रोहड़)**, instead of present spelling **'Ror'**, which is mostly wrongly spelt & spoken by almost every outsider including many from the community, should be selected to be used by all.

* * * * *